Pat Russell

committee Book
MAR. '77

THE WORLD
IN A FRAME

THE WORLD IN A FRAME

What We See in Films

Leo Braudy

ANCHOR PRESS/DOUBLEDAY
Garden City, New York
1976

ISBN: 0-385-03592-6
Library of Congress Catalog Card Number 75–6151
Copyright © 1976 by Leo Braudy
ALL RIGHTS RESERVED
PRINTED IN THE UNITED STATES OF AMERICA
FIRST EDITION

For *Fitz* and *David*—
who were willing to
hear what I had to say

ACKNOWLEDGMENTS

Few books spring fully formed from the author's head. Experiencing and thinking about films, like the process of creating them, is a mixture of solitude and community. The book that follows has been shaped by talk that began with my first Saturday matinee. If I were to list all those companions to whom I was indebted, I would have to recall every grammar-school Saturday, every high-school Friday night, and all the days in between. Let me mention especially Peter Biskind, Dan Menaker, Bob Klein, Howard Darmstadter, Barry Gewen, Ira Brind, Jay Flocks, David Freeman, Ruth Davis, Stuart Pierson, Steve Weisman, Morris Dickstein, Lore Dickstein, Bill Rothman, George Stade, Geoff Nunberg, Ray Buono, and Dennis Turner.

Many of my first thoughts about the problems discussed here were first urged into birth by briefer articles, lectures, and reviews. For the opportunity to begin those explorations, I would like to thank Chick Callenbach and *Film Quarterly;* Gerry O'Grady; Mary Price and the *Yale Review;* Naomi Schor and *Yale French Studies;* Tom Russell and *On Film;* Ron Gottesman, Claudia Wilson, and Prentice-Hall, Inc.; Richard Locke and *The New York Times Book Review.* My classes at Yale, Columbia, the Bread Loaf School of English, and the Film Studies Program at the University of California, Santa Barbara, gave me the occasion and the inspiration to think more acutely and clearly. Bill Whitehead made innumerable helpful observations and gave valuable support for the first draft. Bill Strachan saw it through the next stages with equal calm, assurance, and penetration. Robin Brantley helped check the facts and Michael Silverman supplied many of the most elusive from his own memory. Peter Biskind, David Latt, Steve Weisman, Bart Giamatti, Al LaValley, Michael Silverman, and Dorothy Braudy read the manuscript at various stages and were by turns challenging and sympathetic.

There are no illustrations in this book and therefore no acknowledgments for pictures. A word about this absence. First, many of the most striking stills have already been used in other books. Second, most stills do not represent actual frames from a film; they are the descendants of publicity photographs taken not from the perspective of the camera but from the point of view of a wandering photographer on the set. But my most substantial reason for not using stills arises from my beliefs about the nature of our experience of film. Stills can

x   *Acknowledgments*

be very effective as evocation, to remind one of decor, the features of a particular actor, the static concentration on a single image. They may also furnish the kernel of an illuminating analogy, for example, documenting Ingmar Bergman's admiration for John Ford by two horizon shots: Death leading the players at the end of *The Seventh Seal;* John Wayne leading the Cavalry in *She Wore a Yellow Ribbon.* But stills nevertheless preserve the false notion that a film is x-thousand photographs stretched end to end. As I argue in the first section of this book especially, film bridges the visible and the invisible and makes them whole—what we see and what is implied by what we see. The frame of the still photograph falsifies and limits the possibilities allowed by the frame of the moving picture.

I do not pause very often to argue with other critics in the course of this book. Although the reader familiar with critical controversy will note allusions of agreement and be aware of the positions I may implicitly argue against, such knowledge is unnecessary to the argument of the book. I would, however, like to register the impact of the works of André Bazin, E. H. Gombrich, Parker Tyler, Rudolf Arnheim, Robert Warshow, and Northrop Frye. In my early years of watching films, like so many others, I was nurtured, provoked, irritated, and enlightened by the continuing commentary of Pauline Kael, Andrew Sarris, Stanley Kauffmann, and Dwight Macdonald. Whatever my arguments with them, I would like to pay them tribute.

Finally I would like to thank my wife Dorothy, whose sympathy, interest, and critical eye made her the perfect audience, equal partner in the act of creation.

CONTENTS

THE WORLD
IN A FRAME

INTRODUCTION

Movies in Mind

For instinct dictates the duty to be done and intelligence supplies the excuse for evading it.

Marcel Proust,
The Past Recaptured

In the 1890s three important cultural situations coincided and
began to take shape. The most pervasive was the aesthetic
distinction between clearly separate traditions of serious and popular art, a view that had been fostered by the theory and practice
of the Romantic poets, developed and nurtured by such critics as
Matthew Arnold and Walter Pater, and made a rallying cry by
the fin de siècle aesthetes and the forerunners of modernist literature and painting. Parallel to this effort to discern "true" from
"false" values in art was the entrance of literary studies into the
university. Since, as Arnold had tirelessly urged, literature had
replaced religion, it should be taught to the young in terms of
the timeless values that could be extracted from it, as defined by
the vocabulary of literary criticism. But at almost the same moment, as if to mock the new certainties, was born an art form
whose nature and appeal to its audience defied the modernist separation of elite from popular art, intellectual from emotional response, and meditation from experience, by playing on all simultaneously. Sprung from humble beginnings, considered to be a
magician's trick inferior even to the pleasures of vaudeville, this
new art was of course film.

Although most people would say that the intellectual antagonism to film has greatly diminished over the last ten or fifteen

years, there is still a distrust of film criticism that is the residue of
the early hostility to films in general. While everyone now "ap-
preciates" film and everyone has favorites, "classics," nevertheless
such classics have usually been defined by the way they have transcended the limitations of the form. One can therefore like Bergman or Fellini or Antonioni, and at the same time believe that film
is an inferior medium, compared to the novel, painting, or music,
which are capable of greater intellectual seriousness. Such filmgoers are direct kin to what would otherwise seem to be the opposed point of view: the film buffs, who believe that any criticism
beyond the most anecdotal and allusive "ruins" the effect of a film:
a beautiful and satisfying work of art is destroyed by talking about
it. While the viewer interested in seriousness feels intellectually
embarrassed when his emotions are involved in a film, the mystic
filmgoer embraces that inarticulateness. For both, "escapism" defines a realm where any more complex understanding has no place.
Both would like to separate the experience of film from the experience of the other arts. The first is unable and the second unwilling to bring his or her experience into the discipline and hence
the limitation of discussion, fearful that an emotional response is
somehow either shameful or too sacred to be tampered with.

Modernist theory and university training have tended to make
the audience of art irritated by what moves it emotionally and
proud of what moves it intellectually. No matter how a conservative would like to have a patriotism based on emotive response
and a liberal might want a more rational balancing, when it
comes to art, the educated want seriousness and respectability,
regardless of their political beliefs. In their minds, emotion has become associated with the pleasure that leaves no lasting effect—
escapism—and such transience is not a characteristic of "high art,"
which, they believe, lasts beyond the moment through its appeal
to the intellectual understanding, an escape from the trammels of
personality and time.

Although the literate person can no doubt refer to the emotion
great works of art release in him or her, he or she is made uneasy
by an emotional response to works that are not clearly accessible
to the older categories of critical value. A novelist in his late
thirties told me about the "intellectual demoralization" caused in
him by a youth of going to the movies; a woman studying for

her Ph.D. in English who was very affected by John Frankenheimer's *Seconds* (1966), a film about a man who has been
given a second chance on life, was annoyed that "that bundle of
cliches really kept me up all night." And we have all heard ourselves or someone else say, "I saw a great bad movie last
night." Here in essence is the literate person's belief that the
true appeal of films is anti-intellectual, his separation of the
responses of feeling and understanding, unless the film is one of
the few "serious" works that, like a poem by John Donne, grabs
you by the lapels and cries, "Explicate me. I'm difficult, but
ultimately rewarding." Like the freshman who fears that the
teacher will destroy his favorite poem by discussing it, these
otherwise sensitive people believe that intellectual and emotional
responses, like popular and serious art, are incompatible. The
freshman believes that articulation will destroy an essentially emotional experience; the "sophisticated" moviegoer believes that
works which depend on emotional response can never achieve
the seriousness reserved for works demanding intellectual response.
Neither makes the distinction between the intellectual film and
the film accessible to the intellect, or between the reasons a film
may be a work of art and the reasons it may be compelling.*

We are all involved in this willful blinding of ourselves to an
important area of artistic experience because twentieth-century
western European culture has tended to define aesthetic value in
terms of paraphrasably serious subject matter. Aimed toward
academic study, "serious" art furnished intellectual commodities,
concepts that could be carried away from the context of their
birth. Only artistic experiences that partook of this rarefied in-
tellectual-aesthetic realm could be considered true; all else was a

---

* Since it is possible to give so many different kinds of credit in citing
films, I have generally confined myself here to a reference to the director,
unless special circumstances dictate the presence of other names as well. I
have also generally used the date of release in country of origin, as closely
as possible considering the many contradictions between sources. For foreign
films I have used the most familiar American title, even, in the case of *La
Grande Illusion* for example, when that familiar title is a foreign one as
well. Except when a repetition of the date and director seems called for by
the argument, I usually cite them only once; when neither seems particularly
relevant and their presence might clutter the page, I have omitted them.
Any missing information is supplied in the index.

fleeting and therefore inferior pleasure, the effects of popular art. Wittingly or not, we are the inheritors of the late nineteenth-century belief in art for art's sake—the self-enclosure and self-sufficiency of the art object, unspoiled by any contact with the world of immediacy and ephemerality. Such art disdains the emotional responses that the older arts tried to evoke along with the responses of the intellect. Its meaning arises from an act of complicity between the writer and the reader, or the painter and the viewer, in which the artist initiates the audience into a mystery to which only he has access. James Joyce limits his audience in a way that no writer of novels in English before him even considered. His great innovation was to emphasize method over story, and concept over feeling. Like the Cubists, he and other modernist writers moved more and more toward the expectation of specialized understanding, the arcane fact, the learned allusion, as the basis of community between the artist and his audience, a community that specifically excludes the uninitiated and unintelligent, who must console themselves with the limited pleasures of "popular" art.

Part of the twentieth-century tendency in all the arts has been toward a single-minded theory of their own natures, as if only by purification could they define their separate function and reason for existing, and thereby be considered substantial and serious. Thus the modern novel seeks out itself as a verbal construct; painting emphasizes abstraction, color, the texture of the paint itself; music moves toward sounds; and film becomes a compound of pure images. In terms of the history of each of these forms, such urges toward purity were useful, for they made the artists in all fields aware of the underlying nonrepresentational material of their work, that their methods were not only instruments in the creation of some narrative or anecdotal content, but also artistic definitions of perception. Much early and some recent film criticism attempts to save film "art" from its destructive immediacy by similarly concentrating on the purity and self-sufficiency of the film image as an expression of the essence of film material: the light, the sound, the celluloid itself. Whatever the interest of such experiments, however, their critical urge is to raise an otherwise popular form to aesthetic dignity by invoking the same terms of value used by the aesthetes and the modernists who have attacked, ignored, or condescended to film. Most theories of art from Plato's to the present have tended to be didactic, asserting a necessary relation between the moral and the aesthetic value of a work. The histories of the various arts have accordingly established certain ideals of form and content, and ranked artists by their adherence to or deviation from them. But now, when the distinction between popular and serious art no longer seems so defensively necessary or so critically compelling, film criticism especially seems to be at a point when it can pass from a prescriptive and polemical aesthetic to a looser, more descriptive, and more expansive one, without such masquerading moral imperatives as: films ought to be constructed solely of images; or, sound degrades film art; or, narrative degrades film art; or, film can never achieve the subtlety of characterization possible to the novel.

In the past many aspects of the special aesthetic experience that films allow have therefore been considered inferior to those created within literature and the other arts. I would like to try to see the characteristics of the film experience as a set of principles in themselves, related to but never dependent on the other arts with which they often share so much. Let me apologize in advance if I seem to say that films do something better than theater, novels, paintings, etc. What I mean is that they do it differently. Part of our own obligation in the world of aesthetic experience is to become more open to its variety, and part of the task in creating a coherent film criticism is to understand the special ways film structures the world instead of condescendingly prejudging their inadequacy and airily assuming the superiority of the traditional forms. We need to look as closely and as openly as possible at what film in general has accomplished, instead of assuming that only occasional works of value could come from such a deficient and bastardized process. The history of film is a model of the history of the twentieth century, in which there are an increasing number of things to which the viewer must pay attention. Like all new orderings of human experience, film allows us to re-evaluate the past, to cut across the old divisions between the arts and in the process to create a criticism that ignores the academic compartmentalization of the arts and sciences.

Aesthetically, therefore, I want to expose that false emphasis fathered on us by the aesthetes and the realists of the late nineteenth century: the belief that art—if it's great art—must furnish ideals and purities. For me, the genius of art is the establishment of new continuities and new connections, in itself, and within ourselves. The passivity of the film audience need not be a type of hypnosis or mind control, but an experiment in new possibilities of connection and uncertainty, rather than the ideal of pure principles and idyllic, edenic stasis. Film extends the revolution in art begun by the eighteenth-century novel and its assertion of a continuous form that had to be entered into by the reader, a new conception of art, not as a controller and former of images and principles, but art as a place of testing experience. In Jean Renoir's *La Grande Illusion* (1937) two characters, Maréchal and Rosenthal, have to leave a cottage which has been a place of refuge for them since their prison break. In the last scene of the film we see their two indomitable figures tramping across the blank potential of the snow to freedom in Switzerland. Within the film everyone has a different illusion, and the overarching illusion is the film itself, for all illusions are potential ways of ordering reality. The goal of criticism should therefore be not to destroy illusions but to make us more sensitive to their workings and their complexity.

To consider film as a creative medium equivalent to theater, literature, music, or the traditional visual arts of painting and sculpture therefore threatens several cherished beliefs about the nature and value of artistic creation. I've already spoken about the interrelation of the distaste for the commercial success and the belief that true art is never popular and necessarily has a coterie audience. Similarly the collective nature of film creation— the difficulty of giving any single person total credit—has been attacked in accordance with the Romantic belief that the greatest art is totally original, produced by a solitary figure who stands against the facelessness of industrial civilization. A third attack, on the mechanical nature of film creation and its use of reproductive technology, concludes the implicit defense of the artist in his garret as the only type of creative artist.

The animating force of such objections is a loathing of the twentieth century. To attack the collective and mechanical nature of film, reason such critics, is to attack totalitarian societies with their robotlike masses—and the manipulation of those masses that the mechanical art of film supposedly makes more effective. Once again an aesthetic form has been interpreted morally. But the totalitarian argument lost whatever political cogency it possessed with the waning of the Cold War, and I would even like to argue that the aesthetic nature of films has actually helped to ameliorate the increased mechanization and deindividualization of modern society. Norman Mailer is an interesting contemporary figure here because in his novels he has an almost Luddite view of technology: the cancer of society is most apparent in science; it symbolizes the unnatural, etc. But in *Of a Fire on the Moon,* his book about the moon shot, he makes his peace with technology and sees something mystic in the scientific urge to explore. This new attitude seems to have been fostered by the three movies he has made (*Wild 90, Beyond the Law, Maidstone*), and the need in creating those films to immerse himself in a welter of scientific and technological details, knowledge of which would fuel his creativity instead of stifling or destroying it.

In fact, the ambivalent relation between science and imagination is part of the basic nature of film and a continuing theme. In Fritz Lang's great silent film *Metropolis* (1926), which deals with class conflict in a vast Bauhaus city of the future, there is an important figure named Rotwang. Rotwang is the only character who knows both the managers who live in the high buildings as well as the workers who live beneath the city's surface and make it work. Rotwang is a practical scientist: he creates a robot to take the place of the woman who has led the workers, so that they can be incited to riot and then repressed by the masters. But Rotwang's appearance makes him a curiously mixed figure. His laboratory is totally modern, even futuristic. Yet he himself dresses like a medieval magician, reminiscent of Marlowe's or Goethe's Faust, with a library of mysterious books. He lives aboveground, in a house of curves and softness, a chaletlike mysteriousness that stands against the glass-and-steel symmetries of the city. But, to preserve his intermediary position, in his cellar is a stairway that leads to the catacombs of the workers.

Rotwang is a paradigm of the film director, who attempts to mix scientific knowledge with the primeval magic of artistic creativity, who sympathizes with the masses because they are the basis of his art at the same time that he is tempted to sacrifice them to the managers who give him his livelihood. One is essentially misreading films if one concludes that the reason Frankenstein films and films about mad scientists are popular is only in response to public demands for horrific titillation. In fact, such works perform a twin function, for they both define something of the audience's fears of the twentieth century as well as something essential about the nature of film as a medium and the way in which it caters to, expresses and, by art, allays these fears. Part of my own fascination with films is exactly this way in which film can simultaneously embody some theme that is deeply rooted in the emotions of its audience and at the same time deliver as it were a disquisition on its own artistic nature and why such themes are so suited to it. One could almost reverse the negative attitudes I have been describing and say that the greatness of film is its offer of a potential to achieve creative power and expression within a situation that is commercial, collective, and technological—the forces that otherwise define our anonymity and our frustration. Movies subliminally prove that the new world we live in has not destroyed our dreams, but has made them even bigger, into what Mailer in another connection has called "spiritual technology."

Most theories of film are generative; they concentrate on how films are created. But I would like to begin with the receptive: what films are like in the experience of the audience and how they achieve those effects. The audience for an interesting film should be potentially as mixed as the audience for a Dickens novel, a Hogarth print, or a Shakespeare play. So, too, a responsive film criticism should try to touch on all the possible values a film might have, all the different levels of response it can reach, within an audience or within an individual. The standard of such an approach should be coherence rather than rigid consistency, because our experience of films is often characterized by a sense of fragmentation. In the other arts, we assume coherence and then test for it. But in film we are often content to focus on isolated moments. A member of the film audience can respond to a single element in a film (even though he may generally dislike it) much more readily than he can separate his responses to various elements in a novel. Perhaps this is the reason why arguments over films are much more heated and extreme than arguments over novels. Viewers don't see films as wholes; they are attracted to different aspects and fight violently over those attractions, as if they were the total question. One person is moved by the sense of American adventure in *Deliverance* (John Boorman, 1971) and so loves the film; another sees that, but hates the acting and thinks that the entire effect is too allegorical; a third cannot get beyond the themes of masculine assertion. The film is carved up and evaluated in parts with values assigned to the successful achievement of those parts according to individual taste. One of the great benefits of the auteur theory, which asserts that the director is the main creative force in a film, is that it nominally wants to consider films as whole works, and to take the responsibility for total aesthetic judgment, rather than be content with picking out and exhibiting choice bits. Each art is a variety of care. Arguments against the "seriousness" of an art form are usually arguments against the possibility of a *total or coherent vision:* this was all just slapped together; no one put it there. When we are faced with a film, we should therefore assume everything has meaning because everything is the result of a choice—to write, cast, stage, act, shoot, edit, or score in a particular way—all dictated by formal necessities that in another art could seem disjunctive and fragmentary.

Of course there are good choices and bad choices, choices that enhance a total effect and choices that detract from it. But a film is nevertheless the sum of all its choices, premeditated or improvised, rightly or wrongly delegated, rightly or wrongly included. And the test of a great film artist is like the test of any great artist—the coherence in object and effect of all those conscious, unconscious, and subconscious choices.

Not every movie tells us something about the nature of movies, although I would argue that all of those of any lasting interest do. But, like most other works of art, most films relax within the givens of their form, unself-consciously employ already created modes of expression, and tell their stories without worrying about artistic innovation, whether in style, form, or subject matter. The purities of earlier film criticism fail most conclusively to respond to and explore the actually mixed nature of film, its capacity to absorb and transform—what might be called its narrative indiscretion. No matter how much the novel might imitate sermons, histories, essays, journals, diaries, or other "nonfictional" written forms, no matter how much painting has drawn inspiration from comic strips and computers, music from radio programs and random street sounds, or sculpture from the wavering of leaves or the folds of a paper airplane—film can take and creatively assimilate more. In part, then, my purpose here is not to define limits beyond which film is not art, but to attempt to describe the continuities and new varieties of artistic wholeness film has created, to discover the many worlds possible in films, how they are distinguished and how they cohere. Most of the great novels treat themselves as experiments, in form, in content, or some interdependent combination, as if they were constantly beginning the history of the novel in themselves, perhaps in part because in other literary forms the sense of a past tradition is so strong and compelling. But movies, because their natural impulse is to be without a past, caught in the momentary happenstance of their audiences walking in on them, often find their special nature in the implicit assertion of tradition.† The most unobtrusive or unsuccessful genre film—western, musical, or detective story—can tell us more about the resources of the cinema than the worst comparable novel can tell us about the art of fiction. People truly interested in the aesthetics of an art form will learn more about film from seeing *The Poseidon Adventure* (Ronald Neame, 1972) than they will about the novel from reading Harold Robbins' or Irving Wallace's latest. Discussion about a seemingly insignificant genre or period film can relate it to problems of limitation and strength that all great films in some way share.

Movies are also difficult to appreciate within the standards of the other arts because of the characteristic mixture of eternity and immediacy in any film. In theater and music, there is always a text, a form to which every performance exists at least as a footnote. But in the film the text, the screenplay, is at best the

† Many recent films—such as *What's Up, Doc?* (Peter Bogdanovich, 1971), *Day for Night* (François Truffaut, 1972), and *Young Frankenstein* (Mel Brooks, 1975)—pay explicit debt to previous films. For a discussion of the development of this kind of historical self-consciousness in films, see pp. 114–17.

skeleton from which the film grows, often unrecognizably. Film goes beyond the immediacy of stage performance to express the paradox of specific living beings creating a work once and for all. While a performance of a piece of music may be preserved on a record and a particularly great performance of a play preserved on film, they still remain variations of the original. But a film, however immediate, is an original in itself, preserving all aspects of its performance as necessities of its form. If it is remade— and even if the remake is a better film than the original—the two films have equal status as creations; neither is a variation of some as yet unrealized ideal. Talk about movies therefore demands to exist with an insistence that is not as evident in painting, sculpture, or literature. Only dance and music rival film in the peculiar role talk plays in making the experience last beyond the particular performance. Incidental talk after a screening, fan magazine biographies, and film criticism—all serve first of all to bring the short-lived image into a continuous world of ordinary discourse, to ensure its life beyond those moments in the dark, to make it exist. Unlike the products of the other arts, movies are ephemeral. They aren't available, at least not yet, for easy reference on bookshelves, in prints, or on records. One of the first problems for the student of film is taking notes in the dark—to catch for a moment the rapidly vanishing sound and image. So, too, the aesthetic situation of the movie audience in general is reminiscent of the situation of Homer's first audiences. Once the bard has sung a line, the audience can't demand to hear it again; and so the movie audience is passively drawn from scene to scene, with no ready text or score against which to judge their particular experience, with only the experience itself to generate its own standards, for when movies are repeated, unless you have a video-tape machine and can pirate fragments, they must be repeated in their entirety.

How then do we create that talk known as film criticism and interpretation, with its special obligation to enlarge and enrich our responses not to just one work but to future works as well? Most of the critical standards that any of us have come from experience and training in the older arts, where the principles of value and understanding have been generally established and the principal artists—whose work constitutes a definition of value in itself—

are safely dead. Since movies are such a recent discovery, there is only beginning to be a canon of principles and great men. People may talk about movies or write about them. But such talk and such writing has rarely explored what movies have taught us about themselves—what conventions of form and content we have learned. Following the late nineteenth-century assumption of a hierarchy of the arts, much serious film criticism has either imported a critical vocabulary from already established disciplines or sprinkled analogies to the work of established artists in other art forms. This is a time-honored critical method: Henry Fielding's preface to *Joseph Andrews* half-seriously and half-whimsically attempts to bring the embryonic novel into "serious discourse" under the wing of the already approved and theoretically founded epics and romances. But I doubt whether Robin Wood's references to Mozart, Yeats, Conrad, and Elizabethan drama really convince anyone that Howard Hawks, the nominal subject of Wood's book, is any more serious an artist than they thought he was to begin with. Wood, like so many other, less talented critics, doesn't believe that it is enough to treat a subject seriously to make it serious; he has to make rhetorical gestures of seriousness as well, rudimentary equations of value: X the filmmaker and Y the great writer/musician/painter do the same thing; therefore X is as important an artist as (the already established) Y. Analogies between the arts can be illuminating, and I shall use many of them in this book. But I want to use them as I tried to use the allusion to *Joseph Andrews* above: not to say that movies are important or worthy of notice because similar things happen in them that happen in the more traditional art forms, but to preserve a historical and aesthetic continuity between the arts, to use analogies that illuminate in both directions. The main point of a reference to Shakespeare's dramatic method, for example, should be the increased awareness of the use of adaptation, stereotyped character, or popular motifs in *both* theater and film. A movie method need not be ratified because Shakespeare did the same thing. Any new understanding should potentially illuminate in both directions. The viewer who would understand the true complexities of film must therefore first avoid the distinction between criteria of enjoyment and criteria of judgment, for enjoyment can lead to a new perception of underlying form. Criticism should not try to be a rote promulgation of rules and categories, but an effort to show in as many ways as possible the actual wholeness of the seemingly disparate and discontinuous in aesthetic experience. We can look back at early Renaissance experiments with perspective in painting and call them "primitive" because our conventions of perspective in painting are more sophisticated—but could not have existed without those first efforts. In the same way, we may perceive the "awkwardness" or "bombast" in the narrative of an early silent film or the "obvious falsity" in a *March of Time* documentary without perceiving that we make that judgment because our conventions for narrative and documentary have become more complicated, although not necessarily more true. Art always contains lessons in its own understanding; criticism helps create that understanding by bringing it to consciousness through articulation.

Language helps us articulate, shape, and thereby expand experience. But need it be a special language, invented for the purpose? When I first began thinking about the shape of this book, I conceived of it as an exploration of the validity of critical terms that had been defined in the study of literature, painting, and sculpture: words like "grammar," "symbol," and "plastic." I worried that "audience" referred to a group of listeners, not viewers, and that "spectators" and "spectacle" had debased connotations. Would "vidience" be an acceptable alternative? I also wanted to define what an expanded appreciation of film might be and that project seemed to require a word that could mean "visual literacy." "Visuacy?" "Visionacy?" Would such an enlightened person be "visuate" or "visionate" or perhaps "videate"? What would be the other terms that were peculiarly suited for the discussion of movies?

But as I thought about the problems more and talked to more people, airing ideas, having arguments, I began to think that this preliminary form was too analytic. The talk that attempts to preserve film is also a response to the tendency of films to fragment, to whirl apart before our eyes. The closer one gets to a film to find out the "facts" of its creation, the more fragmented it may seem, as the gradual enlarging of the photograph in Antonioni's *Blow-Up* (1966) serves only to make the meaning more obscure. The urge to purity attempts to cling to some essential element in a film so that the plots and counterplots of eye, ear, and brain—the competing claims for artistic supremacy made by scriptwriter, cameraman, director, and star—can be safely ignored as irrelevant.

Structuring a film book in accordance with a search for proper terminology therefore reminded me more and more of those filmgoers who considered the greatness of films to consist entirely in great "moments" or pure forms, without wondering or caring about the film that contained such moments or the story in which the forms found meaning. Terminology is important, and this book, after all, is a work in words about a medium that is defined in great part by its appeal to the eye. But attempting to find a workable and effective vocabulary is not the same as multiplying categories for every theoretical and terminological distinction. Jargon draws more attention to itself than to what it is talking about. Criticism should allow us to look with refreshed eyes at the artistic materials that gave criticism its pretext for existence. When the creation of a critical language no longer enriches our experience of the works it purports to describe, it has become a self-contained exercise, irrelevant to anyone seeking a larger understanding. My own desire is to show how a familiar vocabulary might be varied and extended so that it will allow us to see more in a work, instead of substituting for it.

In the discussions that follow, I therefore mention but do not deal extensively with experimental films because for my purposes they are too preoccupied with formal problems to the exclusion of story. Like any art that is solely about itself, such films may play brilliantly with the possibilities of their form, but are engaged in a search whose exhaustiveness becomes ultimately repetitious. Many of the experiments that are being carried on now were first proposed (in a somewhat different vocabulary) in the 1920s by Hans Richter, René Clair, and others. The making of experimental films is essential in any film curriculum because it helps the student to understand the rudiments of the art in which he is engaging. But to base a total aesthetic of film on experimental films falls into the modernist assumption that the only end of an art is the exploration of its own materials.‡ It saddens me that, as the study of film has entered the university, it has in-

‡ I might here distinguish between avant-garde films, which usually participate in a self-contained tradition more akin to music than to fiction, and underground films, which experiment with storytelling and whose themes and techniques are often absorbed by the commercial cinema.

creasingly defined itself as a formalist and hermetic discipline, absorbing terms and methodologies from the most academic of European film criticism in order to establish the respectability of its credentials. This kind of defensiveness is as inhibiting to the full understanding of film as are the elitist assertions of aesthetic morality that it tries to placate. The process is reminiscent of the period of the New Criticism, when literary critics sought to defend their "imprecise" ideas against the attacks of the sciences by attempting precision rather than setting up alternate definitions of value. At present the two most obvious examples of what I am criticizing in film are the schools of semiology and auteurism. Christian Metz, whose *Film Language* is one of the main semiological texts, ladles out enough terminology to feed a generation of Aristotles. Andrew Sarris, who has popularized the director-oriented ideas of François Truffaut, Jean-Luc Godard, and other writers around André Bazin's magazine *Cahiers du Cinéma*, is a much looser and more genial figure. But neither should be blamed for the near-religious dimensions that semiological and auteurist methods have taken in many graduate film schools. Both can be fruitful methods of approaching film, but not so long as they are applied with a purified singlemindedness. The methodology of film criticism must finally be brought into the world of story, whether fiction or nonfiction. Experimental films may define the limits of film art, but they say little about the rich complexity of what those limits contain and how the normal experience of films has changed our perception of the world. I think it is difficult to defend any criticism that discusses a popular form in mandarin terminology designed to limit its audience to the initiates. The potential of film to absorb and renew the other arts is reflected in the potential of film criticism to be the crossroads of humanistic study rather than just another outpost. Experimental films, like purely formalist aesthetics, are finally private languages, understood by few, although potentially by many more. But I am interested here in the languages that are immediately understood by many, the commercial film, where private artistic language has been forced to go public. Materials finally end, but the connections of story are infinite.*

*In the same way, I choose not to consider certain kinds of film as art—industrial documentaries or travelogues—even though a teacher of film

I have been at such pains to reject so far any hierarchy of value—moral, thematic, formalistic—as a hindrance to a deeper understanding of films, but let me say before I begin my discussion that there are many value-judgments in the book that follows. Most of these judgments, I hope, will be set in a context of increased understanding rather than an imposed scheme of predetermined standards. I like some films better than others, of course, but I would like to believe that my discussion will enhance the experience of films I don't like as much as those I do. For example: there are two very similar shots in Frankenheimer's *Seconds* and Mike Nichols' *The Graduate* (1967). In the Frankenheimer film a man who has been given a new body and a new life returns home to talk to his wife who thinks him dead. He sees a picture of his old self on her table and picks it up; briefly his new face is superimposed and reflected by the glass over his old. In *The Graduate* the young man and his older mistress are about to make love in her daughter's bedroom, when she is seized by a fit of conscience and rushes out, but not before her face is superimposed on and reflected by the glass over a painting of her daughter on a far wall. There are three possibilities here. First, if Nichols is saying "this is a clever shot that I invented," he's wrong. (A certain hyperseriousness with which the shot is done inclines me to this interpretation; the second or later time such a strong "significant" detail is used should have some tone of irony.) A second possibility is that this is an interesting and as yet unhackneyed way of conveying nuanced visual information that Nichols may be imitating consciously or have devised himself without any awareness of its previous usage. The third, and strongest possibility: if Nichols is consciously using the same shot that Frankenheimer used and invoking something of Frankenheimer's film—mood, interpretation, ambience, moment, the Southern California trap of pseudo-expanded lives—then what Nichols is doing enriches his own film and enriches our appreciation of it, making a link with Frankenheimer's film and possibly provoking us to reflect on the nature of film satire and film attitudes toward the American character.

---

could use them in a rewarding class about how we are manipulated by images, the way a teacher of literature could help a class discover point of view in a supposedly objective news story.

Critically my credo is that we should always try the third possibility first. The more we know about the way it was done, the more we will appreciate how it is done now. Films shouldn't be isolated landmarks, even though that may have been the way they first entered the "higher" aesthetic consciousness. They are both as complete in themselves and as dependent on an artistic tradition as any painting, novel, play, or symphony. I want this book to be as much about what can be done in movies as it is about what has been and is being done. The discussion that follows is based primarily on actual examples, for it is only through seeing what filmmakers have done that we can discover the possibilities of film. Yet discussion of what has been; it leads inevitably to speculation about what could be done and attempts to define potentials instead of being confined to a description of accomplishments. I have called this discussion a descriptive rather than a prescriptive or a polemical aesthetic. But that doesn't mean I don't think my categories cannot be used to make judgments. As I shall try to show, I think they can also be used to suggest why certain films fail as well as why others succeed.

In the book that follows, I have used different critical approaches in different places, according to the three central elements of film experience: its visual and aural form, its context of social myth and reality, and its psychological relation to the individuals in its audience. Following this introduction, the first section considers the place of objects in films and the various ways in which they gain significance. The next section considers genre, the influence of tradition and convention on films, and the special types of themes and characters genre films—especially westerns and musicals—have created. The final chapter focuses on acting and characterization and the varieties of connection we may have with the faces and bodies on the screen. From another point of view, the book opens with an introduction that places the individual outside the film, wondering what critical act would best allow films to release their meaning. Then the first section deals with the patterns of open and closed visual form, the second with narrative and thematic form, and the final with the individual now inside the film: the actors and actresses whose dynamism threatens to disrupt the careful arrays of form. Underneath these divisions is a concern with the history of film that comes up most explicitly in the genre section but also operates as a subtext in the other sections, since the meaning of any film exists within a context of thematic, formal, and even technological development. Finally in each section I also discuss the present state of film in America and Europe and suggest what we might expect in the future. As much as possible, I have tried to make the method of this book eclectic, using formal, sociological, thematic, historical, and other varieties of criticism when I feel they are appropriate—in an effort to respond myself to the variety and complexity of film. To decide that any one of these methods is primary destroys the ability of films to break down so many of our received notions of where aesthetic value resides and what critical method brings those values out most clearly. Most of this book began at the movies, as notes to myself in the dark. I bring these notes together out of the desire to explain and order them for myself, and moved by the critical conviction that every artistic experience is enhanced by the more knowledge one brings to it; the more ways one can understand it, the greater possibilities of perception and appreciation. I hope that people professionally interested in the study of film will find something of interest in what follows. But I write primarily for nonprofessionals who want to watch movies with a greater awareness and understanding of the great art form of our time. This book is less about how to make movies or how they are made or how to evaluate them than it is about how to appreciate better all that they have to offer, how we might become a more active, a more responsive, and therefore a more critical audience. The inclusive nature of film, the way it can bring together the older arts in new and different combinations, its power over our dreaming and waking lives, the process of its evolution, should indicate the flexibility with which we should attempt to engage it. I am sure that every reader will have his or her own favorite example of whatever point I may be making, or perhaps an example that extends the argument further, or a counterexample that could supply a welcome nuance. I have many of those myself, but have tried to restrain my urge to add, vary, and extend so that the basic line of the argument stays clear. The test of any good theory is the amount of space it allows for the participation of the ideas, examples, and insights of others, how it can be used as a possible shape for experience rather than a restrictive enclosure. Perhaps the true model for an aesthetic theory should not be a new terminology or a visual pattern, but a building, created as a possible place, with potential uses and pleasures, but incomplete if no one can enter, occupy, and contribute to the realization of the inside.

SECTION ONE

Varieties of Visual Coherence

"The trouble with you, Robert, is that you make the visible world too easy to see."

> Attributed to Wallace Stevens, after Robert Frost had allegedly complained about the obscurity of Stevens' poems.

A certain selection and discretion must be used in producing a realistic effect . . .

> Arthur Conan Doyle, *A Case of Identity*

Unless a film contains obviously intrusive camera work—flashing lights, rapid montage, striking camera angles—we have difficulty believing that there may be problems in interpreting films comparable to the problems we find in fully understanding the other arts. Because we have gotten so much from a film at first viewing, we often balk at any insistence that the understanding of certain canons, methods, and traditions will help us understand more. But we resist especially because films seem so real and therefore so self-sufficient, without need of any critical interloper to explain them to us. We know, of course, that the plots are usually invented and the characters professionally acted; and no one is slow to criticize plot, dialogue, or performance. But the supposed "reality" of the film—the images of human action on the screen— is not considered a performance of equal artifice and control, un- less the painted sets are so obvious as to be noticed, and even then they might be absorbed as "invisible" conventions, not to be questioned or analyzed, but accepted.

The problem is paradoxical. From one point of view movies are the culmination of an artistic tradition (in the plastic arts, literature, and drama) that tried to help its audience to see better. Joseph Conrad's preface to *The Nigger of the Narcissus* (1897) defined his novelist's task as "by the power of the written word to make you hear, to make you feel—it is, before all, to make you see." Earlier in the century, John Ruskin in *Modern Painters* (1843) had stated the goal even more grandiosely: "The greatest thing a human soul ever does in this world is to *see* something, and tell what it *saw* in a plain way. Hundreds of people can talk for one who can think, but thousands can think for one who can see. To see clearly is poetry, prophecy, and religion—all in one."

But seeing in films seems almost by definition to be too easy. Many casual viewers have even assumed it indicates the absence of art, especially in a culture whose standards for high art have been dictated by the great modernist writers and painters, for whom *mere* representation was a dead style, to be avoided at all costs. Because reality, whatever it was, had to be hard-won, art in the twentieth century has tended to involve obvious self-conscious- ness as part of its subject matter. What James Joyce in *Ulysses* tries to do by irradiating every detail of his work with self-con- scious language and meaning, what Picasso tried to do by ex- ploding and reassembling images, the least cultured or least talented filmmaker can do by turning on his camera. Because the technique is so easy, the art seems easy as well, and therefore de- ficient. As E. H. Gombrich remarks in *Art and Illusion,* "the victory and vulgarization of representational skills create a prob- lem for both the historian and the critic."

Gombrich could have added (and later does add) that it creates a problem for the audience as well. By "vulgarization" he means general acceptance, and therefore general submersion into con- sciousness. When works are representational, the audience thinks that they aspire to the standard of external reality, and if the deviation from that standard is small (there's a rock that resembles rocks I have known; there is New York and that image corresponds to what I expect of New York; there is the Civil War and it seems like the Civil War I have read about), there seems to be no need to search for the manipulations characteristic of "true" art. Some might go further and say that any awareness that we are watching a film destroys most of the effects the film tries to create.

But "reality" and "representation" are concepts as learned as any more obviously artificial ones. Gombrich mentions a South African artist who thought he had learned everything about snow from paintings, photographs, and movies, but was very surprised when he came to England and encountered the real thing: "The strange, crisp, salty consistency of snow was another puzzle. From paintings I had imagined it to be like wax, and snow flakes to be like shavings of candle grease." In the same way we think we have learned the "reality" of perspective in art, when we have actually learned conventions of relationship that may be as artificial, and as undisturbing, as the chapter divisions in novels or the acting style in operas. Brain physiologists have repeatedly shown that the retina is not an organ in itself but a specialized part of the brain, and in the late nineteenth century Helmholtz had already called perception a "conclusion" about the world. Films, like painting and sculpture, therefore both parallel and expand our own ability to interpret the world of visible things. As Raymond Williams points out in *The Long Revolution,* "reality is continually established, by common effort, and art is one of the highest forms of this process."

Too often we accept a film as a window on reality without noticing that the window has been opened in a particular way, to exclude as well as to include. Even today we can't see southern France without looking through Cézanne's eyes or walk through parts of London without feeling the rhythms of Dickens' words. Films also afford this heightened sense of place. If you have ever looked at a part of a city or small town after you have seen it serve as a set for a film, you know that sometimes it has been changed for you forever. The real arrangement of streets in Hoboken, New Jersey, is less visually powerful than the concentrated focus on Hoboken in Elia Kazan's *On the Waterfront* (1954). But in fact, far from accurately recording the spatial reality of Hoboken, Kazan has made his Hoboken by weaving three city parks into one and even including a chunk of far distant Brooklyn, to create a cinematically real neighborhood to which the actual Hoboken must forever subordinate itself imaginatively, in the same way that every decaying small town now exists primarily as a footnote to Peter Bogdanovich's *The Last Picture Show* (1971). Not every piece of visual art can accomplish this transformation of vision. *Bullitt* (Peter Yates, 1968) does little for San Francisco beyond emphasizing its hills, and few people go around Montmartre forever haunted by the images of Utrillo. But the possibility remains for films as it does for painting, dependent on the talent and genius of the individual artist. The movies partly define and partly create the reality of the locations they take for backdrops because they have chosen to look at them closely and use them to tell a story. The actual settings may then in their turn become like those human beings who are movie stars, to be approached with cautious reverence for their new atmosphere of heightened reality.

Representational art in this way always re-creates the world around us as a new form of visual organization. Movies, because they exist in time, expand the shaping possibilities available to painting and sculpture. So influential because in part their methods are so subliminal, movies constitute a generally available method of creating visual coherence whose effect we can see around us every day in paintings, photographs, comic strips, sculpture, life-style, and even the "scenes" our eyes pick up when we walk down the street, across a field, or into a room.* If we can forget for a moment the claims that movies are more "real" than any other art and consider that the world of objects contained in each film is *chosen and transformed in context,* just as are all artistic materials, I think we are on the way to establishing a

---

* For an account of an experiment in attempting to teach filmmaking to Navajos in order to explore the similarities between their ideas of visual language and our own, see *Through Navajo Eyes* by Sol Worth and John Adair (Bloomington: Indiana University Press, 1972). Worth and Adair are especially sensitive to the difference between "our" way and "their" way of telling a visual story and try, often with fascinatingly *un*successful results, to keep their own prejudices out of their teaching. For my purposes in this chapter, I find particularly interesting a passage (pp. 61–62) in which Worth and Adair describe how a Japanese viewer of the finished films "understood" them in a way that was generally inaccessible to the Americans and western Europeans in the audience.

vocabulary that more accurately describes the effects films have upon us and the means at their disposal to produce such effects. Films are not more real than other arts, nor should their realism be taken for granted. This chapter could just as well be called "styles of reality." But that would be a definition of all art. Each film makes some statement about reality, sometimes affirming, usually attacking, but necessarily varying our previous perceptions. They can cue the viewer by reference to a seemingly realistic environment at the same time that their stories bring those responses into question. Unquestioningly accepting and then perhaps moralizing their reality blinds us to the intricacy and vitality of their con game.

A SHORT HISTORY OF THE VISIBLE

What is able to be seen is often what art has taught us to see. However valuable the physiological exploration of the processes of visual perception has been, it leaves out history. Human beings always saw. But how they saw, and the interaction between the visual perceptions of those forerunners we call artists and the visual perceptions of normal human beings is part of a historical continuity. There are always different assumptions about what is worthy to be seen, what is the most acute way of seeing that worthiness, and how that seeing ought to be artistically presented. R. L. Gregory in *The Intelligent Eye* calls the assumptions we make about what we see "stored visual hypotheses." Since our storing comes from our lifetime experience, it must also include the experience of past art and the particular ways that visual art organizes our world. We cannot say with assurance that we see the world the way the Greeks, the Romans, the Victorians, or even the Americans of the 1950s saw it. If we understand the place that movies have in the development of this history of the visible, we can better understand the varieties of visual knowledge that have been one of their prime subjects.

How memorable and important is the visible world? When does one choose to make it memorable and interesting to others by putting a frame around it, whether physical (as in painting or film) or conceptual (as in a sanctioned "picturesque" landscape or the face of a famous person)? Did anyone think a landscape was "picturesque" or "gothic" before there were paintings that brought out and emphasized such qualities, or poetry and fiction that urged one to seek out the visual equivalent of the insufficient words? When was the visible world first appreciated for its own qualities rather than a key to a divine, and therefore less palpable, reality? Without spending undue time on such intricate problems, let me sketch generally what I think are the most important changes in attitude toward the visible world from the Renaissance to the appearance of the first films.

The Renaissance seems to mark the time in the Christian era when visible things began to be valued as much for their surface reality as for the unseen truths that either were contained within them or pervaded them from above and beneath. The increasing secularization that characterizes the Renaissance embodies, therefore, not necessarily a movement away from belief in God, but from earlier assumptions that the world closest and most familiar to human beings was necessarily incomplete and insufficient. Judaism, Christianity, and Neoplatonism had all implied that true meaning was not to be found in the world everyone could see. The opulence of Christian art especially emphasized the far richer world of the unseen. In earlier ages of faith, the invisible art of music had carried much of the weight of emotions that we now feel equally stirred by the visual arts. As Peter Brown has remarked, "When Augustine wept in the basilica of Milan, it was at the chanting of the psalms, not before the still face of an icon." But by the Renaissance the medieval belief in the pervasive presence of God, that is, of invisible meaning, was giving way to a fascination with the possibility of surfaces. Jakob Burckhardt's famous formulation of the Renaissance "state as a work of art" specifies one aspect of this emphasis on the visual. Political structure was not merely an emanation of God's structure for the universe, a necessarily inferior—because human—rendition of the divine plan. It could achieve a completeness, self-sufficiency, harmony, and beauty of its own, akin to the work of art that was also a human production. Of course, the artistic fascination with the invisible world did not disappear with the Renaissance, just as belief in God did not disappear. Historically there still exists a definite prejudice in favor of the greater "truth" of the iconic— which refers outside or beyond itself—over the representational—

which concerns itself with the surfaces of things. Movies are merely the latest manifestation of a historical process of interplay between normal visual perception and the artistic manipulation of that perception, in which the terms of visibility and invisibility weave a complex dialectic. The Renaissance therefore marks a decisive step rather than an unprecedented beginning.

The Renaissance discovery of the possibilities of surfaces and exteriors showed itself in many ways: in the rejection of medieval vocational costume for intricate individual styles, in the increasingly elaborate styles of architecture, and in the choice of more private and domestic subjects for painting as opposed to the religious or mythological (the visible manifestations of the unseen). It also bred an ambivalence about visibility. Surfaces may be beautiful, but the standard of the hidden world implied that visual art could easily become visual artifice and perhaps visual fraud, not as a game but as a reprehensible manipulation of the viewer's visual assent. The standards of the invisible world hung in the shadows. In a more mobile society the change of status made possible by clothes and the knowledge of social forms led to a counterattack against visibility that harkened back to the early Church's refusal to admit pictorial images of divine mystery. In art and literature this ambivalence appears as the motive force behind the explosive development of theater and drama that is one of the most striking features of the Renaissance in England, France, Spain, and Italy; the fascination with the details of society that is evidenced in such nonvisual forms as the picaresque novel in Spain and England; and the personal cosmologies of such writers as Rabelais, Montaigne, and Robert Burton.

Theater and theatricality are specific examples of the general Renaissance conflict between art and artifice, a conflict actually between Siamese twins, each of whom needed the other for self-definition and life. So many dramatists illustrate this artistic paradox: masters of illusion, the messages of their plays tend nevertheless to be the conflict between appearance and reality, with the nod going necessarily toward reality, a flattering of the audience for their need to leave the play when it is over. Even Shakespeare, who, more clearly than most, announces the need for illusion (in a play like *The Tempest*), or Ben Jonson, who is constantly staging prologue discussions between author and actors, finally turn outward to the audiences at the end of the play and, removing their masks, commend their audiences for their greater reality, and their superiority to the illusion to which for a time they had given themselves up.

Once surfaces could be played with, their absolute power to impose was lost. When science began to displace religion as the orderer of the universe, vision became a category of moral choice. The glimpse beyond surface restrictions potentially allowed each person to construct his own world with a freedom defined against inherited conventions. As another such challenge to social orthodoxy, the eighteenth-century novel in England, France, and Germany generally turned its face away from visibility. For all of Henry Fielding's respect for Hogarth, he believes that the novel is superior to the visual arts precisely because it is *not* limited by the hardened surfaces of things. When, for example, Fielding introduces a beautiful woman in one of his novels, he does not describe her in any detail but calls on the reader to think instead of the most beautiful woman he has ever seen and identify that woman with whatever ought to be the physical description of Fielding's character. Laurence Sterne in *Tristram Shandy* similarly rejects the limiting specificities of description and with handy mockery includes a blank page for the reader to draw his ideal woman upon. A novelist like Tobias Smollett, one of the few eighteenth-century novelists who delights in visual detail, preserves the Renaissance attitude toward surfaces in his mainly picaresque works. But the concreteness of his details asserts the necessary separateness of the visual world from his characters as well as his readers, and their inability to control it. In general, the prose fiction of the eighteenth century in its sparse physical description seems almost previsual or nonvisual. Defoe and Richardson describe societies and people who try to escape the limits of their surface appearance because they are searching for the inward reality that will hold them together.

At the same time that eighteenth-century European literature is generally being drained of visual content, the world of painting is expanding. The eighteenth century in England, like the seventeenth and eighteenth centuries in France, witnessed the expansion of the possible subject matter of painting from the religious, mythological, and portrait subjects of earlier periods into landscapes and cityscapes, attempted recordings of a scene that actually existed. But seventeenth-century landscape painting is less localized and specified than it is anthropomorphized and mythologized. Specificity was for recording, not for art. Rich travelers in the eighteenth century, for example, would buy a Guardi to remind them of Venice in the same way that we buy postcards today. The change from Guardi to a postcard may be an artistic debasement, but psychoculturally both works serve the same human impulse and state a continuity between the eighteenth-century attitude toward travel in strange places and our own. As the novel expanded into the world of individual psyches, it often deemphasized and contracted the world of external nature to make that psychological focus more acute; so, too, external nature in painting became gradually more important and the presence of people often contracted. Even a portrait painter such as Sir Joshua Reynolds staged his scenes to bring out special traits of his subjects. A painting like "Mrs. Siddons as Tragedy" indicates his acceptance of a theatrical rather than an individual view of human nature. No wonder then that the great form of English pictorial art in the later eighteenth and early nineteenth century was satiric painting and drawing—Hogarth, Rowlandson, Gillray—the concentration on man as a social being, amid an often chaotic world of objects and individuals, while Blake transformed human beings into visions of the infinite.

Romanticism—as the first self-conscious multinational and inter-art movement in modern times—brought together the visualizing and devisualizing impulses by emphasizing the subjective element in perception. In the realist movement that followed Romanticism, although its theoreticians were at first mainly writers in England and artists in France, all emphasized the same need both to express clearly a more familiar visual world and to reorganize it in either pictorial or literary form. Appropriately enough, photography appeared in the 1820s and 1830s as the tail end of Romanticism with the first experiments of Nicéphore Niepce, Daguerre, Fox Talbot, and others. Now at last the picturesque view, the overwhelming visual experiences of the "sublime," for which literary Romanticism had developed the popular taste, could be the possession of everyone—moments of grandeur, of nostalgia, of record, of a fleeting visual world, frozen for eternity. Photographers could go outside the canons of European art and pioneer new subject matter. At the same time of course there were also many "art" photographers who, through romanticized lighting, soft focus, and theatrical staging tried to "raise" photography into art. They ignored the extent to which the photographic organization of sight was changing the nature of artistic vision as well. Cultural intimidation was as present then as now. Mathew Brady, for example, considered his work to be the raw material from which painters and other "serious" artists could work. But such paintings almost invariably reduced the power of the photograph by idealizing the situation. The fixing of life was not equivalent to the preservation of its vitality.

Nineteenth-century realistic photography found its most enthusiastic support in the movement toward "realism" proclaimed by so many artists and writers. Every avant-garde art movement, whether in literature or the visual arts, took its lead from the Romantics and proclaimed the greater "reality" of its particular mode of expression over the ways of making art that characterized the past. Of course, verisimilitude of detail had played a role in the art of many eras. But the interest in some kind of explicit theoretical statement became essential for the nineteenth-century realists. They aimed to throw off the blinders of tradition and look more closely at the world with the aid of science and technology, to create a new vocabulary for art by reducing the sense of artistic intrusion to a minimum. Specification of detail would confound those who attacked the falsity of surfaces by pointing out the necessity of such knowledge for survival in the modern world. Realistic art and literature, as Linda Nochlin points out in *Realism,* equated "belief in the facts with the content of belief itself." The invisible world seemed to have been banished forever. From such a belief spring both the realistic details of Louis Lumière's early film of a train entering a railroad station or Edison's *Kiss* and *Sneeze,* as well as the seemingly more magical appearing, disappearing, and transforming objects of Georges Méliès. Lumière and Edison exuberantly display the facts of daily life as if by themselves they stated some enormous truth, while Méliès asserts the magic of continuity in a world of flux. When we see silent films now, we may be struck by what to our more demanding eyes seems like an incredible dragging out of detail: why did that scene take so long? don't they know anything about dramatic construction? But we must remember that we have already become jaded to the thrill of seeing familiar and unfamiliar things captured and transformed by film. Early films gave us simple pleasures that quickly became assimilated in a viewing vocabularly, a visual literacy that wanted further challenges. When we watch those silent films we try to—but can't quite—get back to those first joys in lovingly watching the surfaces of things; only the preoccupation with movement in the films of Keaton, Chaplin, and Mack Sennett is still so compelling. Little shadow of this pleasure in seeing things remains for us now, except in the spy and detective films, whose main pretext seems to be the loving display of exotic locales and out-of-the-ordinary milieus, and in those films whose only reason for being is the chance for us to look at someone—Sophia Loren, Robert Redford, or Linda Lovelace—for an extended voyeuristic moment.

When movies first appeared in the 1890s, however, they were not generally heralded as the latest step in the evolution of the most distinctive cultural movement of the nineteenth century. Realism had lost its revolutionary impact, and, where movies were seriously considered at all, at least in the early years, they often became a prime basis for attacking realism itself, especially for those who considered the lower-class appeal of movies to be a further barrier to true art. According to such critics, movies carried to a final absurd extreme the tendency to view reality scientifically and mechanically that more traditional representatives of culture had already attacked in realism. Early twentieth-century painting and sculpture seems to respond to such criticism by becoming less realistic. Literature became more concerned with verbal texture. As Joyce wrote of Stephen Dedalus, "he wanted to meet in the real world the unsubstantial image which his soul so constantly beheld." Photography had seemed to release painting from conventional documentary realism at the same time that it inspired a new look at the external world. In the same way movies seemed to release painting from the analysis of what the eye saw, the effort to capture the present moment that was so much a part of realist doctrine. But, unlike painting, neither photography nor film seemed difficult, and the way of high art was toward greater self-consciousness and more obvious manipulation. Audiences became familiar with assertions about reality that excluded any recognizably representational work, platonic definitions in which detail or the visually plausible was a confinement to be escaped. The Abstract Expressionism of the postwar period developed the tendency of earlier abstract and cubist painting to denigrate visual reality in favor of the artist's insight beyond the surfaces of life. Not a little of the intellectual disdain for film springs, therefore, from its appearance at a time when works of high culture were considered to have gone beyond realism, in the same way that Joyce, James, and Conrad were thought to have transcended the simple realism of the nineteenth-century novel. The literary prejudice against realism has essentially disappeared and the artistic attitude has changed dramatically in the last few years. But the critical prejudice remains, in the refusal to consider movies to be both a natural artistic outgrowth of nineteenth-century attitudes as well as a critical reaction to those attitudes comparable to that embodied in the works of Picasso, Léger, Kandinsky, Mondrian, and Gris. The snideness about Norman Rockwell and Andrew Wyeth may be disappearing in the wake of Philip Pearlstein and Richard Estes, but the representational nature of film is still considered to be a drawback because it is not chosen.

Early film critics tried to get around the seemingly unwilled and uncontrolled quality of film realism by emphasizing the articulation of the image, presenting the filmmaker as a shaper of his materials who worked as obviously as the novelist or the painter. Such director-theorists as Sergei Eisenstein and V. I. Pudovkin often made direct analogies between film and literature. But later critics purged references to the other arts and announced the purity and importance of the film image as the most "cinematic" element in a film, designating montage—the association of images—as the essence of film "language." It was in fact appropriate that such critics worked, or their ideas were formed, when the coming of sound threatened in their eyes to destroy the artistic achievement of the silent film. Sound, they argued, would make the film too close to a transcript of reality, and the only test of art was the extent to which the filmmaker had changed reality. Like the Cubists, film critics such as Rudolf Arnheim, Béla Balász, Paul Rotha, and Raymond Spottiswoode focused on the intervention of the artist in vision, directing the attention of the audience to *how* it saw rather than *what* it saw.

The second stage of film theory appeared in the 1940s and

1950s when first André Bazin and then Siegfried Kracauer began to praise the ability of film to capture a new reality rather than vary an old one. Arnheim, Balász, and the earlier critics had evolved their views in response to attacks against the lack of artistic quality in films. That battle won, Bazin and Kracauer were responding to charges that the world seen in films was excessively artificial. With the impetus of the liberation of France and the almost simultaneous appearance on the world scene of the Italian directors known as the neo-realists, Bazin asserted the essentially "realistic" nature of film in opposition, for example, to the artifice and "expressionism" of the German film of the 1920s. A moral element was added as well, so that no one would think that film theory was returning to nineteenth-century definitions of simple realism. The German films of the 1920s, argued Kracauer in *From Caligari to Hitler* (1947), paved the way for Hitler and Nazism because they were created inside studios, because they were fascinated by architecture and decor, because, finally, they were not realistic. The true end of film Kracauer wrote in *Theory of Film* (1960) was "the redemption of physical reality," which was possible because "films cling to the surface of things." If film distorts visible reality instead of recording it, the result is invariably in the service of bad politics and bad morality. Once again criticism had erected a monolithic standard for what films should be, a fruitless effort reminiscent of the building of the Tower of Babel in Lang's *Metropolis* or the inability of the French and English soldiers to bridge the gap of language in Renoir's *La Grande Illusion*. The theorists of the created image expected the best films to use the materials of reality in order to transcend it (and create for the director a recognizable style); the theorists of the redeemed image expected the best films to find the pure heart within reality (and create for the director a recognizable vision). At the extreme of one view was unqualified praise for the animated cartoon; at the extreme of the other was similar praise for the documentary. Both, in their most polemical forms, tended to ignore or deride subject matter, narrative conventions that could not be discussed in visual terms, and acting.†

† Bazin's criticism is hardly so single-minded. Some of his best passages appreciate the artifice in films, especially his somewhat cryptic essays on Theater in Film. But when he formulates any kind of definitive theory, it is always one that overvalues realistic and undervalues expressionistic elements.

While European critics fretted the problem of where artistic purity in the film could be found, American filmmakers often tended to assert, when they would say anything, that their work had no pretensions to art at all and was only a gaudy and entertaining surface. "I am a camera," wrote Christopher Isherwood in *Goodbye to Berlin* and the implication of his image would be approved by many Americans, filmmakers and audience alike: I am transparent, without ulterior motive, moral or aesthetic. For Isherwood such detachment is a real narrative choice. Realism in literature and painting can refer to either method or subject matter or both. But circumstantial realism in films is hardly ever a methodological choice; if anything, the filmmaker must choose to do otherwise. To call films realistic is similar to calling painting two-dimensional; realism is a necessary characteristic that the whole art grapples with, rather than a particular approach that an artist chooses or disdains according to his cultural moment and his individual will. If realism is to have any use as a critical term, it must be purged of any implication of moral superiority and aesthetic finality, and take its place as a description of a certain range of possibility in artistic construction, which includes subject matter as well as form, history as well as aesthetics. Better than any visual art of the last four hundred years, film has helped articulate the vexed relation between the demands of what is seen and the mystery of what is unseen. Neither the view that the surface is all-sufficient, nor the view that the surface is only the way to less visible truths, satisfies our need to respond to film in as many ways as possible.

THE CONTINUOUS MUSE

Because realistic illusion is so basic to film that anyone who starts a camera can capture a small part of its power, filmmakers often take the route of obvious technique to assert their personal authority. The history of film could be written as a history of technical innovations and the interrelations between those innovations—more sensitive film stock, more mobile cameras, more intense lighting, as well as the more apparent divisions of sound and color and screen size. But such a history must be sensitive to the way style can potentially detach itself from its roots in content to become mere visual technique—a centrifugal possibility basic to films. The knowledge of technical details is, for example, instructive to a film student, but only to a point. It begins to contaminate and confuse when it begins to disintegrate the understanding of film, emphasizing the steps in the filmmaking process rather than the final film and its effect on its audience. Without a sense of context, Lewis Milestone's use of the 360° pan shot in *Rain* (1932) is no different than Jean Renoir's use of it in *The Crime of M. Lange* (1936). It is much easier in film to imitate technical advances, without understanding the way they facilitate and enrich meaning, than it is in any of the other arts. The skill resides in the manipulation of the technique rather than in the artistic perception of the user. Many technical details—a zoom shot, a jumpcut, the use of special lenses, slow motion—have in this way become discontinuous or nonnarrative. When one describes the particular virtues of an early film and the response is "but everyone does that now," this principle of detachable technique has been ignored. Stylistic tricks have now been so traded back and forth between films and TV commercials that no one is quite sure who started them, and Vincent Canby can remark of *The Strawberry Statement* (1970) that it was "directed with all of the nitwit devices usually found in a hair-spray commercial." So the fisheye lens appears in deodorant commercials in the wake of its use in John Frankenheimer's *Seconds* and the association between slow motion and nostalgia first elaborately presented by Sidney Lumet in *The Pawnbroker* (1965) and expanded into an image of heroic loss by Sam Peckinpah in *The Wild Bunch* (1968) becomes a visual signifier for the pastoral world of Salem cigarettes.

Films demand continuous attention. They give us a sense of the uninterruptible, an unflowing of time that we cannot stop, although we can turn away. But if we turn away, we know that we will miss something, and the more we miss of the continuous context a film creates, the more the objects in film detach themselves and return to the "real life" that gave them birth. To our discontinuous eyes, people and things don't necessarily *live* in a film; they *reside* there, they *happen* to be there, even in the most stylized costume drama or *Caligari*-like studio film, with painted perspectives and nightmare trees. It is the continuity of audience concentration and the continuity of visual context and style that hold these potentially discrete and detachable objects together. The essence of reality is its lack of dependence on us, the variable speed with which it can escape our control. Movies interrogate reality not by recording objects, but by establishing a frame in time within which objects can achieve momentary meaning.

This continuity in the definition of its world structurally separates film from the performance-oriented arts of music and theater, and relates it more closely to the novel as a timeless exploration of temporal processes. One could in this way arrange the arts of human presence along a continuum of pattern and movement. From ballet to theater to film, the need to pay attention becomes greater and greater, the threat of interruption more annoying. Except by experimenting with narrative itself (which I shall discuss later in this chapter), film has no structures that allow for interruption. In the theater there is always a sense of potential interruption, and Brecht's effort to break the illusion is less an avant-garde disruption than a disquisition on a basic part of the theater experience. But ballet and theater have ritualized their interruptions into acts and scenes and movements. And to complement the sense of potential interruption of which I have spoken, the historical pattern of their subject matter moves away from realism toward ritual or varieties of ritual realism (like *A Streetcar Named Desire* or *Death of a Salesman*). Consider fighting in ballet, theater, and film. In ballet we know the fight is stylized; in theater the potential for actual disruption (that may include the real personalities of the actors) is markedly greater, and in film the violence may pour out over the audience, even though in viewing the filmed action we are actually the farthest removed from the real people. As the form that accepts narrative interruption the least, movies can include much more intense conflict and violence. The patterns of ritual movement or the form of the proscenium stage that hold together ballet or theater are gone in film, and in their place is a sense of continuity, the invisible connections of film art that hold together the world of visible objects, whose essence seems to be unritualistic, unpatterned, and unpremeditated.

These and other distinctions I shall make between the arts are not exclusive, but a difference in emphasis. Jean Renoir and Akira Kurosawa, for example, will often play between artificial and realistic elements. But, for Renoir to lose his popular theater and Kurosawa to lose his Noh play methods would deprive us of an important source of artistic complexity and pleasure in their films. The stage has used film techniques less successfully; and it tends to use the most stylized and technological, such as the documentary. TV commercials, of course, institutionalize interruption in film and may thereby aesthetically disrupt a commercial film. But, in fact, the uninterrupted BBC film may be a less authentic expression of the aesthetics of television than the American commercial-ridden program. The television image is only one of many visual items claiming our attention in the room, as opposed to the single focus of the movie screen. The continuity of television is not only within its own elements, but also with all the other objects surrounding it. The problem of attracting and keeping attention in television is, therefore, a much greater aesthetic-thematic problem than it is in the normal film. Since the television attention span is usually much shorter than that in any other art, an emphasis on family becomes very important—from situation comedies, to the variety shows with a continuous host and supporting actors, to the talk shows—because then the images on the screen can form a link with the people in the room. The more visually patterned a film is, the better it will come off on television. Horror films, Lang's or Hitchcock's films, and almost any film made in the 1950s are perfect for television. But interruption is infectious; every movie-goer must have noticed how the need to eat, talk, and go to the toilet increases after sustained diets of television viewing.‡

When we look at the world, for a moment it's our own, even though we know we cannot keep it. When we look at a movie, we should know that its world is someone else's, even though it is continuous with and may seem to be the same as our own. In a photograph, reality is captured and partially revealed, but for a

‡ Creative exploration of the special needs and gifts of television is obviously another answer. Many television shows are even now developing techniques—many of them presaged by experiments first made in the 1950s by Ernie Kovacs—that might energize future commercial films or, more probably, point the way toward the independent development of the artistic resources of television. I am here thinking especially of experiments with depth perception, the mingling of live and prerecorded footage, the psychological use of color, and the overloading of visual information in the frame—all of which seem to be fruitful areas of further exploration.

frozen moment. The objects exist, and the photograph will reveal relations, visible and invisible. But the invisible relations are ultimately subordinate to the visible separations. There is a condescension in photographs, no matter how much the photographer may empathize with his subject, because the need to make *one* statement excludes the possibility of other statements. But film, in its images and in its continuities, can make the single statement at the same time that it makes a more qualified statement through juxtaposition with other images.

THE SHAPING EYE AND THE RECALCITRANT OBJECT

What does the filmmaker and the cameraman love the way the writer loves words? Not style, the detachable bits of technique that anyone can imitate, but rather the potential of objects to create a world, the potential of technique to become meaning. Films can be assorted according to their use of montage, their camera style, their status as products of a particular national school, their subject matter, their place in the career of a particular director, and many other variables. But the most characteristic element in any film is the way it presents all its objects— animate as well as inanimate. In films every object has four dimensions—the realities of length and height, the suggestion of depth, and the potentiality of significance. Objects in film gather significance the way snowballs grow when they roll down hills, by the repetition, accumulation, and mere persistence in our eyes. When we watch a play, our gaze may wander away from the center of attention to wonder mutely at the importance of a table or a glass pitcher. When we look at a painting, we are necessarily limited to one angle and one distance. But when we look at objects in films, as when we look at people's eyes, we do not perceive what they are so much as how they are directed, what their regard is toward us. Throughout Jean Renoir's *A Day in the Country* (1936) a storm threatens. Nowhere is the storm emphasized, until the rain actually falls. But the storm is always present— intangible, almost below the level of awareness, until it plays its specific part in the action. In the same way, the atmosphere of films infuses significance into everything they contain, not necessarily high-sounding, specifiable, even symbolic significance, but significance as an indication of *something more,* an invitation to go beyond the face of things, to create a narrative in which meaning often impends, frequently coalesces and solidifies, but just as often may vanish. No film is without such an attitude toward objects, their manipulability, their existence before the camera and away from it, their usefulness in creating not a real, but a believable, plausible, compelling world. It is part of magic of the film experience. It can also be a way to tell the qualitative differences between films, as well as a critical tool for investigating why some fail.

The object has been less often a topic of film criticism than the image, because the image is obviously a construction of the director, whether in the montage of Eisenstein, the analogies to painting invoked by Renoir, or the expressionist sets of Fritz Lang, Robert Wiene, and G. W. Pabst. Unless they are obviously symbolic, the objects within these constructions have usually been taken for granted, as if the objects in a film were not objects of direct choice, only subsidiary choice, like the props on a theater stage, there to lend atmosphere, aura, and occasionally symbolic meaning, deprived of a life of their own. But films create their worlds through their objects. Without necessarily resetting these objects in a new context of plot meaning, they always reset them in a new context of visual meaning and continuity. And while we may forget the specific significance of geraniums in *La Grande Illusion,* or tea boxes in *The Lady Vanishes* (Alfred Hitchcock, 1938), we remember subliminally the new transfusion of meaning the visual world has received from these films. Too often, when objects in films are discussed, they are considered either literarily —how they are significant or meaningful in a paraphrasable way —or formally—how they show the manipulation of images that is the essence of film form. I think both these methods are insufficient because they consider objects as isolated things, the way they are in daily life, either charged with meaning (the literary object) or charged with formal self-consciousness (the imagistic object), or else totally ignored. But film objects can express this kind of meaning and more. No preference need be given to one use of objects or another. Film objects can include those seemingly used only for local color or to define a scene that, taken together, also imply some larger attitude toward the physical world. They can include symbolic objects that are loaded with extrapictorial significance as used by directors such as Ingmar Bergman, Luis Buñuel, and Joseph Losey, or objects that have momentary meaning, but no lasting significance, such as those in the films of Jean Renoir and Roberto Rossellini. They can also be objects whose significance is not the significance of a particular plot or symbolic system, but of a world of nightmarish potential, such as the objects in the films of Fritz Lang and Alfred Hitchcock.

Unlike many symbolic objects in literature or painting, many significant objects in movies lose their special meaning out of context.* The fog in Kazan's *On the Waterfront* is not very much like a literary symbol. But it does add some kind of extraliteral and paraphrasable meaning to the scene: an atmosphere of moral uncertainty imaged as a lack of clarity in our view of the details. On the other hand, the fog in *On the Waterfront* is not as important to the basic meaning of the film as is the fog in the first scenes of Akira Kurosawa's *Throne of Blood* (1957), a fog in which men have literally lost their way rather than one that is a tickling nuance at the edges of our vision. The process is not as marked as the process of symbolization in literature, since objects are already symbolized in literature by being made into words. Nor is it as selective as the process of drama, where objects are mute decor unless they are involved directly or indirectly in the meaning of a scene. Neither of these visual uses of fog is, for example, like the fog in the first chapters of Dickens' *Bleak House,* since part of Dickens' meaning is that his narrator *makes* fog into a symbol consciously. It is there, but its significance is enlarged by a character, a narrative voice that may be wrong. This literary act of consciously imposing meaning is not so much a part of the themes of *Waterfront* or *Throne of Blood,* even though Kurosawa and Kazan of course called forth or approved the fog's presence. When a novelist is self-conscious about his own use of language—like Sterne, like Dickens, like Joyce—language and its abuses can itself be a theme of the novel. But when a film is characterized by self-conscious visual technique—rapid montages, odd angles—and one is consciously forced to notice the aggressive direction of the film, such technical self-consciousness

---

* For the rest of this chapter, I shall speak primarily about nonhuman objects. Section Three will apply these arguments and definitions to human beings, in terms of acting and characterization in films.

often does not reverberate on the thematic level. Technical virtuosity alone has never indicated a truly perceptive use of film. Only by a complex attitude toward the objects within the frame, whatever camera angles or other methods are used to convey these attitudes, can the director express something essential about his craft. From their own resources films lend to twentieth-century visual art the portentousness of detail, any detail, with no specific historical or traditional symbolic scheme to justify it. In the works of Giorgio de Chirico, René Magritte, and other surrealists, for example, we see isolated and arrayed objects whose meaning goes beyond the cultural expectations we have brought to our viewing. The idea of meaning has become more important than the articulation and specification of meaning, and the ability to evoke the dread of unreachable truth more important than the ability to express it with clarity and order. This effect owes its existence to the cinematic attitude toward objects and their invisible potential.

Objects can of course be symbolic in a film, as they can be in all visual art, especially when the director invokes a system of correspondences (for example, those in Christianity or American politics) between specific objects and specific meaning. At some point, however, the movie object detaches itself from the symbolic or significant object of nineteenth-century painting and literature to become something different. "Symbol" in the literary and pictorial sense does not begin to describe the kind of unfocused precision that significant and seemingly insignificant objects have in a film. All that we know of the stone that has fallen into the pool is the radiating circles of its effect. So, too, visual objects spread their nuances through films. They focus our attention less on themselves than on the possible orders that art can give to all the visible world.

This kind of continuity or contextual meaning is often destroyed by the assumption that motif or symbolic object is the deciding factor in film unity. In fact the unity of a visual method determines the selection and elaboration of motifs. Lang's closed doors, Bergman's islands, Hitchcock's stairwells, Renoir's rivers, Rossellini's streets—all lead us back to the basic aesthetic of their films, *if* the motifs are treated as indicative rather than definitive.

Any argument from the existence of the motif—to say, for example, that the eye-level shot in the films of Howard Hawks conveys a sense of democracy—can easily be faulty. The motif itself has been detached from context and used to support a speculation about the meaning of its context. But no object, no motif, in films is necessarily only what it can be defined as in the outside world; it may have a greater or a lesser relation to that definition, but it is never the same. Like Bonnie and Clyde, who hardly believe they exist until they see their names in the newspapers, the objects in films are ratified and defined by the context in which they appear. The analytic and destructive cataloguing of motif draws critical support from the theory of montage, which asserted that meaning grew from the separation and juxtaposition of images, the discontinuous space that was to be filled in by the intelligence of the spectators. By diverting attention away from the continuity of a film to its separate images, montage theory often minimized content in favor of abstract aesthetics and thereby eluded ideological censorship, introducing a pseudo-scientific language for film rather than one based on the audience's experience.

Often films that employ such technique now seem strangely dated, fated to dissolve into great scenes—the Odessa Steps in Eisenstein's *Potemkin* (1925)—or images—the juxtaposition of Kerensky and a peacock in *October* (1927). Such juxtaposition and concentrated focus reminds us of the attitude of the painter or sculptor toward objects. But unlike the art object, which demands special attention because it is framed, moved out of time and continuity into a world of eternal stasis, the film object exists in time, contextually and continually. Some films may emphasize the plot of objects, the intrigue that connects all film persons, places, and things, while others might emphasize the actual contingencies of relationships, the adventitious quality of associations. Yet both depend upon a definition of the context of continuous meaning.

The difficulty of breaking visual attention in a film is exploited by the director who makes all the objects in his world sufficient for the interpretation of it. When we say that "X was too symbolic" in a film, we mean that the context does not support the meaning we think we are expected to extend to X. This problem rarely occurs in painting or sculpture. We do not criticize the use of symbolic motifs in art; instead, we expect it and then decide if the invocation is justified, or we examine the tradition of such usage and compare the new example to that tradition. But the most important tradition of films is structural rather than motif- or object-oriented. There is no equivalent in painting or sculpture to the film sense of continuous context; films may allude to past motifs, as Godard, for example, has Michel (Jean-Paul Belmondo) in *Breathless* (1959) use the upper-lip rubbing gesture of Humphrey Bogart. But the motif must gain new meaning from the new context; unlike an apple or a pelican in a Renaissance painting it will bring in its freight of allusion only if the context justifies it. Thus the Bogart gesture has to be anchored in an understanding of Michel's character. But when James William Guercio sets *Electra Glide in Blue* (1973) in Monument Valley in order perhaps to invoke with nostalgia and melancholy the heroics of all the John Ford films set there, the choice remains an imposition upon the material with no vitality of its own.

The interpretative weight on any one object (at one extreme, to make it symbolic) interplays with the continuous reality, the collection of objects in time, that defines the film. In film nothing exists in itself, only in the way it is used, whether it be a river by Renoir, a crucifix by Buñuel, a gun by Lang, a car by Penn, or a beach by Bergman. Literary symbol hunters often become confused and confusing when they talk about films because they think of their discoveries as isolated things, copses of meaning in a landscape of exposition. But the surrounding world is a necessary part of the meaning of any film object or action. Every film teacher has, I'm sure, felt the tickle of bad faith when he calls attention to significant objects, because to summon them up and dub them with a detachable, cataloguable name can destroy them. It is another example of the tendency of films to fragment once the context of film has been removed. The frame of the film is like the frame of the painting: it gives value by establishing both relationship and concentration (the exclusion of the rest of the world). Because film technique has often concentrated most obviously on the isolation of detail, the film viewer may be unaware of the transforming power of the film context, unless he feels the new reality of a filmed geographical place. But that transformation is an essential part of the methods that film uses to create art. Toward the end of Renoir's *Boudu Saved from Drowning* (1932) the tramp staggers off with a scarecrow on his back, looking very much like a cross. In John Sturges' *The Magnificent Seven* (1960) Yul Brynner sits in front of the crossed bars of a window; his name in the film is Chris. These are not articulatable references in the same way they would be in a static pictorial work or a work of language. They are nuances, and they may even be purposeful nuances, because one of the benefits of film is that such references, if references they are, can be like shadows at the corners of vision, rather than weighty symbols demanding serious attention. To say such films have a coherent religious element would be ridiculous. Their symbolic meaning is in the atmosphere, the wisps of drifting fog.

The real hallucinatory and compelling quality of films lies in their precision, the hard edge of their objects, at the same time that we as viewers are released from our bodies and channeled into our perceptions—visual, aural, mental, and emotional— more fully than in any other art. We may move about, perceive, and feel with our only limit being the recalcitrant, resistant surface of the animate and inanimate objects before us on the screen. Film objects often convey visual complexity through nuance and even throwaway exuberance rather than through the more pictorial methods of motif collection or technical flash. A word like "atmosphere" or "aura" conveys the proper impression of integration with context, instead of the separation of object from context implied by "symbol." But atmosphere designates the meaning that surrounds something. What general words do we have to describe Hitchcock's use of color in *Torn Curtain* (1966) or Ford's use of light in *The Grapes of Wrath* (1940), where darkness comes to mean warmth and community while light implies oppression and injustice? In *Torn Curtain* the audience surrogate, filled with goodwill and confusion, is Julie Andrews, who dresses in earth colors of green and brown, while the malevolent East Germans appear in dark blue, and Paul Newman, the uncertain hero, stays spectrally uncommitted in tones of charcoal green. Does such visual shading forewarn us subliminally of the revelation that Newman is a double agent, finally revealed in an obviously artificial little pastoral park? To mention such matters verges on overstating them, for it threatens to leave out their provisional and playful existence. *Torn Curtain* is after all a comedy. And the worst characteristic of film criticism, or aesthetic criticism in general, is to focus where the artist may want the impression of a blur, to fix what the artist has created to be contingent, and to separate what the artist has worked to cohere.

THE OPEN AND THE CLOSED

There are two major ways in which films present the visible world. Risking confusion with pre-existing terms, I could call them realistic and expressionistic. Paying homage to the two defining practitioners, I could call them the Renoir style and the Lang style. Looking to their origins, I could call them theatrical and novelistic, or pictorial and architectural. Considering their attitude toward all they contain, I shall generally call them open and closed. But, whatever terms I use, they are merely shorthand for two distinct, although often in practice intertwined, ways of confining and defining the objects of the visual world.

I use the names of Jean Renoir and Fritz Lang to characterize what seem to me to be the two most distinct cinematic methods of portraying the visual world because the principal act of film creation has been historically assigned to the director and perhaps subsidiarily to the star or producer (Erich Pommer in the Germany of the 1920s, David O. Selznick, Darryl Zanuck). Recently, through the efforts of Richard Corliss and his magazine *Film Comment,* the contributions of the cameraman and the screenwriter have begun to be studied, or at least brought to the level of conscious awareness. In the evaluation of any particular film, all of these contributing artists should be considered, especially if a critic is making distinctions between the parts of a film that are successful and those that are not. But if we are searching for the aesthetic of film, we must look at the film's entire effect, and that entire effect, whether rightly or wrongly, is in the hands of the director, who must coordinate the contributions

of the scriptwriter, the cameraman, and the stars.† Because I
have provisionally defined the essence of the cinematic manipulation of reality to be in the attitude of a film toward the
objects it contains does not mean that a film without such a
recognizable attitude is a bad film. Often the visual style of a film
is the handmaiden to the script of a film, illustrating it in the best
way possible, telling its story with the highest degree of efficiency
and visual flair. Such a story becomes a film only because film is
the prevalent medium of our time, not because any essence of the
story is best conveyed by a film. Like a novel with a realistic setting, it may be intent on showing the audience a world of which the
audience would otherwise be unaware, or it may be a document of
current customs, like a situation comedy. In any case the visual
world in which its events take place is not an essential part of
its meaning. This is not a dishonorable kind of film; there are
important stories to be told in every era, and they ought to be
told in the most popular and accessible ways.

Often, too, the visual style of a film is noticeably out of key
with the script. The simple soldier-meets-girl story of Vincente
Minnelli's *The Clock* (1945) does not receive any more meaning
from the incredibly elaborate camerawork of that film. The movements of the camera, the surprising setups for various shots, the
constant visual *ingenuity* of the film is a pleasure to watch. But
the pleasure is an analytic one, more attuned to the resources of
film creation than to the potentials of film meaning. If we are
interested in assigning credit, both Minnelli and cameraman
George Folsey should share it. If we are interested in studying the
possibilities of the camera, *The Clock* might have equal place in
a course along with Murnau's *The Last Laugh* (1924), or Welles's
Citizen Kane (1941). But if we are interested in exploring how
movies make meaning in a way that differs from the other arts,
The Clock is at best a curiosity; its visual brilliance has little
meaning in itself, either in contrast to or in support of the story

† "Auteur" has been used by critics who would like to give sole credit to
the director, invoking the analogy with writing and praising especially
those directors who write their own scripts. But perhaps the Spanish "au-
tor" would be a better word, with its implication of the head of a company
or the manager of a group, like the actor-managers ("autores") of the six-
teenth century.

of the film. It exists primarily to show that there is a director present and, in this case, one who considers himself superior to his subject matter. The same situation occurs when the visual style of the film is definitely inferior to the script. *The Heartbreak Kid* (Elaine May, script by Neil Simon, 1972) exemplifies the kind of film totally defined by its script; its dimly conceived visual world illustrates the dialogue and plot with only the thinnest human caricatures and makes so many elementary mistakes of filming (conversations that visually don't seem to be between the people involved, mismatched movements) that the viewer's attention is often distracted from the words and situations. Both *The Clock* and *The Heartbreak Kid* have their pleasures, but they don't really expand our knowledge of what film can do. Unlike *Cries and Whispers* (Ingmar Bergman, 1972), which turns us emotionally inside out, and *The Poseidon Adventure,* which turns us physically upside down, such films tell us little about the special resources of their chosen form.

The open and the closed film are part of a historical and aesthetic continuity, not antagonists but collaborators in the way films have changed our way of looking at the world. My distinction between the two marks different significant points on a continuum, formal methods that have a historical definition and become more and more mingled as films pass into the 1950s and 1960s. The distinction does not explain films, nor is it meant to substitute for them. But it does attempt to talk about films through the way they impose structures of perception upon the audience and how such structures reverberate on levels of meaning and subject matter that otherwise have no visual equivalent.‡ Let me now briefly sketch the contrasting characteristics of the open and the closed film.

In a closed film the world of the film is the only thing that exists; everything within it has its place in the plot of the film—every object, every character, every gesture, every action. In an open film the world of the film is a momentary frame around an ongoing reality. The objects and the characters in the film existed

‡ In the pages that follow, I shall make many distinctions between open and closed films, as well as describe how many films in the 1950s and later mix the distinguishing characteristics of the two styles to create a new synthesis. The special terms of that synthesis will be discussed more specifically on pages 94–103.

before the camera focused on them and they will exist after the film is over. They achieve their significance or interest within the story of the film, but, unlike the objects and the people in a closed film, the story of the open film does not exhaust the meaning of what it contains. Everything is totally sufficient in a closed film; everything fits in. Often a closed film begins with a series of images that defines its nature, teaching its audience how to watch its particular world. The circle of children at the beginning of Lang's *M* (1931), in which one child is counted out, is reflected in the circles of fatality and society throughout the film, the sense of entrapment felt by the protagonist, who is pursued not only by the police and the underworld, but also by the inner self that forces him to molest and then murder young girls. The montage of machines at the beginning of Lang's *Metropolis,* emphasizing their cold rhythmic beauty, foretells the ambivalent attitude toward technology and the future that the film embodies.

The closed film is therefore a purer or perhaps a more schematic form than the open. The open film not only opens outward, but also allows other things into it. Although retrospective analysis will show the intricate relationships in a Lang or a Hitchcock film, within the film itself there is none of the formal self-consciousness, the sense of the other arts, and the sense of making a movie, that is so often a part of Renoir's or Rossellini's story. The opening of *Boudu Saved from Drowning,* in which two of the characters cavort dressed as a satyr and a shepherdess on a stage adorned by a pastoral perspective and a broken column, allows Renoir's characters to make a visual comment on their high-flown romantic relationship in the same way that in the next scene they perform the same actions verbally, in the more realistic setting of a Parisian bookstore. Renoir's theater films of the 1950s, such as *The Golden Coach* (1953) and *French Cancan* (1955), similarly allude to the context of the other arts, with references especially to painting and music. Theater exists, painting exists, dance exists, music exists—and therefore film exists, as an object of aesthetic contemplation as well as a space to visit. But in the closed films of Lang and Hitchcock, any self-conscious reference to filmmaking itself would destroy the illusion of sufficiency, feeling that there is no other world, which is essential to their aesthetic goals. At the moments of greatest intensity, even the audience's awareness of being at a film can vanish, replaced by a sense of enclosed uncertainty about where we really are, the merging of the inside of the film with the inside of our own minds.

In the closed film the frame of the screen totally defines the world inside as a picture frame does; in the open film the frame is more like a window, opening a privileged view on a world of which other views are possible. The closed film definition of its inner space is therefore geometric and architectural, like the Bauhaus sets of *Metropolis,* the bare city street of *M,* the painted walkways of *The Cabinet of Dr. Caligari* (Robert Wiene, 1919), or the interplay between bland horizontal motel and vertical gothic mansion in *Psycho* (Alfred Hitchcock, 1960). In the open film, character plays a more important role than architecture, unless that architecture is the momentary frame inside the film frame: a doorway, a proscenium, a window. The director of the closed film has therefore created his own space, while the director of the open film has found a space within which to tell his story. The closed director is much more autocratic, controlling every detail of production, while the open director is more interested in the possibilities of the filmmaking situation itself and the discoveries that can be made in it. Renoir's world, for example, contains many unobtrusive details that may or may not turn out to be relevant to his story. But Lang's details form a plot in both the aesthetic and the conspiratorial senses; everything is significant. Renoir's camera therefore explores the contexts of the scene, instead of observing it. In *La Grande Illusion,* when Maréchal is hiding from the German soldiers in the castle, we watch them rush by and wonder where he is. Lang might have shot the scene over Maréchal's shoulder or from an overhead point of view. But Renoir watches the soldiers go by and then moves to discover Maréchal behind a post.

Renoir's camera is not identifiable with any character, but is sympathetic to all of them, whereas Lang's camera moves between total omniscience and a claustrophobic identification of our point of view with that of one character. When we watch a film and feel somehow that the camera's point of view is the perspective of the Enemy, personal or providential, we are watching a film in the style of Lang and Hitchcock. When we watch a film in which the camera stands alongside the characters as another, inquiring spectator, peering down corridors and through doorways to discover things of interest, we are watching a film in the style of Renoir and Rossellini. Kurosawa's camera in the first scenes of *Hidden Fortress* (1962), for example, stays close to his characters not to confine our vision but to surprise us (and them) by what else is in the world. Even when he employs a totally studio-built set (in *Diary of a Chambermaid,* 1946, for example) Renoir's style makes it difficult for the viewer to become claustrophobic. Even when Lang shoots out-of-doors (in parts of *Spies* and *Man Hunt,* for example), his style makes it difficult for the viewer ever to feel expansive and free. If Lang's films express a world of totally enclosed and self-sufficient meaning, Renoir's exhibit a garden of potential flowers and weeds alike. Lang is God as the head of the spy ring and Renoir is God as the chief gardener.

These distinctions imply attitudes toward the audience as well. The audience of a closed film is lured into its world or just as often pulled in, as, for example, when the traveling camera at the beginning of Hitchcock's *Psycho* pulls our attention over the rooftops of Phoenix, Arizona, and through a hotel window where we are to watch a noontime tryst between two people whom we meet for the first time. In the open film, on the other hand, the audience is invited in, as the audience is explicitly invited into Renoir's *The River* (1950) by several smiling people who are drawing a traditional Indian invitation to enter a house on the floor before us. The difference may be the difference between finding a world and creating one; the difference between using the preexisting materials of reality and organizing those materials into a totally formed vision; the difference between an effort to discover the orders independent of the watcher and to discover those orders the watcher creates by his act of seeing. Voyeurism is a characteristic visual device of the closed film, for it contains the proper mixture of freedom and compulsion: free to see something dangerous and forbidden, conscious that one wants to see and cannot look away. In closed films the audience is a victim, imposed on by the perfect coherence of the world on the screen. In open films the audience is a guest, invited into the film as an equal whose vision of reality is potentially the same as that of the director. Renoir's themes often involve the creation of a community that could include the audience, while Hitchcock's may involve the entrapment of an innocent bystander, the guest betrayed. Lang makes moral judgments difficult because we are implicated in the weaknesses he exposes, another victim along with those in the film. Renoir makes moral judgments difficult because we are being asked to include so much in our understanding. Renoir's camera may be my friend, but Lang's is often me. Lang teaches us about ourselves; Renoir teaches us about the rest of the world.

Once inside the closed film, the audience experiences a story in which plot and pattern seem imposed from above, while in an open film story is defined as a movement generated by the characters, without necessarily neat results. A characteristic of the closed film is therefore the false summary or the "happy ending," in which form itself supplies an answer, whether it is the hand of Justice at the end of *M,* the camera's discovery of the meaning of "Rosebud" in *Citizen Kane,* or the explanations of the psychiatrist in *Psycho.* The open film ends instead by focusing on the irresolvable in relationships and stories. Maréchal and Rosenthal walk away from us through a snow-covered Swiss Valley in *La Grande Illusion,* the partisans drop into the Po in Rossellini's *Paisan* (1946), the Bengalis drive back to Calcutta in Satyajit Ray's *Days and Nights in the Forest* (1970)—all escape the frame of the film without escaping the conflicts that it has helped to articulate. In *The Rules of the Game* (1939) Renoir even has two endings: the closed solution of Robert de la Chesnaye in which an accidental murder is covered over with social form, and the more somber and open-ended farewell of Marceau the poacher and Octave the failed lover—a fitting ending to Renoir's last French film before the outbreak of World War Two. Renoir is more concerned with the boundaries he hopes men can cross, the frontiers that are political rather than natural, while Lang is preoccupied by the limits, from without and within, that can never be escaped. In the closed film there is nothing offstage. As in *The Thirty-nine Steps,* theater is no refuge from violence; it must either attempt to combat evil (as do the Polish actors when they fight the Nazis in Ernst Lubitsch's *To Be or Not to Be,* 1942) or be destroyed by its own inner compulsions (like Hitchcock's Mr. Memory or Lang's Haghi). But the open film likes to explore the tension between offstage and onstage (Renoir's

Nana and *The Golden Coach,* Rossellini's *Open City* and *The Rise of Louis XIV*); theater there may be a potential refuge and source of value, a frame *within* the film that implies a conscious limitation and focus of interest. Lang and Hitchcock are often criticized for their happy endings, but it is the open film that considers the truth of a world outside the self. The truth of the closed film is the truth of subjectivity. Only the open directors could make a truly picaresque film; only the closed directors could make a film that truly explores the obsessions of the individual. Renoir and Rossellini rarely frighten us; Lang and Hitchcock almost always do.

FRAME AND CONTEXT

The motion picture frame of a closed film makes a statement about the inclusiveness of the film. All the characters and all the objects in such a film are controlled by outside forces, ultimately by the director himself. Whereas Renoir's frame implies a momentary inclusion, a provisional statement, Lang's frame subtends an entire world. In the closed film there is no escape from the logic of actions and events, while in the open film characters may walk off the frame to some section of the world the camera specifically does *not* define. In Antonioni's *L'Avventura* (1961), for example, characters are constantly walking into the frame, undercutting any belief that the scene focused on is the only possible reality, even for that moment. In *The Passenger* (1975) Antonioni takes this willful disruption of the order of the frame even further by allowing the camera in several scenes to be so interested in unpeopled areas of wall or natural scenery that it is only reluctantly pulled away to photograph the unraveling of the plot. Like Renoir, Antonioni places his frames inside the visual field instead of identifying them with it. In contrast, Stanley Kubrick in *Barry Lyndon* (1975) constantly pulls his camera back from his characters to subordinate them to the more inclusive vision of the director and the formal beauty of the landscape.

The films of Lang and Hitchcock are filled with deadly coincidences, and the entrapment of innocent bystanders. The closed film director does not elicit order from the world; he imposes order upon a world perceived basically as a chaos of people and things. The imposition may resemble ritual, allegory, fantasy, romance—or dreams. Often an entire Lang film is presented as a dream. In *The Woman in the Window* (1944), for example, a university professor of criminology first denies that murder can be accidental and then is enmeshed in a set of circumstances that force him to commit one himself. At the end of the film, the murder is revealed to have occurred in a dream that visited him while he dozed in a chair at the faculty club. Many critics at the time objected that this ending was another cop-out, some odd form of happy ending. But Lang's basic aesthetic emphasizes the truth of such dreams. Once again, we are entrapped by the frame. The film convention in which the beginning is an end and the content of the film is flashbacks (for example, *The Power and the Glory,* William K. Howard, 1933; *Citizen Kane; Double Indemnity,* Billy Wilder, 1944; and *Mildred Pierce,* Michael Curtiz, 1945) emphasizes the fatalism of the story. Alfred Hitchcock's lying flashback in *Stage Fright* (1950) and Billy Wilder's flashback told by a dead man (*Sunset Boulevard,* 1950) have pushed the convention almost to self-parody. But the paranoid point still has power; as at the end of *Caligari,* in which the narrator is revealed to be an inmate of an insane asylum, the dream does not qualify our identification with the film—it enhances it.* Although we may be fascinated by the character who accidentally commits a murder, we do not necessarily identify with him. But when we discover that his murdering was a dream, we become more identified with him through our own half-perceived, dreamlike impulses to violence. Hitchcock's use of psychiatry in various films has similarly been criticized (*Spellbound,* 1945; *Psycho;* and *Marnie,* 1964, for example). But once again the emphasis is on dream rather than explanation of detail. Psychiatric explanation in all Hitchcock films reduces the power of dreams

* Kracauer in *From Caligari to Hitler* says that Robert Wiene was forced to put a frame story around *The Cabinet of Dr. Caligari* and thereby undercut what could have been a savage attack on German society after World War One. Fritz Lang, who was the first director approached about the project, has said that the frame story was present from the beginning. But, even without this historical testimony, the frame story, as in all closed films, intensifies the impact of the film instead of qualifying it. Kracauer, like many anti-expressionist critics, tends to consider the psychological to be an attack on the political. But in closed films—and in films in general —they work together.

to words and formulas. Whatever falsification of actual psycho-analytic methods one might object to in such films, the symbolic point, the way in which Hitchcock has absorbed psychiatry into his aesthetics, remains clear. He uses external intellectual systems with the pure opportunism of the true artist.

The cinematic assertion of the power and reality of dreams that is typical of closed-film directors comes from that aspect of the film experience that is dreamlike, and the sense in which films appear to the audience as waking dreams. Susanne Langer has philosophically popularized the film-as-dream viewpoint. But she considers the dream element in films to be escapist. The closed film actually raises the fear of never waking up. In a television film, *The Deadly Dream* (Alf Kjellin, 1971), Lloyd Bridges plays a scientist who has made the discovery that DNA can be changed inside a living person. In his dreams he is being beaten up for discovering this way of manipulating people. When he awakes, the scars from the dream beating are real, and finally he is killed in his dreams. Even closed films desire to have consequences outside themselves. They are not voyages into the impossible so much as they are, in the words of the title of a Méliès film of 1903, *across* the impossible, and then necessarily back to tell the tale. Lang's professor waking from his dream is the audience waking from the film, with the same hope that the experience has changed them, that it has not been mere escapism, to be easily compartmentalized, catalogued, and then ignored. Hitchcock's films like *Psycho* draw neither power nor authenticity from any Freudian analogues. They lure us with the depiction of a dream within a dream, and the possible consequence that, as the Red King's sleep implies, a dream within a dream is real. By asserting the one-to-one correspondence between outer and inner reality, the visible world and its invisible connections, closed films imply that both dreams and films have consequences, and that both film satire and film propaganda can work.

The counterpart in closed films to the inner framing and chosen framing of open films is the involuntary enclosure, the physical prison and the prison of the self. Both Lang and Hitchcock are fascinated by the courtroom, the closed context of judgment in which the audience and the jury are identified (*M; Fury,* 1936; *The Paradine Case,* 1947; *I Confess,* 1952). The accused in

the courtroom, the traveler in the haunted house, the innocent in
the prison or the insane asylum, the victim in a natural disaster—
all are variations of the basic closed-film situation. Like such
characters, we in the audience are trapped without the possibility
of transcending or understanding why this has all happened, unless we identify with the director who has brought this world into
being. Thereby we become both defendant and jury, blind victim
and malevolent God. The tight social worlds of 1930s comedy,
with their stylish safety, the prison films of the 1950s, with their
microcosms of social repression, the disaster films of the 1970s,
with their blindly unleashed natural forces—all place the individual within an environment of rules he has not made. Their
aesthetic is closed, with its emphasis on the similarity of the
movie-screen frame, hostile society, gloomy architectural enclosure, and the frail human mind. The comic view of society
in the closed films of the 1930s, so often set in hotels, ocean liners,
or otherwise isolated structures, requires that the world of forms
be rejected by a combination of love and personal style. But the
later closed forms are more powerful. The upside-down claustrophobia of *The Poseidon Adventure* which occurs in the middle of
the unavailable openness of the ocean outside, is only the contemporary version of a paranoia about our helplessness before
events that has been the special subject of closed films since the
earliest days of cinema. There will be survivors. But the greater
truth is that nature and society are in league to bury us alive, in
the same way that we have passively submitted ourselves to the
world defined by the huge screen before us. Even when that
screen has shrunk to the size of a television set, the totally
organized and internally consistent visual form of the closed film
can be enough to rivet our attention and involve our feelings.
Lang's and Hitchcock's films are almost always effective on
television; Renoir's and Rossellini's films are rarely so.†

† Television in the past few years has increasingly experimented with natural locations, although often the story itself has the structure of a closed
story. The counterpoise to the entrapped situation in the closed film is often
the community of the isolated. The aesthetic of the closed film therefore has
special affinities with stories about or including circuses—*City Streets* (Rouben Mamoulian, 1931), *Freaks* (Tod Browning, 1932), *Saboteur* (Alfred
Hitchcock, 1942), *Nightmare Alley* (Edmund Goulding, 1947), *The Greatest Show on Earth* (Cecil B. DeMille, 1952), *The Naked Night* (Ingmar
Bergman, 1953), and *Some Came Running* (Vincente Minnelli, 1959) being
an interesting handful in the sound period.

Because frames limit space, they can arouse a feeling of inarticulate foreboding in the audience. There is, for example, much
more weather in open films than in closed films. When weather
does appear in a Lang film, for example, it is another indication
of malevolence, for example, the fog in *Ministry of Fear* (1944),
not the eruption of a chance world into the lives of the characters,
as in Renoir's *A Day in the Country*. There is very little sky in
most Lang films. One of Hitchcock's most brilliant scenes
occurs in *North by Northwest* (1959), when Cary Grant stands
in a flat midwestern landscape under a broad sky, seemingly safe,
but soon to be hunted down by a crop-dusting plane, previously
just another seemingly benevolent and irrelevant detail in the
open landscape. Lang may leave out the sky, but Hitchcock
plays with the expectations of openness that the sight of the sky
invokes. Renoir, Rossellini, or Satyajit Ray regard nature as a
reservoir of potential in which they and their characters can find
personal meaning. But nature for Lang, Hitchcock, or Kubrick is,
like the frame of the film itself, an imposition of destiny, even
death, on the character caught inside; it is a magic book whose
clues are open only to the director and the audience. The so-called
"humanistic" impression given by Renoir's films derives from the
open and contingent relation between people, places, and things
within his narratives; the frequently attacked "inhuman" quality of
Lang's films derives from his insistence on a total visual schema
of every person, place, or thing in his films. Renoir defines the
possibility of the world; Lang explores its thwarting of potential.
Renoir's films are experiential because they allow us to live in
situations not our own; Lang's films are experiential because, no
matter what the situation, he enforces the absolute identification
between our own position as spectators and that of the characters.
The open film indicts society for its public face, its day-to-day
brutalities; the closed film indicts society for its oppression of the
inner life.

Open and closed are distinctions rather than absolute differences, a revolving door of visual meaning. The great directors
can therefore set for themselves a dialectic of confinement and
release. Vehicles are obviously confinements of a sort and each
type of film uses them in a characteristic way. Since the closed
film is so concerned with the atrophy and weakness of the will
faced by constraints and limits, it is attracted to the train, a

vehicle that subordinates its passengers, whisking them along into adventures that may be unwilled and undreamed of. When the camera looks outside the train that takes prisoners to an internment camp in *La Grande Illusion,* we see only the rapidly moving countryside, never the frame of the train window, and the structure of the film is the effort, finally successful, to escape. The closed films that take place primarily on trains—such as *Shanghai Express* (von Sternberg, 1932), *The Lady Vanishes, The Narrow Margin* (Richard Fleischer, 1952), and *The Sleeping Car Murders* (Costa-Gavras, 1965)—restate the paranoid premises of enclosed films in general: there is no escape, and yet all the answers are here as well, if you are wise enough to look for them. No one is a real prisoner on these trains because everyone in the film is a prisoner of its universe.

Because open films are concerned with problems of freedom and self-definition, trains tend to take a subordinate place to cars, unless the trains invoke a sense of social and personal fatality (as in Renoir's *Toni,* 1935, and *La Bête Humaine,* 1938). Whereas cars in closed films tend to be out of control (as in Lang's *Dr. Mabuse* (1922) and Hitchcock's *North by Northwest*), cars in open films indicate the direction of a character's will. In two Rossellini films of the 1950s (*Voyage in Italy,* 1953; *Fear,* 1954), the increasing problems of a marriage are visually expressed by the wife driving the car while the husband is the passenger. So, too, in open films a car can embody the cultured insularity of the Bengalis in *Days and Nights in the Forest* or the mingled assurance and uncertainty of the upwardly mobile hero of *The Middle of the World* (Alain Tanner, 1975). In the 1950s especially the car was used as a metaphorical extension of identity; in *Rebel Without a Cause* (Nicholas Ray, 1955) the ability of the hero (James Dean) to use a car properly is part of his initiation into the high school community, involving life and death. One of the most elaborate uses of vehicles appears in *The Great Escape* (John Sturges, 1963), in many ways a visual elaboration of *La Grande Illusion,* in which a whole camp attempts to escape rather than two men. The choice of vehicles here almost explicitly involves a special nuance: the English prisoners reveal their willingness to subordinate themselves to authority by taking trains and buses (and finally getting caught and killed), while the more anarchic spirits take more personal vehicles—a boat, a bicycle, a motorcycle—

and either escape or are returned to the camp alive. A more complex use of the car appears in *Bonnie and Clyde* (Arthur Penn, 1967). The enclosure of the gang's car, so essential to the success of their robberies, is finally fatal to them. Many scenes are concerned with being trapped in the car, either as a stranger picked up by the gang or as Bonnie and Clyde themselves are in the final ambush; the most persistent image in the film is the car with its inside lights on, rocketing over a darkened prairie at twilight (imitated by Terrence Malick in *Badlands,* 1973). Penn, as befits a director who made his first film in 1958 (*The Left-Handed Gun*), mediates his interest in enclosure with a sense of the potentially open world that his characters cannot achieve. In a few of his early films Lang had included small details that had little to do with the plot, in order to emphasize the inclusiveness of what remains. In *Spies* (1928), for example, a small boy asks a nightclub doorman for some money and, when he gets it, somersaults and runs off the left side of the frame. His presence indicates another world at the same time that it highlights the self-absorption of the master spy Haghi and his official antagonists, which is the main content of the film. In *Bonnie and Clyde* Penn expands this contrast. On the periphery of the film he has placed other characters, often blacks, walking by, leaning against a building, watching with bemused grins while a holdup is in progress or a gang member tries to get his car out of a tight parking space. They define the interior of the film because they are what is omitted: an outside world whose existence the obsessed main characters have failed to acknowledge. Penn gets much of his strength as a director from his stage experience, his ability to extract performances from actors. He is attracted to characters obsessed with breaking out of some confinement: Billy the Kid from his mind (*The Left-Handed Gun*), Helen Keller from her body (*The Miracle Worker,* 1962), Alice Brock from her age (*Alice's Restaurant,* 1969), and Jack Crabb from all of these (*Little Big Man,* 1970). But the visual strength of his films springs from his implicit understanding of the dialectic between open and closed, visual freedom and visual confinement.

What happens when a director does not "understand" the different claims of the open and the closed worlds? John Schlesinger seems to me to be a good example of a director whose films often break apart because he seems neither explicitly nor implicitly aware of the effects of those claims on what he is trying to express. In Schlesinger films such as *Darling* (1965), *Midnight Cowboy* (1969), and *Sunday Bloody Sunday* (1971) what I have been describing as a complex interaction between openness and enclosure becomes a destructive paradox. Specifically the conflict is between the accurate observation of the facts of social reality and the exaggeration of those facts for the purposes of satire. In *Midnight Cowboy,* for example, Schlesinger constantly undercuts our belief that he is accurately observing New York lowlife by including such unnecessary exaggerations as a scene in which a man lies on a Fifth Avenue sidewalk while crowds stroll obliviously by. Why does Schlesinger pick one of the least likely places in New York for this scene to happen? The film gets much of its power from its realism of milieu and character, but the man on the Fifth Avenue sidewalk is not a human being. He is a bit of satiric business, a mechanical joke that makes us wonder about the realistic claims of the rest of the film. Satire in films has often been presented either as a form of social reportage (*The Rules of the Game*) or as conscious farcical distortion (*Doctor Strangelove,* Stanley Kubrick, 1963). But Schlesinger is always confusing the two. When *Sunday Bloody Sunday,* for example, concentrates on the emotional intricacies of the three-way situation (woman, bisexual man, homosexual man) that is its subject, and when it includes such well-observed scenes as that at the Bar Mitzvah, it becomes very effective drama and satire of the social observation sort. In these parts of the film Schlesinger and Penelope Gilliatt, his scriptwriter, present with taste and tact and without sensation a human situation that in the films at the time was fairly uncommon. There are details of character that could be called satiric, but they are well integrated with our ideas of the specific nature of the three people at the center of the film. Even in this film, however, there are satirically exaggerated depictions of minor characters that may make the audience wonder about the reality of the central situation. The party with an aggressively arguing husband and wife, the permissive socialist parents and their pot-smoking children—both seem like situations precut for polemic reasons. In response to this imbalance, the audience may wonder about the sloppiness of Glenda Jackson's character, the concentration with which Schlesinger has detailed how she grinds out cigarette ashes on her rug. Is that a real or a satiric gesture? Is it part of her character or part of Schlesinger's interpretation of her character? Is Jackson's effort to create a plausible character in conflict with Schlesinger's desire to make a satiric point? With the appearance of such questions the coherence of the film, its effort to represent a continuous and consistent world, is lost once again. Although we are expected to view the situation as open and comparable to one that could appear in our daily life, the characters are treated like objects or sight gags by Schlesinger's urge to propagandize. Instead of learning more about the characters and their world, we may wonder why the director hates them.

Satire in film demands an agreement about limits. What distortions of recognizable reality are we willing to accept to further the satiric ends of the film? Film satire is therefore very different from, say, musicals or science fiction films. Those films say "accept my world and its standards totally or don't accept them at all. It is irrelevant to apply the criterion of recognizable reality to what's going on here." But film satire constantly asks the viewer to *compare* what's going on with a recognizable reality. How else would it be an effective satire, if the satiric and the real were not in constant interplay? Schlesinger's problem (and, I would say, the problem of such films as Milos Forman's *Taking Off,* 1968, and Lindsay Anderson's *If . . .* 1967) occurs when the picture of a morally deficient reality does not enforce but actually conflicts with a more stylized satirization of abuses. The existence of satiric exaggeration undercuts the documentary assertion of real abuses by allowing the viewer the possibility of dismissing them as yet another exaggeration; the director's moralism sinks his storytelling. Mike Nichols is a satirist with similar problems. *The Graduate* (1967) works because it immediately establishes that the film's point of view corresponds to the point of view of Benjamin, its main character. The subsequent satire of his parents and their milieu is easily understood as his idea of them, and finally his own point of view is in its turn satirized. But in *Carnal Knowledge* (1969) the nostalgic reportage of the first sections slides imperceptibly into exaggeration and stereotyping until the viewer feels betrayed. Candice Bergen, who plays the only mysterious, potentially complex character, disappears from the film, and two-dimensionality, *mere* satire, takes over. Because there is no implicit perspective the film falls apart in search of the easy successes of shock and verbal wit. Schlesinger and Nichols both have trouble sorting out the human from the satiric in their characters. But Nichols is put in jeopardy by words as well. In *Carnal Knowledge* and *Catch-22* (1970), he brings the word play of Jules Feiffer and Joseph Heller to the screen and leaves the characters behind. Lured by the discontinuities of verbal wit, he attempts to hold his films together with visual tricks (especially in *Catch-22*), but the result is a shambles of incompatible tones. *The Graduate* in retrospect seems more like a lucky coincidence than an accurate perception of how film satire works. Like *The Fortune* (1975), its strength is less dependent on wit or profundity than on comic movement and stylized characterization.

Essentially, Schlesinger and Nichols never knew or have forgotten the importance of the frame around movie reality. Satire especially needs the frame to be successful. When, for example, people are to be regarded as objects of ridicule, the audience must have already committed itself to the film's special perspective; otherwise, what is meant to be satiric or comic will seem only cruel. The frame may be the perspective of a single character, a pervasive tone of exaggeration, a distancing into history, or many other possibilities. But there must be a frame, because our appreciation of the satiric point is bound to our belief that the director knows how to manipulate the terms of the artifice he has chosen. Richard Lester in *A Hard Day's Night* (1964) uses the frame of the music of the Beatles to bind together an assortment of semidocumentary scenes of the group on tour, verbal jokes, and absurdist antics. *Help!* (1965) is less successful because the plot is farcical, the Beatle songs more set pieces, and the comic bite therefore more episodic. The satire of *A Hard Day's Night* has become a series of one-liners, a method that has been successful in film only when, as in a film like Olsen and Johnson's *Hellzapoppin* (H. C. Potter, 1941) most of the jokes are made at the expense of the medium itself.

Another problem in the creation of film satire is the different effects of black and white and color. Open films imply that the world outside us is complex, difficult to understand, but basically benevolent; closed films imply that it is understandable, usually malevolent, and virtually impossible to escape from. So long as all films were in black and white, the distinct transformations of the visible world represented by the open and the closed film could have equal perceptual weight. When films first began to be made in color, it became clear that black and white was more conducive to presenting a closed and self-sufficient world, while color implied potential openness, in part because an older technique always implies a conscious choice of aesthetic limitation for effect. *The Wizard of Oz* (Victor Fleming, 1939), while not the first color film, illustrates the new aesthetic problems the technical advance brought. Normal life in the film (Kansas) is in black and white; fantasy (Oz) is in color. The theme of the film is be happy with what you have: the Scarecrow is already smart, the Tin Woodsman already has a heart, the Cowardly Lion is already brave. The magic of the Wizard is just a series of illusions and he, like Dorothy, would be better off back in Kansas. But Kansas is in black and white. However secure and satisfying life there is, it does not match the heightened reality of color. When color became the standard visual method of a majority of films, the world of black and white seemed even more confined and limited. Mario Monicelli in *The Organizer* (1963) therefore uses black and white to invoke a nineteenth-century past. Color had become the easy choice. With the added inducement of Cinemascope, lesser directors moved away from cities and toward location shooting and milieu setting in the same way that their aesthetic ancestors thoughtlessly used studio sets and shadows in the era of black and white.‡

The realist urges of color therefore press Lester as they press Schlesinger. Since *A Hard Day's Night* is in black and white,

‡ Neither Lang nor Renoir makes a total commitment to color. Lang uses it in westerns (*The Return of Frank James,* 1940; *Western Union,* 1941; *Rancho Notorious,* 1952), a costume drama (*Moonfleet,* 1955), and a war film (*An American Guerrilla in the Philippines,* 1950). But his heart seems to belong to the purer world of black and white. After 1950 Renoir's films are mainly in color, with a return to black and white for a Jekyll and Hyde horror film (*The Testament of Dr. Cordelier,* 1959) and a prisoner-of-war film (*The Elusive Corporal,* 1961).

while *Help!* is in color, more emphasis on the frame should have been necessary rather than less. Lester's sense of satiric form (and subject matter) fragments even further in *How I Won the War* (1967) and *The Bed-Sitting Room* (1969). Like Mike Nichols, he seems to think that inventiveness, whether in technique, situation or dialogue will make up for the lack of coherence. Lester's control happily does return in *The Three Musketeers* (1974) in which the satiric and the realistic elements work smoothly together because the frame is the glorious past and the way we have perceived it in countless swashbuckling films. Slapstick can exist here because it has some standard to play against. In fact, it more than exists; it becomes another element of the film's complexity. When Lester's musketeers miss no opportunity to kick an opponent in the groin to win a battle, when his Louis XIII forgets which side to stand on to begin the minuet, when a character falls comically into a well and gets hurt—the audience believes that these situations are probably more true to the way it really happened than are the myths of historical romance, in which everyone in the past knows all its rules. Without a sense of frame, we know neither the rules nor the deviations. The James Bond films are successful satires because they play Bond's flawless personal style against an editorial-cartoon version of world politics. Satires of Bond films succeed only at those points where the original slips and takes itself seriously. Otherwise they are like people who make a career of imitating impersonators.*

Until fairly recently, the successes of film satire tended to be in what in the seventeenth century was called tragical satire (as opposed to comical satire). The perspective in tragical satire is melancholic, focusing on the necessary limitations of human aspiration by the rhythms of nature and society. Unlike comical satire, which deals in exaggeration, tragical satire can be totally

---

* Lester's recent disaster film *Juggernaut* (1974) similarly ruins the effect of its situation (bombs have been planted on a ship at sea and demolition experts have to be flown in to find them) by fragmenting our attention between the ship and London, where the operation is being coordinated. We have no empathy with the leader of the experts (Richard Harris), at most only an admiration for his technical expertise. By drawing our attention to his own manipulation of the visual world of *Juggernaut,* Lester loses the claustrophobic power of such films as *Lifeboat* (Hitchcock, 1943) or *The Poseidon Adventure* and turns the final defusing into a petty triumph rather than a grand finale.

realistic, even surrealistic in plot, because the satire both attacks and employs the aesthetic and social forms that define it. Comically exaggerated satire works best in a written form, where the presence of the narrator mediates between the exaggeration and the reality to which the exaggeration refers. In film, where there is no narrator, or rather, where the narrator has to be consciously brought in (like a voice-over), the audience can lose sight of the line connecting reality and exaggeration. Ernst Lubitsch therefore played against the frame of social form and Preston Sturges often worked against the context of the small town. It is fitting that the most successful films of the later, more surrealistic satire should be made by directors whose basic aesthetic is that of the closed film: Stanley Kubrick's *Dr. Strangelove, 2001* (1968), and *A Clockwork Orange* (1971); John Frankenheimer's *The Manchurian Candidate* (1962) and *Seconds*. Kubrick fits definitely into the tradition of Lang and Hitchcock because of his fascination with aesthetic limits, whether those of the crime film (*The Killing*, 1956), the war film (*Paths of Glory*, 1957), or the science-fiction film (*2001; A Clockwork Orange*). His increasing interest in decor in *2001* and *Clockwork Orange*—his total control of the details of his set—further illustrates his affinity with them. Once we have accepted the standards of his totally enclosed world, we can accept everything inside it, even the somewhat disruptive verbal wit of Terry Southern's names for the characters in *Strangelove*. Instead of the archness with which we view the world of Ratso Rizzo and Joe Buck in *Midnight Cowboy* we realize that everyone in *Strangelove* is deadly serious; it is the world itself that is insane. Schlesinger is worried about emphasizing details that the audience might miss; Kubrick realizes that once he has established his control of the film's visual world, all the details will fall easily into place. *Barry Lyndon,* with its moralistic narrator and its oppressive preoccupation with decor, shows how unsuited Kubrick's style is for expressing individual vitality. Since all must finally be subordinated to the director's vision, the film can only gesture at the supposed energy and complexity of the central character. Casting the weak Ryan O'Neal as Barry completes Kubrick's aesthetic ascendancy.

Both *The Manchurian Candidate* and *Seconds* have this same combination of a serious context for surrealistic occurrences. But John Frankenheimer came to an understanding of the aesthetic of the closed film from a somewhat different route than Kubrick. Frankenheimer began his career in television, which, although it had no direct inheritance from the Lang-Hitchcock tradition, offered an obviously compatible visual situation. (*Alfred Hitchcock Presents,* begun in 1955, has been one of the most long-lived of television successes.) If any subject matter is typical of television drama as it developed in the 1950s, it is the effort to characterize familiar, lower middle-class and middle-class milieus, in short to document a new reality, in the Philco Television Playhouse and Playhouse 90, in the work of Paddy Chayefsky, Rod Serling, and Robert Alan Aurthur. But the *situation* of all these characters was an entrapped one, whether in a job, marriage, or personal nature. Born in black and white, the television aesthetic was an enclosed one, and so its subject matter dealt with varieties of enclosure, no matter from what ostensibly naturalistic source the material seemed to be derived. The film directors who had television experience— Frankenheimer, Arthur Penn, Sidney Lumet—therefore learned how to deal with enclosed space, learning as well the subject matter that suited their methods. Their careers grew as a dialectic of method and subject matter, each pushing the other a little further each time. Documentary method and personal intensity are the hallmarks of this period in television, and, as part of their re-energizing of American film, the television directors brought documentary and subjectivity together. Better than directors like Schlesinger or Nichols, who are confused between open form and closed subject, they can integrate the objective impulse of documentary with the subjective impulses of the television emphasis on closeups and personal problems. From such elements comes the power of films like *The Manchurian Candidate* and *Seconds.* Frankenheimer uses them to create a kind of satire that is both plausible and unbelievable at the same time, an interplay between psychic and physical confinement. It is a visually oriented satire because it mingles objective realism and subjective distortion without compromising either. Frankenheimer followed his interest in enclosed spaces into two prisoner films—*Birdman of Alcatraz* (1962) and *The Fixer* (1968)—and a classic vehicle film, *The Train* (1965). But his ability to handle satire is dimmed in *Ninety-*

nine and $^{44}/_{100}$% *Dead* (1974), where an effort to merge comic-book violence with realistic situations breaks apart on the same rocks that doomed Schlesinger and Nichols. The problem is partially due to the star, again Richard Harris, whose visual presence conveys a shallow nastiness that fails to hold together the disparate styles. Frankenheimer is much more successful in *French Connection II* (1975), where he has a strong central character ("Popeye" Doyle played by Gene Hackman), whose paranoid vision of the world connects the episodes of the film with a steely spine. Satire that is uninterested in character, like that of Stanley Kubrick or Richard Lester or Mike Nichols, needs paranoia to be effective, and paranoia is easier in black and white than in color.†

MAGIC, SCIENCE, AND RELIGION: CONNECTING THE VISIBLE

The meaning of objects in the world often depends on the system of invisible connection we have chosen to explain them. The meaning of objects in a particular film depends on the kind of continuity the director creates according to his aesthetic leaning toward the open or the closed form. The visual world of the open film gives the audience an incomplete message because it asserts that there are always more details to be considered. The visual world of the closed film gives a complete message because it asserts that all details are the expression of an invisible order. In the broadest sense all art and all films are the product of enclosure; the way a director creates meaning within his film must be the product of prior decisions to limit his material, his treatment, his methods, and his setting. But, within this general context of artistic reordering of the world, the

† There is a slowly growing tradition of comical satire, represented especially by *The Graduate*, Howard Zieff's *Slither* (1973), and the films of Paul Mazursky. These films typically have a picaresque narrative that winds through various social settings; their subject is American life, whether seen by the student in *The Graduate*, the ex-convict in *Slither*, or the retired English teacher in *Harry and Tonto* (Mazursky, 1974). Since the structure of the film is defined by a particular character, the satiric vision of the director and the scriptwriter becomes part of his nature instead of being an imposed interpretation. Luis Buñuel's success in satiric films also comes from an acute sense of the disjunctures possible with narrative in color and a surrealistic feeling for the potential of objects. See pp. 71–74.

aesthetic motion in a closed film can be described as a burrowing inward, an exploration of inner space, an effort to get as far as possible into the invisible heart of things, where all connections are clear. The comparable movement in an open film is more dialectic, an interplay between artifice and the reality that refuses control, which escapes interpretation not by its mysteriousness but by its simplicity. The house and the vehicle may entrap characters in closed films, but the more pervasive visual settings in open films are the street and the river, which come from outside the frame, pass through it, and continue on.

Film occupies the shadow area between the scientific, accumulative, and objective perception of objects, and the magical, deductive, and subjective use of objects. Science tries to describe and thereby preserve the solidity of objects, while magic works to transform them, to reveal their inner potential. Science seems to search for isolated detail, but actually tries to consider each detail as part of a system of total meaning. R. L. Gregory has pointed out that scientific advance has led to the greater and greater symbolization of the world, as each object takes its place in and refers to a larger system of explanation. Magic attacks science because it does not seek to explain publicly, nor do its explanations have a democratic validity. Magic is aristocratic science, open only to the initiate and the true perceiver. It places less weight upon the interrogation of objects themselves than upon their connections in the invisible world beyond the physical. And it has the ability to change one object into another. Films are equally fascinated by scientific laboratories and the dark catacombs of the magician. Figures like Lang's Rotwang (in *Metropolis*), Victor Frankenstein, Dr. Jekyll, and Dr. No bring the scientist and magician together in a typically cinematic conflation.

Both magic and science meet in the significant object, whose meaning reveals a usually malevolent pattern in the world of things. The connection between objects in a closed film is not their existence in the world, but their existence in a pattern of visual significance created by the director. Since characters are a part of this inner space, the meaning of objects and situations in closed films is transmitted directly from director to audience, often leaving the character ignorant or unmoved. In

Fritz Lang's *Destiny* (1922), Death enters an inn where a newly wed couple are having a honeymoon drink out of the inn's special wedding glass, shaped like a linked pair of hearts. Death orders a beer and silently watches the young couple. The young man's gaze wanders to Death's beer glass, which changes into an hourglass. In horror, he drops and breaks the heart glass. Who makes these objects mean something beyond their physical nature? Death makes his glass change into an hourglass for the moral improvement of the young man; the young man inadvertently but appropriately drops the heart glass for the director and the audience. The young man does not have to interpret the change into an hourglass, but we have to make an interpretation, admittedly minimal, of the breaking glass. Natural objects, with their continuous connection to the world around them, have been transformed into separate significant objects. No innkeeper comes out to berate the young man for destroying a cherished possession—and even if he did, it would only ironically illustrate the transformation from object to symbol the glass has undergone. Similarly, in *Metropolis* the young son of the manager of Metropolis descends to the huge machines and thousands of workers in the heart of the city. There he watches workers toil up a long stairway where a central machine roars. All of a sudden the machine turns into a giant mouth, while the workers become Egyptian slaves toiling up the stairs between its mighty legs. "Moloch!" the young man shouts. He has seen this vision, but it is not his alone. It is a vision of the machine world that the audience is to share, not an insight into the young man's fantasies or character.

Although the symbols in these films are seen by characters, they still exist more definitely in the world of some larger meaning—equivalent to the visual structure of the film—of which the characters are at best only dimly aware. Characters in closed films travel in trains at night, with small knowledge of what goes on in other compartments and none at all of the nature of the engineer. Any vision of the transformed meaning of things is a vision of the true order of the universe, the fatalistic linkages of meaning that make the world whole. The closed-film director knows that meaning and his objects are subordinated to it. Like the guns in Lang's gangster films of the 1950s that are so often

seen in closeup, such objects have taken on a sacramental meaning, transubstantiated within the film's total form into something
more than themselves. Every laddered venetian blind in the
Lang-influenced American films of the 1940s and 1950s carries
with it the same aura of fatality, of the omnipresent evil in the
world that flows effortlessly into objects and needs only a suitable
situation to emerge.

In open films characters create their own space. Instead of
being internally consistent, therefore, the objects in open films
express a continuity with their three-dimensional fellows outside
the frame. The shock of isolated significance is rarely part of
their effect, and often it is only in retrospect that they raise
themselves out of the ambience of plot and scene. Whereas the
objects in a closed film may appear to us as significant immediately, the objects in open films become clearly significant
always through the conscious choice of the characters. Both
Rossellini's *The Miracle* (1948), with Anna Magnani, and *Stromboli* (1949), with Ingrid Bergman, end with long climbs, as
Magnani ascends to a monastery to give birth to a child she
believes was fathered by St. Joseph, and Bergman climbs over
the volcano of Stromboli trying to get to another town and
escape from the island. Neither of these climbs is "symbolic" in
the sense that the character does not understand the supraliteral
meaning of her action. Magnani climbs to the monastery to find
the solace and community she has been refused in the town.
Bergman is a Scandinavian refugee who marries an Italian soldier
primarily to get out of an internment camp. But the island turns
out to be just another prison. Her climb is no more imper-
sonally symbolic than is the fact that in the film she almost
always wears shoes, while her husband goes barefoot. Bergman
chooses to wear her shoes: the meaning of her act is part of her
personality and part of the fabric of the film. In the same way
she tries to liven her house by painting a tree on the walls. Her
husband enters and asks why she wants a tree in the house.
The world is not just there, implies Rossellini; it requires a
viewpoint to make it live. Facts are mute and morally neutral
until the eye gives them meaning. Rauffenstein cuts a geranium
in *La Grande Illusion* when Boeldieu dies. He has already said
it is the only flower in the gloomy prison-castle. He makes it

into a symbol of Boeldieu's life, just as he has stylized himself with white gloves and a tightly fit uniform. His choice of symbol is Renoir's way of showing us his character, specifically because the choice is a conscious one. In open films such details tell us more about the insides of the characters than they do about some hidden substratum of the film of which the characters are unaware.

GODS IN THE FILM

Film is potentially the most atheistic of the arts because it resembles the novel in the substitution of the artist for God the creator. Even the fatal forces that control the world in the closed film are less a statement of Manichean fatalism than an embodying of the director's personal pessimism. The religious phase that appears in the careers of open directors like Renoir and Rossellini calls upon the incantatory use of real objects, without recourse to the magical transformations of the closed film. The objects are still solid, still themselves, but in a religious context they are infused with extraphysical meaning, just as in other films by these directors the characters impose meaning upon their world. Religion for the open-film director is equivalent to the painted and enclosed sets of the closed-film director; both imply a total context of meaning for the otherwise inert facts of the world. Religion functions for the open director like the elusive peripheral characters function for the closed director; the one indicates a way toward total, nonhuman explanation, the other a way out of such explanation. While Lang and Hitchcock presuppose the malevolence of the natural order, Renoir and Rossellini believe it is either benevolent or neutral. Their religious films therefore have a strong tone of pastoral myth, perhaps best represented in Rossellini by the first scene of *The Little Flowers of St. Francis* (1950), where St. Francis and the brothers walk down a road and cross a stream, singing and talking, all in a pouring rain; and in Renoir by the purification of technology-tainted relationships in *Picnic on the Grass* (1959) accomplished by the presence of a Pan-like bearded wanderer, complete with goat and pipes. Depending on the director's degree of self-assertion—the place in his personal aesthetic of

the definition of his own role as creator—the order of the
world in the plot of the film is either imposed or discovered as
the imposition of God (in a director interested in religion) or
some total force opposed to God (in a director who is interested
not in the question of belief but in the question of order). Unlike
Renoir's goatherds, poachers, and impresarios, Lang's metaphysical geniuses Dr. Mabuse and Haghi expect and receive fanatic
loyalty from their underlings, who would rather die than betray
them. They repress any physical desire or the more generalized
reaching out to another in order to further the aims of the
Organization. Obviously Lang's world is Manichean; God has
vanished, to be replaced by His modern equivalent, the spy
organization that knows everything and exists everywhere, with
a mysterious omnipotent figure at its head.

Ingmar Bergman is a director whose attitude toward religion
seems dependent on the aesthetic of the closed film, especially
in his early works. But Bergman is from a later film generation.
He began his film career in the late 1940s and what is aesthetically assumed in the films of Lang and Hitchcock has become
much more problematic, crossbred with attitudes more typical of
the open film.‡ Bergman's treatment of visual objects springs
from the heightened meaning that natural objects achieve through
religion, the imposition of God's providential meaning upon the
things of the world, either to form a definite pattern or because
God sees these objects, events, and people and thereby justifies
their existence. But Bergman is such a successful "symbolic"
director because he rarely uses symbolic objects in isolation. His
characters believe in the symbolic resonance of their own worlds
and they transmit their belief to the audience. If the meaning of
actions, objects, and characters in a film like *The Seventh Seal*
(1956) were imposed by the director, the whole experience
would have a hollow feeling to it. But Bergman's characters are
engaged in their world and gain substance from it. Like characters in an open film, they assent to or resist the meaning of events
in their world instead of being unconsciously controlled by them.

Like Lang and Hitchcock, Bergman perceives the world to be
an array of otherwise disparate or even chaotic things on which

‡ For further discussion of the interweaving of the open- and closed-film
styles after World War Two, see pp. 99–103.

meaning has to be imposed through fantasy, allegory, ritual, dream, paranoia, or religion. But Bergman departs from Lang and Hitchcock by blaming God directly for the need to create such meaning. Unlike Lang, Bergman in his films up to *Winter Light* (1962) is fascinated by belief—belief expressed specifically as the desire to understand the things of the world to be meaningfully connected. Bergman's world in these films does contain a mysterious figure, akin to Lang's Mabuse or Haghi. But he is more often expressed as emptiness, the "spider God" of *Through a Glass Darkly* (1961), the false illusions of *The Magician* (1958), the impersonal fatality of *The Seventh Seal,* the tank of *The Silence* (1963), whose title stands as an image of the motif of empty search that preoccupies Bergman up to the early 1960s. The writer in *Through a Glass Darkly,* who observes his schizophrenic daughter in order to gather material for his novels, is Bergman's image of the heartless creator, absorbing the life forces from others to make them into art—a simultaneous image of the film director and God. No matter what shape a director like Renoir or Rossellini makes of the world outside himself, he believes that the order of nature from which he has drawn the details has a life and a continuity of its own. But for Lang, Hitchcock, von Sternberg, and the early Bergman, aesthetic form is both a salvation from the chaos of things and an assertion of personal ego and demonic control. As Bergman has said, "The religious problem is an intellectual one to me: the relationship of my mind to my intuition." But simultaneously he must attack the way "the individual has become the highest form and the greatest bane of artistic creation" and remind himself that "I am really a conjuror," who in later films such as *Persona* (1966) calls attention to the film frame and the process of film creation itself in order to free himself from the pretense of the sufficiency of the medium.

The kind of God, the kind of control, that forms part of a film director's themes is therefore almost inseparable from his aesthetic vision of the way to make films. The film that utilizes religious symbols or imitates the religious process of symbolization is a special case of the closed-film definition of the world because it draws upon Catholic and Protestant ideas of the mixture of matter and meaning, solidity and significance, in an object.

Luis Buñuel, although his personal beliefs are militantly anti-religious, is as aesthetically influenced as Bergman by religious attitudes toward the meaning of the visible world. Surrealism in Buñuel's early films is defined by a variety of transubstantiation —the change of wine and wafers to blood and flesh—but worked by atheists rather than believers. The fluidity of objects in *Le Chien Andalou* (1928)—the way breasts will change to buttocks, a hairy armpit to a hole with ants crawling out—states surrealistically what Buñuel constantly rephrases in his later films on a more narrative level: nothing in the world exists in itself, but also as a reference to something else, and therefore every object, every person in the world, has the potential of changing unexpectedly. Every shoe fetishist in Buñuel's films has the power of accomplishing what God or the director can do: transform the meaning of physical objects by personal choice. (What was buzzing in that box in *Belle du Jour?*) Fetishism, surrealism, and Catholicism exist for Buñuel in an aesthetic continuum. Symbols can be applied to anything, even their literal opposites. With a beard and a rough cloak, the Marquis de Sade becomes Christ. The episodes of *The Discreet Charm of the Bourgeoisie* (1972) and *The Phantom of Liberty* (1974) extend to the level of narrative the belief that no order or meaning is innate. Buñuel's subject is less the story than the expectations of the audience about film form, how a story is told, what objects mean, and what suspense leads to. Buñuel uses an association of images, a plot of objects, to cohere what his characters separate. The bourgeois obsession with food, money, and language that the films so wittily document is exactly that kind of meaning that Buñuel has condemned from the beginning of his career. His hatred of the bourgeoisie springs not so much from any concerted political philosophy as it does from an aesthetic one, founded on the belief that religious modes of patterned meaning and bourgeois modes of possessive meaning are oppressions of the eye, the mind, and the spirit. Institutionalized belief is not belief but tyranny. Buñuel's characters, like the couple in *The Phantom of Liberty* who call the postcards of Sacré Coeur and Notre Dame "obscene," force meaning on the world. But the true freedom is the director's play with meaning, his ability to indulge his whimsey at the expense of the hard surfaces and rigid ideologies of the world.*

Whether the context is Protestant or Roman Catholic, Bergman or Buñuel, consubstantiation or transubstantiation, the mixture of matter and meaning in film objects fascinates the religiously oriented director, no matter what role religious belief plays in his own life. What role can belief play when everything is already there? Coleridge's concept of the willing suspension of disbelief is irrelevant to film because the problem is not to believe in something that you normally do not. No act of will is necessary. If there is any problem, it is extracting yourself from the cinematic illusion that is so much more believable than your normal life—Coleridge in reverse. How could he ever anticipate the extent to which the ideas that people have of themselves and their relationship to others and to the world could be influenced by an art form? Bergman and Buñuel explore through their films the special way religion has influenced our view of the physical world. And we might not know that religion has had this effect without their films.

Buñuel and Bergman basically explore the mystery of infused objects. Does the director, with his commitment to the visual world, discover God's meaning in objects or impose his own? Few of their characters, like few of Lang's characters or few of Hitchcock's, achieve any understanding of their worlds in the way that Renoir's often do. Most of their films end with a kind of blankness, for the characters as well as spectators, like the staring ostrich at the end of *The Phantom of Liberty,* about to plunge its head into the sand. The final vision remains the director's. In each film Buñuel has further explored his own premises; his career is in its way as pure as Lang's or Renoir's, and the films of his old age much more impressive than theirs in their experimentation and control. Bergman, as befits a younger artist, has changed more definitely, following the subjective implication

* Alexandro Jodorowsky's *El Topo* (1971) merely imitates Buñuel's manner without his meaning. The Buñuelian images of decadence and degeneracy have become mere symbols, isolated and sensationalistic—and the anticlericalism that is often one of Buñuel's themes because it expressed his ambiguous feeling about Roman Catholicism has in *El Topo* become an adolescent business of using Bibles for toilet paper.

of the closed view of the world to its logical next step in the psychological film. *Winter Light* is Bergman's final attempt to examine the truth of the religious or theistic assertion of meaning. His main character, a minister, cannot prevent a despairing man from committing suicide, because his own faith is so weak. The final scene, in which the minister decides to preach in a parish church even though the only people present are the sexton, the organist, and the minister's mistress, implies that meaning finally is personal, not divine. We find our own truth in things, not God's truth. Accordingly Bergman's films after *Winter Light* concentrate more and more on psychological and personal modes of meaning. The piece of glass that is first placed and then stepped on in *Persona,* the photographs in *A Passion* (1970), even the footage from *Shame* (1967) that is included in *A Passion* have meanings made in collaboration between the characters and the director. One of the most lasting images from Bergman's films places formally dressed people, often in period costumes, within an out-door setting—human order and style within the lushness of nature. Color also has its thematic effect on Bergman. Its tendency to give objects a firmer surface allows him to concentrate more on actors than on himself or God, and, in *Scenes from a Marriage* (1974) he has also attempted to work with the less restricted narrative forms allowed by television. God is finally gone for Bergman, whereas Buñuel, who never thought God was there to begin with, can continue his dialectic combat, using God's terms but coming to opposed conclusions.

The increasing number of enclosures in Bergman's later films— the island, the many houses—show his need for an inner frame once the frame of the divine has been removed. John Ford accomplishes the same effect through the frames of geographical space and historical perspective. Ford can make picaresque films, like *Stagecoach* (1939) or *Cheyenne Autumn* (1964), because the frame of Monument Valley is a naturally enclosing and stylized setting within which the characters are free to define them-selves and their community. In *The Searchers* (1956) the terms are reversed: the creation of inner space amid the grandeur of western nature images the confinement and fear of the ranchers. The doorways of the cabins shut out the possible complication of the world outside. Such visual rhythms in Ford's works help ex-plain why a director usually considered to draw so heavily upon the West and its scenery and its sense of physical expansiveness could also make films like *Sergeant Rutledge* (1960) or *The Man Who Shot Liberty Valance* (1962), in which the elements of theatrical stylization—obviously false sets, artificial lighting, heavy makeup—are so strong. Ford's sense of film space needs an enclosure to define it. It forms part of a continuum that includes Bergman's islands and Hitchcock's use of trains, courtrooms, and such theatrical pieces of geography as Mount Rushmore or the Statue of Liberty.

The vision of the director—his choice of a space and its framing pattern—must be apparent to the spectator in these films. Often the patterning observer is himself part of the film, for example, in Joseph Losey's *Figures in a Landscape* (1970). Losey is a director whose basic images include many varieties of enclosure—the house in *The Servant* (1963), the past in *The Go-Between* (1971), or the genre in his early gangster films. His style was developed in the 1950s, in America and England—the final flowering of the closed-film style before the triumph of color and the wide screen. *Figures in a Landscape* begins with Robert Shaw and Malcolm McDowell running with their hands tied behind them over a rough landscape reminiscent of southern Spain. To the viewer familiar with Losey films the scene at first seems strange: how could there be a Losey film with so much space and sunlight and freedom? Of course the men are tied, much too long for any plot necessity, and then the larger confinement appears. Shaw and McDowell are being watched and throughout the film will be followed by a helicopter, whose point of view we share. The ambivalence is clear. We are related sympathetically to the men on the ground. But the helicopter is our point of view because it is Losey's. At the end of the film we stay not with the men on the ground but with the helicopter in the sky, morally compromised but aesthetically pure. Instead of a parable of totalitarianism, Losey had made a parable of the ambivalences in his own directorial point of view, perhaps politically committed to the underdog, the men of earth, but aesthetically tied to the God's-eye-view of the director in the sky, who connects all things and abides all questions.†

† There is a vogue for helicopters in European films of the 1960s. But the point of view is usually from the ground up. We look up at the helicopter in the beginning of *La Dolce Vita* (Fellini, 1959), outside the hospital

The aesthetic paranoia of the closed film often produces the paradox of a personally liberal director whose chosen style is implicitly authoritarian. Losey and Lang are only two such examples. Kubrick's *Barry Lyndon* similarly aligns the director with the doom that awaits Barry rather than his personal energy. Open-film directors rarely use overhead shots, let alone an established overhead point of view, because the world their characters inhabit is only part of a continuous environment that extends beyond the confines of the film. If the character can leave the film, if the object has an irrelevant meaning, the total scheme —whether rational or irrational—that a closed-film director explores is destroyed. When the helicopter herds Shaw and McDowell in the Losey film, when the helicopter descends to pick up the mentally disturbed Karin in *Through a Glass Darkly,* when Lang views his characters from high overhead in films such as *Spies* and *M,* the detachment of the director implies the possibility of an invisible transcendence made visible for a moment. This presence is almost necessarily malevolent, for it invokes a connecting deity who is detached from the plot of the film, inaccessible to the intelligence or perception of the characters. They can only flounder about in a world whose meaning was created by someone else. Behind Bergman's God who answers no questions is Lang's Mabuse or Haghi, who runs his organization totally and firmly, brooking no revolt or personal assertion.

THE THEME OF THE OBJECT

Unlike novels and paintings, where the world is totally and obviously created by the artist, in films, no matter how much control the director and the set decorator have over every object in the scene, we may still feel that the objects are there by chance and may at any moment vanish or extend themselves into the life

---

window in *La Notte* (Antonioni, 1960), and in the Bond films the identification of helicopter with an authoritarian point of view, especially in *From Russia with Love* (Terence Young, 1963), becomes explicit. Kirk Douglas, as the outdated cowboy in *Lonely Are the Brave* (David Miller, 1962), manages to shoot down the helicopter chasing him, but is later killed by a truck filled with toilets while crossing the main highway. Here is a "symbolic" situation in which the most explicit symbol ruins the effect of the others. Compare my earlier discussion of vehicles, pp. 55–57.

beyond the frame. Thus, more than novels or paintings, films have the capacity to present an enclosed world of total meaning at the same time that they offer the possibility of another reality outside these momentary limits. Just when the world seems most totally explained, when its pattern is about to become visible, the centrifugal force of objects, their escapability, threatens a return to chaos and separateness. The different efforts to control and order the elements of a film must constantly face the knowledge that facts escape, that objects have another life outside the film which feeds the life within, and that paranoia may vanish once you leave the theater. Renoir's attitude toward objects highlights their freedom. But, while his style is loose and episodic, his themes are often those of confinement and limitation. In contrast, Lang may count and cohere his objects with paranoid precision, but his themes often deal with the uncataloguable, the ungraspable, the invisible.

This seeming paradox becomes a dialectic within the frame of the audience's undivided attention, the viewer's urge to make his experience whole. The simultaneous fear and courtship of the invisible characterizes closed films much more than open films. Open films make no final claim about the eternity of their orders. Nature, religion, theater—all are frames for awakening meaning rather than defining it. But with the greater visual control of the closed film comes a greater apprehension about failure. The elusive fact and the ominous situation are an essential closed-film counterpoint. All detective stories in which there is some answer, some fact to be discovered, some specific time to be somewhere, some person who is the key to the mystery, parallel the necessities of the film of enclosure, in which everything in its world is part of a total truth. Bad detective films dissipate tension and empathy by making the world too open, too filled with objects and characters on missions of their own that imply other, distracting, possibilities. Whether the movie is *M, The Maltese Falcon* (John Huston, 1941), or *Goldfinger* (Guy Hamilton, 1964), the hidden hook of its allure is at that place where public fantasies and movie obsessions meet: the search for the object, the key to the mystery of time and identity.

Consider, for example, Orson Welles's *Citizen Kane* (1941) and Rossellini's *Paisan* (1946). Both are films about the effort to tell a story: in *Kane,* to patch together from reminiscences and documents the real story of Charles Foster Kane; and in *Paisan* to tell the story of the American invasion of Italy through six episodes set in different parts of Italy and interspersed with documentary footage and animated maps. But the patchwork stories of *Kane* and *Paisan* are told in very different visual styles, with different attitudes toward the material and different narrative methods. Welles's camera induces significance by focusing with great moody weight on everyday things, interrogating them to see if finally here or there is the key to Charles Foster Kane; the most emphatic example is the "solution" of the problem of Kane by the camera's discovery of the sled "Rosebud" at the end of the film. Rossellini's camera, on the other hand, never dwells on any object. His search for meaning is in the connectives, the efforts of the individuals, Italians and Americans, to break down the barriers of language. Accordingly Welles's world is nightmarish and enclosed, while Rossellini's is much more open, so open that the film threatens to fragment into its episodes, and the inadequacy of the documentary frame becomes more apparent with each interruption by the announcer's voice. Since Welles's business is with the meaning he hopes to find in objects, the sled "Rosebud," the "March of Time" documentaries, and the memories of Kane's assistants are equally important, all to be subsumed into the unceasing enclosure of the film. Since Rossellini's meaning resides principally in his effort to make connection, his own narrative is more fragmented, a mirror of the efforts to bridge gaps, to cross boundaries, and to establish relationships that preoccupy his characters. Like Lang, Welles doesn't worry about connection, because his film is already connected through an intricately ordered visual form. Like Renoir, Rossellini searches for connection through the more associative and thematically oblique connections between episodes. No character in *Citizen Kane* can make the discovery of the "true" meaning of Rosebud that is revealed by the camera, and that meaning is itself suspect because it is so flatly factual. The characters of Lang and Welles never achieve any solution, no matter how a specific crime or puzzle might be solved, because they remain isolated; the characters of Renoir and Rossellini justify themselves despite the lack of solution because they have made some kind of connection, however fragile.

In Hitchcock's *The Wrong Man* (1956), the life of Manny Balestrero, a Stork Club bass player, has been almost ruined by his arrest because of mistaken identity. But his final exoneration does nothing to preserve the sanity of his wife, who has had to be institutionalized because of the ordeal. In the last scene we are left with the image of Balestrero (Henry Fonda) trying fruitlessly to comfort his plainly unhinged wife (Vera Miles). Then a superimposed title tells us that she fully recovered and they began to lead a normal life again. But Hitchcock's aesthetic assumes that objects and objective answers never do solve anything; the questions and solutions exist only within the minds of the characters. At the end of *Psycho* the tension is clearer. While the psychiatrist "explains" what has happened, the camera takes us back to the cell of Norman Bates (Tony Perkins) and we hear him in the voice of his mother on the soundtrack and watch a fly crawl over his motionless face. The human reality mocks the tidiness of the explanation; the psychiatrist becomes a bad director. In open-ended films, on the other hand, the continuity of the film itself builds up meaning in the object. In the early scenes of Eric Rohmer's *Chloë in the Afternoon* (1972), for example, the main character buys a green plaid button-down shirt, when he is actually looking for a turtleneck. He is flirted and wheedled into the purchase by a salesgirl, who has an anticipatory resemblance to Chloë, a character who has not yet come into the film. I say "anticipatory" because her looks form a residue in our minds that recalls the previous situation: she gets him to buy the shirt by telling him she doesn't care whether he wants it or not. When he later wears that shirt in meetings with Chloë, its presence recalls his willingness to be imposed on by women, his general passivity, his strong response to women who say they don't care what he wants. Meaning in such a film is therefore created somewhat below the level of consciousness, but still within the character, not in a separate collusion with the audience, as, for example, when Hitchcock imposes a special meaning on neckties in *Frenzy* (1972) or showers in *Psycho*. In Lang's and Hitchcock's films the quest for the elusive micro-dot presupposes that the aesthetic order defining the search is itself suspect. The illusion that there is a secret which, once discovered, will explain everything parallels the search for a vanished God, now replaced inside the film by some paranoia-spawned Organization or outside the film by the director. Lang, Hitchcock, and Welles all focus on the faces of objects as if they will finally yield up their meaning. Lang's camera tracks past varieties of cigar butts, salamis, and jewelry in *M;* it examines the enlarged fingerprints and maps the police are using to track down the child-murderer; it details the elaborate search of the criminal gangs through every room of a large building—but no visual method can finally penetrate the heart of the psychotic main character, whose "M" is an allusion to the pattern on everyone's palm.

Light creates the separateness of objects, and light in closed films usually represents a malevolent clarity and control: Rotwang in *Metropolis* pinning Maria to the wall of the catacombs with his flashlight beam, or the headlights and flashlights that oppress the Joads all through Ford's *The Grapes of Wrath.* The preoccupation with the object is matched by an almost mystical belief in its insubstantiality and ultimate irrelevance. Dana Andrews in Lang's *Beyond a Reasonable Doubt* (1956) protects himself from being suspected of a murder by planting circumstantial evidence to accuse himself, and many of Lang's American films from *Fury* (1936) on explore the problem of factual evidence that is not true. Hitchcock has called the factual pretext for his films the "McGuffin"—the missing object, the vital set of plans, the one character who knows what is going on and must be discovered and questioned. Although it pretends to be vital, the McGuffin is always a diversion from the real truth. Hitchcock himself is his most prominent McGuffin, appearing personally in his films to allow the audience to step away from a world in which all ordinary objects and people seem suddenly ominous and threatening. A belief that everything in the world fits together can be the source of satire or melodrama, and Hitchcock has worked both possibilities. But Rosebud explains just as little as any McGuffin; the earrings in Max Ophuls' 1953 film *The Earrings of Madame De* . . . are the trivial links in a fatal chain of circumstances; and the possession of the robe of Christ will not cure the insanity of Tribune Gallio (in *The Robe,* Henry Koster, 1953) until he changes his state of mind as well.

Because the meaning of objects is so problematic in the closed film, blindness may appear as a relief or at least an intriguing

way to cut through the atmosphere of invisible menace and escape
the vulnerability of being seen. Lang, especially, seems fascinated
by blind characters. In 1939 Lang and Jonathan Latimer wrote a
script in which an international spy ring searched for the inventor
of a new secret weapon that destroys sight. In the final scene the
blind inventor and the blinded master spy fight it out. The film was
never made, but the early scenes of *The Day of the Triffids* (Steve
Sekely, 1963), in which the entire population of London has been
blinded by monster plants, gives a little of the flavor, as do scenes
from Lang's *Man Hunt* (1941), in which a group of blind crim-
inals stalk the streets of blacked-out London, ominously tapping
their canes in unison. By implying that blindness frees one from
the trammels of sight, Lang continues the general expressionist
attack against the sufficiency of the visual world. Renoir and Rossellini might think that there is enough ambiguity and complexity
in nature for endless exploration. But Lang and Hitchcock imply
that such ambiguity is a reason to look beyond the surface of
things because for them the visual world is filled with deception.
Hitchcock's interest in voyeurism is the perfect mirror to Lang's
interest in blindness; both constitute a post-Christian attack on the
truth of surfaces, in which the invisible cosmic order has been
identified with individual sexual and psychological darkness. By
degrees Hitchcock implicates first his characters (like James Stewart in *Rear Window,* 1954) and finally his audience as well
(especially in *Psycho*) in the act of irresponsible seeing we call
voyeurism. "Through a glass darkly"—the title of the first film in
Bergman's trilogy of personal isolation—could stand as the closed
film's motto for its entire enterprise.

Seeing for Renoir and Rossellini is a pleasure to be understood;
seeing for Lang and Hitchcock is a prison from which we must
escape. Sound offers one escape from the all-sufficient image.
Welles overlaps distinct sound with noise to convey a chaos of
connection, while sound in von Sternberg's *The Devil Is a Woman*
(1935) swells from the next scene even before the present one is
over. The character who "solves" the crime in *M* is a blind
beggar who recognizes the murderer's whistling of Grieg's "In the
Hall of the Mountain King"; a blind man's dog traps the killer in
The Naked City (Jules Dassin, 1948), a film that is almost a
catalogue of closed-film motifs. Renoir generally considers sound

to be a vehicle for the varieties of human relationships, the possible completion between human objects. Different national languages in *La Grande Illusion* (French, German, English, and Russian) are barriers to understanding until they are recognized to be as artificial as the frontier between Germany and Switzerland. Like the Italian and American spoken in *Paisan,* they are ways of testing human connection, while Lang's Babel in *Metropolis* expresses the immutable differences between people. Dialogue for Lang is not nuanced in Renoir's way, but emblematic and foreboding. Renoir may believe that human feeling can infuse sound and language with meaning, even when the words are mispronounced or misunderstood. But for Lang, sound may be another example of the invisible forces that threaten to destroy the world. The open film therefore uses music for connection and comment, while the closed uses it for punctuation, to accent the fatality of events. The sound in *M* is divided into two types: the whistling of "In the Hall of the Mountain King" that finally traps the murderer, and the endlessly uninformative dialogue about how to trap a murderer that is characteristic of both the police and the underworld gangs who are after him. Lang's sense of sound is therefore more abstract than informative, the complement to his patterned visual form. In contrast, in Renoir's first full-length sound film, *La Chienne* (1931), the story of a Sunday painter who falls in love with a Montmartre prostitute and later murders her, the sound is used for characterization and mood, to define the different speech rhythms of the characters and the music of the streets. The search for Beckert (Peter Lorre), the murderer in *M,* ends finally in the storage attic of a large building, filled with things people no longer need but won't throw away, dumped like Beckert himself into a no-man's-land of useless objects. At the end of *La Chienne,* the framed self-portrait of Maurice Legrand (Michel Simon) is loaded into a car, while the real Legrand obliviously leaves the frame of the film to have a drink with a friend. Open films make us wonder about what we've seen and the values of things in themselves; closed films make us wonder about the act of seeing and the kind of automatic value we assign to objects. Both, by their different interrogations of the visible world, attempt to give things back to themselves and transmute both divinity and demonology into what is more fruitful—different ways of seeing.‡

FACT-GATHERER AND FACT-CREATOR

The metaphysics of facts is therefore an essential part of film, whether the emphasis is on their potential separate existence or on their place in a total pattern of explanation. But it is the closed film especially that has explored the ambiguous attitude toward seeing that is at the heart of the detective and the spy story. When literary historians mention that the detective novel in the twentieth century is a natural development of nineteenth-century novelistic realism, they seem to assume that the tradition has degenerated. But film, because of the interpenetration of the detective themes and style with the visual necessities of film form, has carried on the themes with a vitality and complexity the novel often lacks. Only the weakest detective films, like the weakest detective novels, concentrate on facts exclusively. The best look as well into character. But only in films is the *conflict* between character and facts, between continuity and stasis, portrayed dynamically. So often in Lang's films there is a conflict between a policeman and a criminal genius, and through these two exemplary characters the film splits its allegiances—to the world of cataloguable, self-existing, and self-justifying facts on the one hand, and to the world of magical connection, mystical meaning, and invisibility on the other. In films like *Dr. Mabuse, Spies,* or *The Last Testament of Dr. Mabuse* (1933) the policeman is often an unimaginative manipulator of facts; his part of the film is a police procedural, with blown-up fingerprints or detailed semidocumentary scenes of

‡ The purest example of the urge to see the final undeniable fact is of course the pornographic film. Since intercourse itself cannot be totally filmed, at least by present methods, makers of pornographic films have tended to concentrate on more clearly visible activities. But the concentration on detail loses sight of the whole, and the exploitation of outlandish physical abilities or proportions blocks the efforts of the audience to empathize. Pornography has rarely if ever explored the narrative and visual flexibility of film. Instead of including the sexual scenes within the context of normal situations, pornographic films might experiment with them in the way Buñuel uses objects, not as things in themselves so much as focuses of reference, fragments of surrealistic ritual.

police investigations. His antagonist is the criminal scientist, the master of magic, like Mabuse perhaps a psychiatrist, or like Rotwang, a Faustian scientist. Their interplay reassorts the archetypal relation of Sherlock Holmes and Professor Moriarty, the metaphysician of clues and the mathematician of crime.*

Great detective novels, like Ross MacDonald's *The Chill* can also present this conflict as one between two characters (once again a detective and a psychiatrist). But in film the conflict also forms part of the visual structure. The detective generally leads a dull life. The case is the most interesting thing he does, yet he destroys it by solving it. Obsessed with method, he wants to refine his technique rather than find the answer. Facts become a way of keeping away feelings, an image of the directorial preoccupation with style. As most good detective films make clear, the details of police procedure exist primarily in contrast with some other reality. The station-house life of the police detective may be contrasted with his family life (the basic tension of the TV show *Dragnet,* descendant of so many similar films of the 1940s and 1950s) or the drab office of the private detective with the glamorous lives of his clients. In greater films the contrast between facts and connections becomes more intricate. The famous confusion over who committed one of the murders in Howard Hawks's *The Big Sleep* (1946) wryly emphasizes the way in which the lure of that film is created by Humphrey Bogart, who plays Philip Marlowe, a character who doesn't really care about facts. In one scene, for example, Marlowe has a brief dalliance with the clerk of a bookstore; totally irrelevant to any solution, it is completely essential to our feeling for Marlowe's character. Like Hitchcock in *The Wrong Man,* Hawks shows that the procedures and truths of investigative realism are *opposed* to the truths of character and audience empathy. Excessive concentration

* Arthur Conan Doyle was an eye doctor who could not make a living and began writing the Holmes stories to fill his time. Holmes often refers to his method of identifying with the mind of the criminal in order to solve the crime. The double death of Holmes and Moriarty at the Reichenbach Falls in 1893 (Holmes was resurrected in 1904) is another coincidental prelude to the appearance of movies: the private eye goes public. (The first Holmes film, according to William K. Everson, is the 1903 Biograph *Sherlock Holmes Baffled.*) For further discussion of the theme of double identity in films, see pp. 226–35.

on circumstances can threaten to destroy the mystery of human nature and identity.

Another typical character of the American films of the 1930s, 1940s, and 1950s is the reporter, like the detective or policeman a professional gatherer of facts, but one who looks more for the story than for the single fact that will complete the story. By the nature of his job, the reporter is usually a manipulator of facts and therefore human lives. In a quintessential reporter film of the 1940s like *His Girl Friday,* human beings are always subordinated to the scoops, the facts. No one seems to notice or care when the criminal's girlfriend jumps out a window, and the escaped man himself is hidden in a rolltop desk, like any other secret file. Detectives and reporters generally subordinate themselves to the world of facts; the plot of their films often allows them to discover a moral nature as well. A reporter like the character played by Barbara Stanwyck in Frank Capra's *Meet John Doe* (1941) at first occupies the same status as Edward Arnold's demagogue in the same film: both are variants of the God's-eye director who manipulates his world with much greater effect; both must either be punished or find enlightenment. The interest in the manipulative reporter seems similar to the interest in the character of the corrupt lawyer or cop: in their search for truth, the public guardians of society have lost their principles. In novels we can identify with the detective or the reporter who stands outside the pattern in order to see it. But in films, because their visual world is laid upon us, we have at least equal sympathy for the victims. The character of Superman (created in the late 1930s) attempts to solve the problem by identifying the timid reporter with the powerful but good alien, allowing him to mediate external power with inner sensitivity. He is the fantasy parallel to the reporters I have already mentioned, whose manipulative exteriors often turn out to contain hearts of gold if not muscles of moral steel.

The search for the essential fact is therefore a displacement from the search for the controlling vision, and the one who controls the facts in such films is either the director or his surrogate within the film. All the detectives and lawyers in Hitchcock must finally bow to the director himself, who may choose to reveal the truth only to a character who can discover it by accident. But a character potentially more equal to the director creates facts more often than he searches for them. He is a kind of impresario of the real. Lang's films, especially the silents, often center on characters like Mabuse (four films, two silents and two sound), Haghi (in *Spies*), and Rotwang (in *Metropolis*) who are controllers of the entire world of things. Mabuse is the head of an enormous gang of counterfeiters and gangsters; Haghi is both the president of a large bank and the head of an elaborate spy system that transcends those of all the official countries; Rotwang has created the technology that allows the ordering of society by the masters of Metropolis. They create the order of objects; much like the director, they are masters of inner space, Gods within the film. But not Gods outside the film, for in the end—like the similar characters played by Orson Welles in films such as *Citizen Kane, Mr. Arkadin* (1955), *Touch of Evil* (1958), and *The Immortal Story* (1968)—all either die or lose their power. Lang and Welles, the directors, remain supreme.

In open films the counterfoil to such characters is the man of theater, or display, who makes facts and life itself jump through the hoops of art: Renoir's Danglard in *French Cancan* or Rossellini's della Rovere in *General della Rovere* (1959). In *Jean Renoir* I have written about the way in which Renoir's films of the 1950s, especially *The Golden Coach, French Cancan,* and *Elena et les Hommes,* elaborate this figure of a detached impresario, a producer of popular spectacle, who manages and heightens reality for his audience. Such a figure is equivalent to the mystic gangsters of Lang, whose sense of the need to impose order is much more determined and fatalistic, without either a sense of play or a belief that any world exists outside their forms. A later director like Elia Kazan, whose work interestingly mingles the open and the closed, may characterize such a figure as a priest. Costume is part of spectacle and clothes, for example, are very important in *On the Waterfront*. Characteristic of the open film, Joey Doyle's jacket means something because everyone in the film has explicitly decided that it has meaning: the kids consider it to be the mantle of a new hero; the dockers see it as the emblem of the fate that will come to Terry Malloy (Marlon Brando); and Terry himself puts it on for the last sequence to indicate how he has taken on its cloak of responsibility. Everyone in the film is constantly talking about clothes: Terry's brother Charley is a "killer in a camel's hair coat"; Terry designed the jackets for the Golden Rangers; Edie Doyle (Eva Marie Saint) wears a dress that is almost a habit—the uniform of the Catholic girls' school at Tarrytown where she is a student. But Father Barry, the priest (Karl Malden), is not content to allow the jacket to accumulate meaning naturally. In a way reminiscent of Buñuel's play with transubstantiation, Father Barry's effort to symbolize ignores the individual and reaches for the universal. At the end of the film he tricks Terry into zippering up his jacket and walking onto the dock. Barry tells Terry that Johnny Friendly (Lee J. Cobb) is laying odds against him, but his real goal is to make a symbolic gesture, at whatever personal cost to Terry. Like Kazan himself, Barry stands back from the real action of the film, yet manipulating events as much as possible. He cares little for individuals, only for large gestures and significance. Kazan's directorial sympathy is split between Father Barry the manipulator of images and Terry Malloy the victim. The director's desire to organize meaning must bow to the actor's desire to embody a character. Barry believes that something great has been accomplished by the end of the film, while the audience knows that there are bigger villains that remain totally untouched (the faceless man who turns off his television and instructs his butler not to receive calls from Johnny Friendly anymore). Barry stays inside and Kazan remains outside, his visual style subtly qualifying the closed attitude toward objects and the implicit belief in society's justice that the priest represents.†

When a film concentrates on a ruler, we have an almost pure exploration of an impresario of the real who, at least in stature, can potentially rival the director. Within films the ruler's mastery is often most effectively expressed as a mastery of decor, since the way decor articulates and defines cinematic space can serve as an image of social power as well. In early films decor was the cutting edge of the visual, a world of things the viewer could luxuriate in and roll around himself. But decor in most costume films became an end in itself, mere detail, with no integral relation

† For a further discussion of the conflict between the director and the actor as creators of meaning in the films of the 1950s, see pp. 241–44.

to the plots, visual and verbal, the film could express. Costume films, like nostalgia films, place too much weight on merely being in the past. *Cromwell* (Ken Hughes, 1970), *Paper Moon* (Peter Bogdanovich, 1973), and *Stavisky* (Alain Resnais, 1974) are equally at fault. They offer an escape from the present that does not bring us back enriched. Our attention wanders from the film to meditate on the details of decor because the details have become detachable: was *Cromwell* really shot in the Fen country? is that really the site of the battle of Naseby? isn't Peter Bogdanovich great at casting minor characters? is that authentic period music? what really happened during the Stavisky riots? In *The Birth of a Nation* (1914) D. W. Griffith was so interested in the process of historical reconstruction that several of his intertitles tell us that the previous scene has been modeled on a famous painting or authenticated by reference to a standard work on the Civil War—the film equivalent of footnotes. Perhaps in this documentary way he harks back to the Biograph practice of placing their corporate logo conspicuously on some part of the background scenery—to prevent other studios from pirating those sequences. But without Griffith's controlling point of view the documentary or detail-oriented side of films separates from the fictional, the connective tissue. Decor becomes mere embellishment, like the fancy camera angles and cutting of the latest film by the newest young genius director.

To present a ruler as the master of decor preserves the true genius of film—the integration of detail with continuity, of object with meaning. Joseph von Sternberg's *The Scarlet Empress* (1934) and Roberto Rossellini's *The Rise of Louis XIV* (1966) illustrate how the analogy between film director and decor-controlling character functions in first a closed and then an open film.

Sternberg's Catherine lives in a world whose style pre-exists and for a time controls her. Even though she is played by Marlene Dietrich, a dynamic presence in her own right, we see her first submerged in the forms and ceremonies of her native Prussia, facing the world like a doll, lower lip hung open and few words emerging. She ceases to be a little girl only when she learns how to manipulate the world of Russia, with its strange style of baroque primitivism. Huge statues, mixtures of gothic distortion and Rodin-like size, people the halls of the imperial palace, often dwarfing the human figures. In several scenes, when characters sit in chairs carved in the shapes of these figures, it takes a few seconds before the eye can pick out the human figures amid the gigantic ones. The decor of the imperial palace, with its atmosphere of a gargantuan and surrealistic ski lodge, is always about to overwhelm its inhabitants. People dress in oversized clothes that threaten to smother them, as Tsar Peter is finally smothered by his pillow in the prelude to Catherine's seizure of the throne. In a more comic elaboration, Sternberg includes shots of a door so massive that it requires six chambermaids to close it.

Catherine must escape being swallowed by the decor and avoid having her individuality obliterated by the forms and desires of others, becoming a doll or a statue rather than a person. Catherine's control primarily asserts itself through her sexuality. She has been brought to Russia by the Empress Elizabeth to furnish an heir to the dim-witted Peter and is constantly associated with horses, even called a "brood mare." But, by the end of the film, in her successful move to power, she rides a horse herself up to the throne. The secret of control, like that in Lang's films, necessitates a submersion of the inner self and a manipulation of appearances. The choice presented by *The Scarlet Empress* is either to become immobile and decor-like or to get behind the decor, to use it for your ends and thus become self-moved. In the key scene, when Catherine is shown the secret staircase to the Empress' bedroom, she is simultaneously being introduced to what on the visual level is the way behind decor and on the thematic level is the secret sexual power that ties people together. All the baroque world of the palace and all of Russia become organized around this bare and secret stairway. After Catherine discovers that the man she thought loved her is a backdoor lover of the Empress, her road toward power involves an increasing coldness and distance, even as she makes herself more sexually accessible. After a fascinating scene in which she reviews a group of soldiers to see who would be both a new lover and a political supporter, she leaves, a white face shrouded in darkness, physically and personally removed, accepting and rejecting new lovers as she tries on new costumes. Did Catherine

really become Empress through making herself sexually available to anyone whose services she could use? The conviction
that such an anecdotal explanation carries is due entirely to
the way we see, in cinematic terms, Catherine's physical nature
to be equivalent to the decor of the film, and her control of that
physicality to be equivalent to the director's control of the film's
visual world. Lang may have to kill off Mabuse, Rotwang,
or Haghi because they are weaker competitors, but Sternberg
allows Catherine to live, move, and succeed because outside the
film he believes he has created the star personality of Dietrich
herself.

While Catherine gradually moves behind the decor and makes
its meaning into her own, Louis XIV in Rossellini's film actually
creates the details, the decor, by which he keeps his power. At
the heart of movies is the maxim that the king is he who looks
like the king. But, unlike Dietrich, Rossellini's star, Jean-Marie
Patte, has no previous screen image; he is a nonprofessional who
rarely changes his expression throughout the film. Sternberg
basically approves the manipulation of self and decor that in-
sures Catherine's rise, while Rossellini is more ambiguous about
its effect on Louis personally. Catherine uses the established
meaning of objects, but Louis must impress his personality
upon otherwise insignificant objects. Unlike the secret Catherine,
the secret Louis therefore becomes one of the problems of the
film, consciously imposing a façade upon himself and others.
Part of the reason for the difference is that Sternberg's basic
mode is romance, while Rossellini's is documentary; Sternberg
elaborates his story through impassioned intertitles and montages
of tortures, while Rossellini takes pages from sober history books
and includes the comments of middle- and lower-class characters
on Louis' actions. *The Scarlet Empress* is a myth; *The Rise of
Louis XIV* tries to be history. Sternberg's details are the elab-
orations of baroque fantasy, while Rossellini's are the facts of
historical documentation. But both work, as films must, through
individuals, the cold vivacity of Catherine, the blank passion
of Louis.

Rossellini's unobtrusive recording of the details of everyday
life in the seventeenth century (at least as it was passed in royal
households) firmly anchors the moments recorded in the history

books. Sternberg's details are the multitudes of drapes, veils, furs and feathers, wall hangings, and icons that encompass and determine the life of Catherine. Rossellini's are common details of normality, otherwise unnoticeable, that, through the emphasis of the camera, become fascinating and important. All of Rossellini's historical films play upon that virtually untapped desire we all have to see the normal life of the past, not its great events. In an early sequence, for example, a lady-in-waiting gets up from the mattress on which she sleeps outside the king's bedroom, enters the room, takes the king's and queen's clothes from a large chest, lays them out, and then opens the curtains of the bed so that the crowd of apprehensive courtiers who have begun to enter the room can see the now-wakened royal couple. The mortar of *Louis XIV* is just such in-between moments: the incessant walking between places, the opening of doors, the passageways, the insistent clack-clack of wooden heels on wooden floors, the echoing announcements of "Le roi!" Such details, unlike the psychic emanations of *The Scarlet Empress,* are not significant individually, but they do bring up the nature of detail itself, leading us to the problem of Louis' privacy in a world where the most intimate, habitual, and personal events are always on public display. Until Louis is alone at the end of the film, there is virtually no private moment; everything and everyone is always on stage.

The main visual plot of the film details the way Louis self-consciously manipulates this world in which objects have no hidden significance and every private fact must fit a public ceremony. We hear some complicated explanations of the economics and politics of it all. But what remains in our memories is the image of Louis seizing and mantaining power by forcing his nobles to place more and more *explicit* value on appearance and public show. Many a costume film depicts the past as merely the present dressed in funny clothes, with the praise for the film being more appropriate for the costumer and set designer than the director. Sternberg transcends this problem by making his own directorial style the object of his main character's attempts at control. In *Louis XIV,* on the other hand, clothes are reality; Rossellini's theme is the commitment of the past to its own style. The everyday detail of the lady-in-waiting laying out the king's clothes at the beginning of the film has by the film's conclusion been elaborated into a theory of government. Rossellini's specific exploitation of film aesthetics—the concentration on the object—has told us more about the social realities of the Grand Siècle than any disquisition on its politics or more abstract forces, just as Catherine's attitude toward decor makes more psychological sense of the Empress than would an account that made her into an atheistic, sexually driven *philosophe*. Late in the film Louis XIV walks through the court at Versailles and we are shown how the most casual expression of courtesy to one courtier makes that man's fortune, not by any benefits that may come as a result of the king's pleasure, but through the way people interpret that gesture of courtesy. It may mean nothing, but Louis creates the meaning and others have to interpret, whereas Catherine manipulates the meaning others have already accepted.

Catherine never changes things; she uses brilliantly what is already there—the decor of Russia, the necessities of the studio set. Her aim is to place herself in the dynamic line of succession; unlike Louis, she does not worry about establishing her legitimacy. So, too, comes the contrast between their final triumphs: she rides into the throne room on a white horse, at the head of a troop of her supporters; he sits at a large banquet table, while his courtiers watch him eat. Hers is a triumph of action and sexuality, his a triumph of intelligence and appearances. She has become the master of an inner world of decor and ceremony; he has created a world of ceremony so that he can be master of it. In his world there is always an outside, a world of others, with which he must deal, whereas in her world there is nothing else, only the self-sufficiency of the studio set and the self-absorption of her own nature. In the last scene of *Louis XIV* the king enters a private room, takes off his costume, and reads la Rochefoucauld's maxim about the power that appearances have to impose themselves more heavily than merit or birth. Louis defines himself in *Louis XIV* as a creator of appearances; Catherine defines herself in *The Scarlet Empress* as a manipulator of appearances. Both entrench their personal natures well behind the lines of their power. Allied with their creators, Louis is like the open-film director, who imposes a perception on the world outside himself, while Catherine is like the closed-film director, who works within a pre-existing world and controls it by knowing what lies behind it.

Neither Catherine nor Louis XIV, neither Mabuse nor Octave, nor any such figure within a film, is finally equivalent to the director himself, who uses such characters to distance and thereby examine aspects of his own artistic role. Movies often define a literary creator as the reality behind his fictional creation. Minnelli's *Madame Bovary* (1949) is framed by Flaubert's trial for obscenity, focusing on his famous remark, "Madame Bovary, c'est moi"; Elsa Lanchester plays both Mary Shelley and the Bride of Frankenstein; and the play-into-film, *Man of La Mancha* (Arthur Hiller, 1972), presents Cervantes acting out *Don Quixote* to a rabble of prisoners of the Inquisition. The early film directors were impresarios, simultaneously inventors, artists, and businessmen. Combining the talents of the barker and the magician, they embodied the ambivalence in their films: illusion in the service of a supposedly clear and distinct reality. Somewhere between Mabuse the psychiatrist and Rotwang the magical scientist is Lang himself, immersed in the detailed technology that filmmaking demands and yet in touch with the artistic intelligence that controls the hidden and magical connections between the things of the world. Hitchcock's casual appearances in his own films—always on the periphery of the action, a disinterested passerby—emphasize his detached control. We and his characters are anxious to figure out whatever the specific mystery of the film may be, while he, the creator and controller of the mystery, with bemused concentration loads his bass fiddle onto the train. Missing Hitchcock is like missing some key to the film's total mystery; seeing him moves you outside to a brief identification with the creator rather than his creations, the manipulator rather than the manipulated—a comic relief from Lang's more unrelieved submersion of the audience. Once again, the contrast between closed and open films helps us to make some distinctions. Since the closed-film director's aesthetic involves the formation of objects into a work that competes against the normal world of the audience, the directorial character within the film may be a scientist, magician, or detective who ineffectually attempts to bind together the meaning of things.

Such a director might never appear in his films (Lang), create a special relation to his star (von Sternberg), or impersonate that kind of character himself (Welles in *Citizen Kane, Mr. Arkadin, Touch of Evil,* and *The Immortal Story*). Renoir, on the other hand, appears in his films as a character who attempts to make connections of feeling between the other characters. He plays the role himself as Octave in *The Rules of the Game,* Père Poulain of *A Day in the Country,* and Cabuche, the falsely accused poacher in *La Bête Humaine,* while in other films it is assigned to Renoir-like characters, Charles Laughton in *This Land Is Mine* (1943) and Charles Kemper in *The Southerner* (1945). When Renoir appears as himself, to introduce the segments of *Le Petit Théâtre de Jean Renoir* (1969), he further illustrates how the open film allows a continuity between director and scene, unlike the closed-film detachment of director from scene. Renoir may be a better Octave in the same way that Lang is a better Mabuse or Rotwang, but Lang needs to kill off his film selves while Renoir allows Octave to learn his deficiencies. Until the end of his career, therefore, Lang must continue his conflict with Mabuse, whereas Renoir can absorb Octave and move on to the more benevolent impresarios of *The Golden Coach* and *French Cancan.*

OPEN WORLD AND ENCLOSED STORY: NEW FORMS IN THE
1950s AND 1960s

Most of my discussion in this chapter has been based on the distinction between open and closed styles of filmmaking. Lang and Renoir have been my great exemplars, but the difference I see between their work is much more in degree than in kind, much more in emphasis than in exclusion. The closed style is potentially more static and pictorial and thus was the perfected product of the silent-film period, even though the open-film acceptance of detail seemed to further the experiments of literary realism and artistic impressionism. Sound, by individualizing the actor and connecting the film scene by yet another element to a world like the audience's, allowed the open style to develop while the closed style could refine its gifts of claustrophobia and context. With color and the wide screen, further possibilities of the open film presented themselves for exploration. Through lighter equipment and more sensitive film stock the inner space of film could be expanded to farther and farther horizons. The technological situation and therefore the aesthetic as well had been reversed. Until the 1950s the closed-film tradition had been dominant. Whereas the open films often had to counter the conventions of the film without sound or color, the closed film developed and flourished. The 1950s represent the last full flowering of the closed-film style as I have defined it. The "normal" experience of film was becoming an experience of the open style. Neither Lang nor Renoir made very many films after 1959. (Renoir made two and Lang one.) The distinctions between their methods and visions of the world were breaking down as directors, writers, and cameramen struggled to find a new synthesis, a new way of telling stories, that could eclectically mingle the best of the open and closed styles in the light of technical and cultural change. The 1950s ushered in an era of flux in film style, an era that I think we still inhabit, in which all the old canons are being re-evaluated.

The closed style received perhaps the most severe revaluation. The concentration on architectural decor as an evidence of the special vision of the director and the articulation of that decor as the most direct expression of a film's meaning lost impact with the increasing use of color and the movement of Hollywood production out of the expensive studios and onto less expensive locations in America or abroad, with cheaper technicians and actors as well. A truly enclosed film began to have a touch of the archaic about it. Charles Laughton's *The Night of the Hunter* (1955), for example, tells a story that underlined the significance of detail so elaborately that the main character's fingers were tattooed "LOVE" and "HATE." The detail is in the original novel, but its prominent place in the film could only serve notice that much of the power of the closed form had evaporated, turned almost to parody. To make an enclosed film was at that moment a choice in the face of the greater expansiveness that was possible. *The Night of the Hunter* succeeds as a child's vision of a nightmare world rather than an adult's. Hitchcock's work continued its power, but changed. *Psycho* was a brilliant achievement in its articulation of audience involvement and complicity. But in the 1960s Hitchcock increasingly uses color and his great films of this period become more and more problematic, unless like *North by Northwest* they have obvious comic elements, or like *Vertigo* (1958) they verge on being psychotic case studies.

The first mingling of the traditions seems to occur in America, perhaps in part because both Lang and Renoir, like many other European directors, came to work in Hollywood during the war, and influenced the directors who were then seeking a personal style that might be defined more eclectically. Elia Kazan, Robert Aldrich, Nicholas Ray, Samuel Fuller, Douglas Sirk, Joseph Mankiewicz are among the great names of this period, and their work historically moves directly into the mixed forms of the French New Wave, mingling the influences of Renoir and Rossellini with the more enclosed world of the American genre films. The influx of new American directors from stage and television, like Frankenheimer, Lumet, and Penn, brought a special sense of the aesthetic possibilities of confinement to the American film. Within a confined visual field, they took a more fluid attitude toward inner meaning, mixing the characteristics of open and closed cinematic form.

But the popular recognition of the change had to wait for European validation. Neither Lang nor Renoir was a direct beneficiary. Renoir always had some reputation, but his public stature as an artist seemed excessively dependent on what the audience conceived to be his liberal, antiwar, or anti-aristocratic point of view, not the way in which that point of view was expressed. In the late 1950s cultural approval was given first to directors like Bergman and Fellini, who, like Eisenstein in the 1920s, made films that were obviously "significant" while at the same time they did not, like Lang, go in for the intellectually dubious pleasures of spectacle or genre. "Serious" filmgoers praised Bergman because in a certain sense they could read him better than they could other directors. The American film tradition, which tends more toward genre and the self-effacing director, was ignored in favor of the star directors of European cinema, or the occasional star personalities, like Welles and Hitchcock.

After the introduction of sound it seems to me that the most important change in filmmaking and film appreciation occurred in the late 1950s and early 1960s with the international impact of five directors: François Truffaut, Jean-Luc Godard, Federico Fellini, Michelangelo Antonioni, and Ingmar Bergman. These directors strikingly affected the general cultural understanding of films because they made audiences aware of films as aesthetic problems that they might not be able to figure out (the typically modernist way of determining aesthetic value). The New Wave, especially Godard and Truffaut, had a self-consciousness about film practice that drew equally on the serious and the popular traditions of film through their background as film critics for André Bazin's magazine *Cahiers du Cinéma* and their love of the American genre film. Bergman's praise of John Ford also had its effect, and for the first time audiences who had picked and chosen the film "classics" and ignored or despised the rest discovered that their new idols—the young European directors —admired American films they had never even heard of or had catalogued in their memory as trash or self-indulgence. The effect on the film audience could only be healthy. For the first time the understanding of film could be related to an under- standing of all film, not just what was considered to be "serious" films. The self-consciousness of the director in making his film extended to a self-consciousness about the tradition in which he was working. He no longer had to be either a commercial hack or a diamond in the rough, whose success had nothing to do with his understanding of the medium, just his own innate talent, flourishing in the unsympathetic field of filmmaking. The celeb- rity of the New Wave directors, the second wind of the neo- realists, and the appearance of Bergman marked the end of a cultural era in which there was a moral distinction between the serious and the popular film, between elite and mass culture.‡

In national terms, the closed-film tradition could be described as German-English-American, while the open was primarily French-Italian. Joseph von Sternberg, Erich von Stroheim, and

‡ The incommensurability between the artist and his art was a typical at- titude toward film among American and British intellectuals. W. H. Auden's praise of James Agee's film reviews for *The Nation,* while he admitted that he didn't like and rarely went to films, is a classic example. Even now, any book by Pauline Kael is sure to get a review like that of Saul Maloff, proudly emblazoned on the paperback cover of *Kiss Kiss Bang Bang:* "Reading her is better than going to the movies."

Alfred Hitchcock parallel Lang in their elaboration of the closed aesthetic. Their greatest heir, appropriately enough in nationalistic terms, is the Englishman Ken Russell. Renoir, Rossellini, Visconti, De Sica, Antonioni, Fellini, Satyajit Ray, and Akira Kurosawa elaborate the possibilities of open film. The young directors of the late 1950s drew equally upon the German-American school of studio-genre films and the French-Italian school of naturalist-milieu films. Truffaut, with his double allegiance to Renoir and Hitchcock, is only the most visible of this group in his tastes. At various times he worked with Rossellini, wrote a book about Hitchcock, and edited Bazin's essays about Renoir. Godard's heritage was just as complicated, indebted equally to a neo-realist sense of milieu, an American feeling for genre, and a Langian interest in enclosure and the varieties of suspense. Drawing genealogies for the New Wave and post New Wave directors (like Bernardo Bertolucci) would be a fascinating project, but it might become almost unmanageably complex. Even before directors were interested in exhibiting their explicit relation to the directors of the past, the quick adaptability of methods and the sense the director, unlike the solitary artist of Romantic myth, had of working in a collective tradition complicated the play of relationships. Some directors, like Dreyer, Bresson, and Ozu seem purer because they are more self-contained (and perhaps therefore considered to be "truer" artists by the critics in search of unindebted sensibilities). But most film artists are influenced by everything they think is valuable. "I am made of crumbling sands," says Renoir, "and everything around me influences me very much." There is an obvious interplay between Lang and Hitchcock, for example; von Sternberg's early work seems very influenced by Lang and Eisenstein. But, with *The Scarlet Empress* he seems in his turn to influence Eisenstein's *Ivan the Terrible I* (1944). When self-consciousness becomes an explicit part of a film's content, the combination of traditions can be even more tangled. Godard's closed-film heritage appears in his taste for flatness, for gangster milieus, and for faceless characters, like Eddie Constantine in *Alphaville* (1965). Like a good post-Langian, Godard also believes that the most effective way to complicate his narrative texture is by speaking directly to the audience, playing against the fixity of attention the closed film had drawn upon for its greatest effects. Godard expands the appearance of Hitchcock—the momentary stepping back—into an aesthetic of narrative disjuncture (such as the titled episodes in *Vivre sa vie,* 1962) and whispering voice-overs. Following closed-film morality, he makes his work explicitly didactic, with an obviously superior director. Truffaut, on the other hand, follows the more open placing of film within the context of the other arts. His self-consciousness often appears as a self-consciousness about making a movie, the explicit story of *Day for Night* (1973), in which he himself plays the director, while the director of Godard's film-within-a-film (*Contempt,* 1963) is Fritz Lang himself, a gnomic emissary from the glorious film past.

In the next chapter I shall consider the re-evaluation of film genre conventions that the work of the late 1950s and early 1960s allowed. But, in terms of the formal and visual considerations of this chapter, the basic characteristic of the new films being made in the late 1950s and early 1960s was their efforts to consider closed-film themes within an open style. Renoir and Rossellini influence the New Wave more in terms of style, while Lang and Hitchcock influence them in subject matter. The New Wave directors turned against the architectural and decorative impulses and the single-frame beauty beloved by the studio-set directors. Instead of framing and reframing characters in a scene, as would Lang, to articulate some hidden thread of relation, Truffaut and Godard moved their cameras more erratically, catching a part of a face here, allowing the body to extend beyond the frame in an invocation of that "extension" that is characteristic of the open film. Furthermore, they helped break film away from an Aristotelian form of narrative, with a beginning, middle, and end. Following the looser constructions of Renoir and Rossellini, they played against the necessary continuity of the film situation by introducing disruption into the narrative, disappointing and varying the audience's expectation of how a filmed story should be told. Alain Resnais' *Hiroshima, mon amour* (1959) and *Last Year at Marienbad* (1961) explored the closed-film definition of memory as a suffocating trap, while *Muriel* (1963) and *Stavisky*

applied the same analysis to history. Godard structured *Vivre
sa vie* in silent-film episodes and *La Chinoise* (1967) with sim-
plistic politics and primary colors. Antonioni, a neo-realist who
began his career somewhat earlier, directly attacked the closed-
film search for meaningful data by constructing in *L'Avventura*
(1959) a film that willfully disregarded the structure of plot for
the structures of character; unlike in closed films, the missing person is never found. Antonioni has probably been most polemical
in this way, but the tendency was present in all the neo-realist
directors, even such traditionalists as Visconti and De Sica. Behind Antonioni was Fellini's *La Dolce Vita* (1959), one of the
first films to have excited violent arguments over meaning. But
Fellini's theme was the way imagination creates meaning in objects
where it may not exist. The episodic, associative narrative was a
testimony of good faith in open forms of meaning. The vision of
Christ in the Campagna by the two children and the resulting
stampede and carnival is balanced by the dead fish at the end
of the film—the blankness of religious and aesthetic meaning.
In *Blow-Up* (1966) Antonioni carries the attack still further
against both the significant objects of Lang and the religious,
atmospheric symbols of Bergman. The main character is a photographer (David Hemmings), a collector of objects, an imprisoner
and imposer of meaning, who disguises himself and goes into
flophouses to capture reality. In one scene he wanders into a
club where a rock group is playing and watches the lead guitar
player attack and destroy his instrument as part of the act, whipping the audience into a frenzy. Hemmings carries the guitar neck
out of the club and drops it on the street, where some passersby
pick it up and treat it for a moment as an object of significance.
But for them it has lost the contextual meaning it had before; it's
only a piece of a broken guitar. So, too, his own search for the
fact, the truth of the murder in the park, is doomed. The more
and more he blows up the picture, the less and less he understands about what has happened. Like a Langian or a Hitch-
cockian character, he has a secret no one knows or believes
while he searches for some kind of answer that will make everything rational again. The jeep full of commedia dell'arte figures
who play tennis without a ball mock that same search. Shortly
after the photographer picks up the invisible ball to throw it back,

to show he has learned nothing, he, too, disappears and we are left with the green grass and the continuities of nature, the meaning that rests in persistence rather than in significant facts wrested from any human context.

The master image of the new aesthetic is the last shot of Truffaut's *The 400 Blows* (1959)—the open sea and the frozen face of Antoine Doinel (Jean-Pierre Léaud), potentiality and stasis, the possibility of both open extension beyond the frame and closed constriction within the frame. The basic vision seems more open because it points to the special personal vision of the director, while the closed aligns the director with the impersonal fate that rules the universe. Often these films of the late 1950s and early 1960s deal with characters who are limited in some way, especially a weak, male observer—a character who appears in one form or another in *Shoot the Piano Player* (Truffaut, 1960), *Breathless* (Godard, 1959), *La Dolce Vita, L'Avventura,* and *The Seventh Seal*—within an open, potentially liberating context. The effort to break down and expand the traditional film narrative appears variously in Kurosawa's use of the genre conventions of the American western; in Buñuel's alternation of stylized episodes with resolute walking down an unspecified open road in *The Discreet Charm of the Bourgeoisie;* and in the efforts of Satyajit Ray in the Apu trilogy to go beyond the single-film story.*

* Still photographs in film often function as a concentration of meaning. Early filmmakers, such as Sergei Eisenstein, considered the photograph to be a conventionally established symbol for the world. Later theorists, such as André Bazin and Siegfried Kracauer, defined the photograph as a casually related *index* to the subject matter, the seed of film form. But between the art photograph and the documentary photograph developed the candid photograph, which attempted to deny the paraphrasable significance of its subject matter, preserving the moment rather than any specific meaning. André Derain had said that the Fauves emphasized color to release painting from a reliance on the photograph. But the extension of the body beyond the frame typical of the paintings of Bonnard and Vuillard invokes the candid photograph against the art or documentary photograph, the incomplete world against the complete. The invention of the Speed Graphic camera in the 1920s no doubt encouraged the concentration on reporters and facts in American films: the analysis of otherwise too rapid action. But the most extensive use of photographs that correspond to the film frame occurs with the exploitation of the freeze frame after *The 400 Blows.* Crime films use stills to try to identify the dead or missing person, but films such as *Bonnie and Clyde, Butch Cassidy and the Sundance Kid* (George

Recent American road films, like *Easy Rider* (Dennis Hopper, 1969) and *Slither* (Howard Zieff, 1973), have tried to exploit the tension between closed car and open landscape, free individual and confining society, by playing Cinemascopic mobility against the uniformities of roadside life, the seemingly bland but potentially malevolent continuities of Holiday Inns and local prejudices. *Easy Rider* combines the politics of *The Grapes of Wrath* with the episodic camaraderie of the Hope-Crosby *Road* movies. But the effect is almost totally fatalistic: stable society is hostile to the traveler, even to the point of killing him. *Slither* is more complex. By fostering the feeling that there is a large organization of evil men out to get the hero (James Caan), no matter where he wanders in the United States, it draws upon the aesthetic of the enclosed film, even to the darkly malevolent recreational campers that loom on the horizon when least expected. But the film's brilliance is its upending of the conventions of Hollywood-created paranoia. The Organization is a group less organized and less effective than the main characters; their malevolence is only ordinary greed; there is no treasure after all; and the terrifying vans collapse like cardboard while the final revelations are being made. The road is really open after all. Hal Ashby's *Harold and Maude* (1971) similarly turns conventions around and builds a human story inside a cliché, principally through the self-consciousness of his characters, the roles they play, and the shiftings between the roles. Ashby's *The Last Detail* (1974) summarizes many of the new tendencies of American films, the effort to place older, more limited worlds in a new context; to view the closed film, so long our main definition of what film can be, within the larger world made aesthetically accessible by color, the wide screen, lighter equipment, and the technology of miniaturization. Even the title of *The Last Detail* invites a double reading: the final scene of actual imprisonment within previous more subtle kinds of imprisonment; the sending of a prisoner on the road where for the first and last time the prisoner can savor the details of life he had never experienced before; the

---

Roy Hill, 1969), *Repulsion* (Roman Polanski, 1965), and *Blow-Up* use the photograph not to solve a mystery but to define one—a public face of character, time, and setting that can never quite be penetrated, no matter how much it is specified.

film's effort to get familiar details of normal life—the trains and train stations, the normality of things—into a story.

The formal force of most important films since the late 1950s has been in the intensity of open *and* closed, the crossing of the barrier between film and the world, and, as I shall argue, between high and popular culture as well. Both Lang and Renoir ended their careers by returning to older themes and recapitulating past methods.† But the new directions of film narrative and style involved further experimentation and innovation. The formal and spatial analysis I have used in this chapter must give way when we come on forms so resolutely committed to mixed form and unlimited space. Another perspective is now necessary, one that will involve the most familiar, supposedly the least "artistic" of all types of film—the genre film. Fellini, Bergman, and Buñuel have their strolling players and episodic narratives, but the greater innovation of Godard and Truffaut was to introduce film audiences to the place of genre in film—the inner frame of convention that could contain a story beyond itself, perhaps the most unique contribution of films to the history of art, after the cinematic articulation of vision itself.

† Appropriately enough, Lang's career may be called circular, since in his last films, *The Indian Grave* (1958) and *The Thousand Eyes of Dr. Mabuse* (1960), he returns to the themes, situations, and even characters of his first. Renoir's final work, *Le Petit Théâtre de Jean Renoir* (1969), more a summary than a restatement, is an overview of all the styles, theatrical as well as naturalistic, in which he has worked.

Genre:
The Conventions
of Connection

Actually I do not think that there are any wrong reasons for liking a statue or a picture . . . There *are* wrong reasons for disliking a work of art.

E. H. Gombrich,
The Story of Art

No part of the film experience has been more consistently cited as a barrier to serious critical interest than the existence of forms and conventions, whether in such details as the stereotyped character, the familar setting, and the happy ending, or in those films that share common characteristics—westerns, musicals, detective films, horror films, escape films, spy films—in short, what have been called *genre* films. Films in general have been criticized for their popular and commercial appeal, seemingly designed primarily for entertainment and escape rather than enlightenment. Genre films especially are criticized because they seem to appeal to a pre-existing audience, while the film "classic" creates its own special audience through the unique power of the filmmaking artist's personal creative sensibility. Too often in genre films the creator seems gone and only the audience is present, to be attacked for its bad taste and worse politics for even appreciating this debased art.

The critical understanding of genre films therefore becomes a special case of the problem of understanding films in general. Genre films offend our most common definition of artistic excellence: the uniqueness of the art object, whose value can in part be defined by its desire to be uncaused and unfamiliar, as much as possible unindebted to any tradition, popular or otherwise. The pure image, the clear personal style, the intellectually respectable content are contrasted with the impurities of convention, the repetitions of character and plot. We undervalue their attractions and inner dynamics because there seems to be no critical vocabulary with which to talk about them without condescending, and therefore no aesthetic criteria by which to judge them, no way of understanding why one horror film scares us and another leaves us cold, why one musical is a symphony of style and another a clashing disarray.

Critics have ignored genre films because of their prejudice for the unique. But why should art be restricted only to works of self-contained intensity, while many other kinds of artistic experience are relegated to the closet of aesthetic pleasure, unfit for the daylight? Genre films, in fact, arouse and complicate feelings about the self and society that more serious films, because of their bias toward the unique, may rarely touch. Within film the pleasures of originality and the pleasures of familiarity are at least equally important. Following Marcel Duchamp and Antonin Artaud, Andy Warhol in the early 1960s announced "no more classics." In painting and sculpture this meant an attack on the canonization of museum art and the acceptance of previously unacceptable, often popular, forms. For films, the problem has usually been the other way around. "No more classics" for film might mean no more films defined as separate from the popular forms that are the great energy of film, artistically as well as thematically.

The modern prejudice against genre in art can be traced to the aesthetic theories of the Romantic period. In the later eighteenth century the older idea of poetic inspiration began to be expanded into a major literary theory by works like Edward Young's *Conjectures on Original Composition* (1759). Poetic "imitation," the building of creativity on the achievements of the past, began to fade as the standard of personal vision became more important. Only conventions that could be understood literally survived, and the eighteenth-century unwillingness to accord imaginative sympathy to convention received its most famous expression in Samuel Johnson's attack on John Milton's *Lycidas,* a poem in the form of a pastoral elegy, which drew upon a tradition of lament that went back to Theocritus and Vergil. The English and German Romantic writers consolidated this trend by establishing originality not only as a criterion of art, but, in their crudest statements, the *only* criterion of art. Art could owe nothing to tradition or the past because that debt qualified the power and originality of the individual creator. The poet was inspired by what he saw and experienced, and the intervention of any prior categories for that experience doomed the work to secondary value unless the forms that intervened were primitive forms—the folktale or the ballad —that had none of the hated sophistication of the art of the previous age. Any use of genre and convention as such necessarily debarred a work and its author from the status of true art. If poetry were defined as the spontaneous outpouring of strong feelings, how could a work that employed stock characters and stock situations, stock images and stock resolutions, have any art or originality in it? Folk art or popular art could be used because it was generally assumed that serious art was the purity of which popular art was the degeneracy, and that purity necessarily precedes degeneracy.* Poetic inspiration and self-sufficiency occupied the higher peaks of art, while hack work and despised formulas inhabited the more populated and bourgeois valleys. Genre and convention were the fare of the multitudes, while originality and storming self-assertion, without a past, without any controls, was the caviar of the truly aware audience.

---

* Ballad-collectors like Bishop Percy or Sir Walter Scott could therefore argue that their rewritings were an effort to restore the ballads to the form in which the "Bard" originally created them, before they were passed on to the fumbling brains of the folk. Pop Art has revived this theory in a somewhat different form. Ostensibly making us look at the common objects of the world with new intensity, Pop Art also conveys the idea that serious art and artists make popular themes and motifs worthy (read "self-conscious") by putting them into museum settings and charging high prices. Warhol may have first done this to satirize the whole elitist-popular division, but the joke seems to have run thin.

Until the eighteenth century, artists had generally been distinguished by their class, their education, and their patrons. But, with the growth of a mass society and a mass culture, the hierarchy shifted from distinctions in genealogy to distinctions in sensibility. Almost all of the great eighteenth-century English novelists and essayists had spent some time in Grub Street, that world created to serve the new hunger for the printed word. But the Romantic sensibility turned Grub Street into a synonym for the convention-ridden enemies of art. The true artist was noncommercial, struggling on the fringes of human existence, with neither society nor companions (and hardly any publishers), alone with his indomitable self. Only Byron, the most eighteenth-century of the Romantics, could have said, "I awoke to find myself famous" (on the publication of *Childe Harold*); such an obvious interest in the approval of a book-buying public was disdained in the Romantics' image of their calling. And Byron himself preoccupied much of his writing with the depiction of solitary heroes, striding mountainsides to challenge gloomy fates. The Romantic artist tried to make his work unique to escape from the dead hand of traditional form. The only serious use of the past was the contemplation of vanished greatness, to raise the artist out of what he believed to be an uncultured present and establish for himself a continuity with what has been best before the triumph of modern degeneracy. Like T. S. Eliot in *The Wasteland,* the serious, unpopular artist was the only one in a corrupt age who could summon up the artistic Eden of the past and collect its fragments into some coherence.

Such absolute creativity is finally a fraud because all art must exist in some relation to the forms of the past, whether in contrast or continuation. Both the generic work and the more self-contained work expand our sense of the possibilities of art. But the nineteenth-century stress on literary originality and freedom has inhibited our responses, both intellectual and emotional, to works that try to complicate our appreciation of tradition and form, works that may in fact embody a more radical critique of the past than those which ignore it. More people dislike westerns or musicals because such film genres outrage their inherited and unexamined sense of what art *should* be than because the films are offensive in theme, characterization, style, or other artistic quality. Every lover of musicals, for example, has heard the complaint that musicals are unrealistic and the viewer gets embarrassed when people start singing or dancing. But the relationship between realism and stylization is a central issue in musicals, not an absurd convention. When auteur critics applaud the studio director for triumphing over his material and point to the glimmers of original style shining through the genre assignment, they may awaken us to the merits of an individual artist. But they also fall into the Romantic trap of searching for only what is obviously original and personal in a work. In auteur theory, genre directors with large popular audiences become transformed into embattled Romantic artists trying to establish their personal visions in the face of an assembly-line commercialism. Frank Capra has pointed out the opposite possibility: in the days of big studio monopoly, there was a great deal of freedom to experiment because every film had guaranteed distribution, whereas now, with increased independent production, films have become more uniform and compromised, because each has to justify itself financially. Underground and avant-garde films, with their emphasis on the individual creative sensibility above all, are naturally enough the most hostile to genre. But the bulk of films fall between pure personal expression and pure studio exploitation, mingling the demands of art and culture, creativity and talent. By their involvement in collective creativity, film directors have, at least practically, moved away from the image of the isolated Romantic artist, no matter how they may indulge that image in their public statements.

Instead of dismissing genre films from the realm of art, we should therefore examine what they accomplish. Genre in films can be the equivalent of conscious reference to tradition in the other arts—the invocation of past works that has been so important a part of the history of literature, drama, and painting. Miró's use of Vermeer, Picasso's use of Delacroix are efforts to distinguish their view of the proper ends of painting. Eliot's use of Spenser or Pynchon's of Joyce make similar assertions of continuity and difference. The methods of the western, the musical, the detective film, or the science-fiction film are also reminiscent of the way Shakespeare infuses old stories with new characters to express the tension between past and present. All pay homage to past works even while they vary their elements and comment on their meaning.

Perhaps the main difference between genre films and classic films is the way that genre films invoke past forms while classic films spend time denying them. The joy in genre is to see what can be dared in the creation of a new form or the creative destruction and complication of an old one. The ongoing genre subject therefore always involves a complex relation between the compulsions of the past and the freedoms of the present, an essential part of the film experience. The single, unique work tries to be unforgettable by solving the whole world at once. The genre work, because of its commitment to pre-existing forms, explores the world more slowly. Its hallmark is less the flash of inspiration than the deep exploration of craft. Like Ford's *Stagecoach* or Aldrich's *Ulzana's Raid* (1972), it can exist both in itself and as the latest in a line of works like it, picking and choosing among possible conventions, refusing one story or motif to indulge another, avoiding one "cliché" in order to show a self-conscious mastery of the cliché that has not been avoided. After all, the reason that an artistic element becomes a cliché is that it answers so well to the experience, intelligence, and feelings of the audience. Subsequent artists, perceiving the same aptness, want to exercise its power themselves, even in a potentially hostile new context, to discover if all the possibilities of the form have thoroughly been explored. The only test is its continuing relevance, and a genre will remain vital, as the western has, and the musical has not, so long as its conventions still express themes and conflicts that preoccupy its audience. When either minority or majority art loses contact with its audience, it becomes a mere signpost in history, an aesthetic rather than an art.

Genre films affect their audience especially by their ability to express the warring traditions in society and the social importance of understanding convention. When Irene Dunne, in *The Awful Truth* (Leo McCarey, 1937), disguises herself as Cary Grant's (fictitious) sister and arrives drunk and raucous at a society gathering where Grant is trying to establish himself, we can open a critical trapdoor and say that the other people at the party, who already know her, don't recognize her in her flimsy disguise because of the necessities of plot and comic form. But we must go on to say that this particular convention, used with all its force, allows McCarey, without dropping the general humorous tone, to point out that she is unrecognized because the upper classes base their estimates and knowledge of character on dress, voice, and manners—a theme supported by the rest of the film as well. The conflict between desire and etiquette can define both a social comedy like *The Awful Truth* and even a more obviously stylized genre work like *Dr. Jekyll and Mr. Hyde* (Rouben Mamoulian, 1932); it parallels in the plot the aesthetic contrast between the individual film and the conventions to which it plays a complex homage.

Genre demands that we know the dynamics of proper audience response and may often require a special audience because of the need to refer the latest instance to previous versions. But response is never invariable. Convention isn't only whatever we don't have to pay attention to. Explaining Shakespeare's use of soliloquies by observing that the practice was an Elizabethan dramatic convention tells us as little as saying that Picasso used blue because it was cheap or that Edward Everett Horton appeared in so many Fred Astaire-Ginger Rogers films because comic relief was needed. Why a soliloquy *now?* What does Horton's presence mean *here?* The possibility exists in all art that convention and comment coexist, that overlapping and even contradictory assumptions and conventions may be brought into play to test their power and make the audience reflect on why they were assumed. The genre film lures its audience into a seemingly familiar world, filled with reassuring stereotypes of character, action, and plot. But the world may actually be not so lulling, and, in some cases, acquiescence in convention will turn out to be bad judgment or even a moral flaw—the basic theme of such Hitchcock films as *Blackmail* (1929), *Rear Window* (1954), and *Psycho*. While avant-garde and original works congratulate the audience by implying it has the capacity to understand them, genre films can exploit the automatic conventions of response for the purposes of pulling the rug out from under their viewers. The very relaxing of the critical intelligence of the audience, the relief that we need not make decisions—aesthetic, moral, metaphysical—about the film, allows the genre film to use our expectations against themselves, and, in the process, reveal to us expectations and assumptions that we may never have thought we had. They can potentially criticize the present, because it too automatically *accepts* the standards of the past, to build subversion within received forms and thereby to criticize the forms instead of only setting up an alternate vision.†

Through a constant interplay between the latest instance and the history of a particular form, genre films can call upon a potential of aesthetic complexity that would be denied if the art defined itself only in terms of its greatest and most inimitable works. Because of the existence of generic expectations—how a plot "should" work, what a stereotyped character "should" do, what a gesture, a location, an allusion, a line of dialogue "should" mean—the genre film can step beyond the moment of its existence and play against its own aesthetic history. Through genre, movies have drawn upon their own tradition and been able to reflect a rich heritage unavailable to the "high" arts of the twentieth century which are so often intent upon denying the past and creating themselves totally anew each time out. Within the world of genre films one finds battles, equivalent to those in the history of literature, drama, and painting, between artists who are willing to reproduce a tradition through their own vision because they believe it still has the ability to evoke the emotional response that made it a satisfying artistic form to begin with, and those who believe the form has dried up and needs an injection, usually of "realism." Poets, for example, may contrast the city and the country because that opposition answers to some real beliefs in their audience and because the choice of the rural virtues of the country satisfactorily resolves the conflict. Others might question the authenticity of the traditional materials: did shepherds really play their pipes in singing contests? isn't

† The three main American critics who appreciated such films before the New Wave popularized them critically—Otis Ferguson, James Agee, and Manny Farber—were less interested in them for their formal qualities than for their action and unpretentiousness, aspects of energy related to their formal self-consciousness. But both Agee and Farber (and Pauline Kael is their true heir in this) wanted to protect at all costs their beloved movies from any charge of art. As far as the definition of art they were attacking goes, they were right. But to continue such attacks now confuses where it once illuminated. One virtue of the French New Wave critics was that they didn't have to defend themselves simultaneously against pompous ideas of high art, the myth of the American tough guy artist, and the specter of Hollywood commercialism.

the elaborate language untrue to rural idioms? or, to extend the analogy, did cowboys really respect law and justice so much? do people really break into dances on the street when they're happy, and does the neighborhood automatically join in? The later generations may feel an emotional pull in the form, but they might want to destylize it and make it more real. The directors of the "adult" western of the 1950s accepted the vitality of the western but thought that a more realistic treatment would strengthen its inherent virtues. If controversy were part of film tradition, we might have an argument between John Ford and Fred Zinnemann on the essence of the western like that between Alexander Pope and Ambrose Phillips on the pastoral, Ford and Pope arguing for the value of form and style, while Zinnemann and Phillips press the need to make the characters of art as close as possible to the real persons who live or lived in that place.

Genre films share many of the characteristics of the closed films I have described in the previous chapter. But, instead of being framed visually, genre films are primarily *closed by convention*. Of course, they may be visually enclosed as well, as, for example, are horror films and 1930s musicals; but the more important enclosure is the frame of pre-existing motifs, plot turns, actors, and situations—in short everything that makes the film a special place with its own rules, a respite from the more confusing and complicated worlds outside. The frame of genre, the existence of expectations to be used in whatever way the intelligence of the filmmaker is capable, allows freedoms within the form that more original films cannot have because they are so committed to a parallel between form and content. The typical genre situation is a contrast between form and content. With the expectations of stock characters, situations, or narrative rhythms, the director can choose areas of free aesthetic play within. In genre films the most obvious focus of interest is neither complex characterization nor intricate visual style, but pure story. Think about the novel we can't put down. That rare experience in literature is the common experience in film, where we stay only because we want to, where we often must be intrigued by the first five minutes or not at all, and where we know that once we leave the spell is broken.

Like fairy tales or classical myths, genre films concentrate on large contrasts and juxtapositions. Genre plots are usually dismissed with a snide synopsis (a process that is never very kind to drama that employs conventions, like Shakespeare's plays). But, amid the conventions and expectations of plot, other kinds of emphasis can flourish. To the unsympathetic eye, the pleasures of variation are usually invisible, whether they appear in the medieval morality play, the Renaissance sonnet, the Restoration comedy, the eighteenth-century portrait, the Chopinesque etude, the horror film, the romantic comedy, the musical, or the western. When we can perceive the function of vampire-film conventions in *Persona* or boxing-film conventions in *On the Waterfront* as clearly as we note the debt of Kurosawa's samurai films to American westerns, or that of the New Wave films to American crime films of the 1950s, then we will be able to appreciate more fully the way in which films can break down the old divisions between elite and popular art to establish, almost unbeknown to aesthetics and criticism, a vital interplay between them.‡

Genre films strike beneath our intellectual appreciation of high art and make us one with a large mass audience, often despite our more articulate and more elitist views. To understand genre films properly, we must often translate from the vernacular and bring to light our own less articulate feelings and beliefs. Otherwise, we fall into the kind of confusion exhibited by Nora Sayre when she calls *Airport 1975* "a really rotten movie that's entertaining just because it's so bad" or when Pauline Kael says of *The Exorcist* (William Friedkin, 1973) "A critic can't fight it, because it functions below the conscious level." Such criticism considers emotional manipulation to be a characteristic of bad art, refuses to examine its appeal, and thereby

‡ The way in which television "cannibalizes" material therefore has less to do with its constant demand than with the speed with which such material becomes outdated. When the audience accepts material as generic and ritualistic—situation comedy, talk shows, sports, news, weather—the form can include an infinite variety of nuance. But when the paradigms are no longer emotionally appealing, formal variety will do no good and there arises a desperate, cannibalizing, attempt to discover the new form of audience solace, whether the subject matter is Dick Cavett or the Vietnam War. Thus the whole process of cultural history is speeded up through successive purgations of used-up subject matter and style.

becomes more its victim. Kael says of *Don't Look Now* (Nicholas Roeg, 1973), "It's not that I'm not impressionable; I'm just not as proud of it as some people are." But genre films draw much of their force from simplifying emotion, not to reduce it, but to make it more powerfully direct. Jan Deregowski has pointed out that physiologically there is a continuum between reflex and reflection, not an antithesis. Emotional response is no less varied a world than intellectual response, and the more its varieties can be critically articulated, the more complex it will become. Condescending to the audience (and to the part of oneself) that takes pleasure in certain conventions can never purge unappealing emotions, and may even strengthen them. An aware appreciation of genre film allows the viewer to enjoy his own participation in the historical flow of forms and conventions instead of using the canons of high art to dismiss such works. If Siegfried Kracauer had been able to write *From Caligari to Hitler* during the Weimar Republic rather than thirty years later, and empathized with those films and that audience instead of attacking them, history might have been very different.

SELF-CONSCIOUSNESS AND STORY

From its earliest days Hollywood has made films about itself and the process of filmmaking, usually with a comic tone. The self-consciousness of high art tends to be the self-consciousness of *the existence of a creator;* the self-consciousness of a genre film is of *the existence of a historical method and form.** Within genre films I would like to distinguish two further varieties: the implicit self-consciousness of plot and the explicit self-consciousness of form. Implicit self-consciousness is a property of every genre film: the knowledge that previous films like it already exist. Such knowledge can create a complicated response to a film like *Bend of the River* (1952), in which Anthony Mann and his scriptwriter Borden Chase comment on *Red River* (1948), directed by Howard Hawks and also written by Chase. No explicit consciousness of the existence of *Red River* ever

---

* When films become more self-conscious in the late 1950s and early 1960s the two begin to merge, especially in the works of Godard, Truffaut, and Fellini.

appears in *Bend of the River,* even though there are many
similar situations, relationships, and speeches. The generic framework of the western is still sufficient to enclose an examination of
values of individuality and community that in the earlier film
were stated and resolved quite differently. The critical approach
comes not from without but from within, long before criticism
itself is aware of the problem. In a similar way, in *His Girl Friday*
(1940), Howard Hawks remakes *The Front Page* with a woman
(Rosalind Russell) playing the main character, originally a male
role. Although *His Girl Friday* is self-contained, the audience's
knowledge of the original play and its appreciation of the changes
and adjustments constitutes an important part of the potential
effect of the film: a reflection on the importance of women reporters in many other films of the period; the knowledge that
The Front Page was a play of the 1920s and the change between
that period and the 1940s setting of the film; and its relation to
other films, such as Raoul Walsh's *The Roaring Twenties* (1939),
that look back to the world before the Depression.

His Girl Friday gives a charge of energy to the image of the
reporter in the same way that *Superman* does, by making the
role self-consciously allegorical. The commitment to a life of
action for the public good is shown satirically in *His Girl Friday*
and with debased seriousness in *Superman* because the real possibility for such disinterested service no longer exists. For those
who appreciate the genre traditions, a historical development
has been implied. When Francis Ford Coppola casts Fred Astaire
in *Finian's Rainbow* (1968), he both evokes the history of the
movie musical and also seems to say that the world and values
defined by musicals has vanished, that Astaire is the only remnant,
the golden bough, we have to help us return to them. A truly self-
conscious use of genre does not mock the form—as, say, *Cat
Ballou* (Elliot Silverstein, 1965) mocks westerns or *The Long
Goodbye* (Robert Altman, 1973) mocks the detective film. It
draws upon the history of a form to involve the audience that once
appreciated it. It does not allow the audience to be superior to
the form, but reveals the depth of its previous emotional participation. Both explicit and implicit self-conscious uses of genre can
reveal our previous assumptions in a new perspective. The self-

consciousness of a genre film is gentler and perhaps wiser than the more raucous self-consciousness of avant-garde theater in the 1950s and 1960s, which broke through the proscenium to attack the audience, but still remained a performance. The New Wave directors may have helped inspire the convention-breaking of the recent past in theater, art, and music. But the awareness of genre traditions does not destroy its inherited form so much as it uses the old to build the new. The great artists in film genre are like literary ironists, creating their effects from nuance and relationship rather than from grandiose assertion. But when the emotional commitment of neither the audience nor the filmmaker is present, such variation creates merely formal pleasures. The form becomes a formula, the effects are merely mechanical, and "aware" film-makers decide to juice up the old stories with a contemporary mockery.†

Until Truffaut and Godard showed the way, it was difficult for an audience brought up on traditional high art to appreciate the special self-consciousness of genre films, so often intent on hiding rather than displaying their creators. Genre films and conventional forms are generally deceptive because they are so accessible. If you haven't seen them before, you still have a good chance of having culturally absorbed their aesthetic canons. We have all learned many things unconsciously about viewing films. We accept certain ways of telling a story that are not real but only a generally established means of referring to the outside world. Audiences have learned the conventions of film form very rapidly over the history of film so that effects—ways of telling a story visually—that were impossible twenty years ago can be used freely now, just as types of convention acceptable then— the obvious dramatizations of the *March of Time* documentaries, for example—seem obvious and absurd now. The seeming "primitiveness" of the early films is neither aesthetically nor intellectually naïve, merely the first form of awareness. After a while it no longer sufficed only to *see* something—a human face, an odd situation, a strange setting—the audience asked for more com-

---

† An extreme explicit self-consciousness may in fact proclaim the end of the ability of a genre to express the issues that most touch its audience. But strong genres can take parody in their stride, and poking fun at genre conventions has been a staple of Hollywood slapstick from Mack Sennett through Abbott and Costello to Mel Brooks.

plex pleasures. When one of the bandits in *The Great Train Rob-bery* (Edwin S. Porter, 1903) fired his gun at the camera at the end of the film, audiences shrieked. But no one really imitated the exploitation of the form until the 3-D films of the 1950s. That one scene had virtually exhausted the potential of the new technology to shock and intrigue an audience. But the western itself continued to adapt and change over the years, to establishing a continuous tradition in which the simpler satisfactions of the past could be glimpsed in a more complex context, much as we see the medieval morality play in *King Lear* and *Othello,* or Restoration comedy in Sheridan's *The Rivals* and *The School for Scandal.* The admiration of Godard and Truffaut in their early critical pronouncements for westerns, musicals, horror films, and gangster films was in fact an admiration for this quality of implicit artistic self-consciousness. While serious films exist in themselves, genre films are so conscious of their audience and their manipulation of that audience that the feelings of the viewers of such films can often be their most important subjects. Convention consciously employed can therefore affect the daily life of the audience much more than the demanding original film, where response is so concentrated and rarefied that the experience seems more self-contained, more artistic in a hermetic sense, and therefore less applicable to the normal activities of any member of the audience. Can works that affect us so deeply be denied cultural status by calling them formulaic? Whatever the intellectual disdain for genre stereotypes, for the popular Hollywood film, those conventions have had a profound effect upon our ideas about society and ourselves, not only, as is usually argued, to the ends of corruption, but also to those of purgation, enlightenment, and enrichment.

ENCLOSED SOCIETY AND OPEN SPACES

The visual equivalent of the enclosure of story and convention may often be architectural: in horror, detective, and spy films it can be the crypt, the city, and the master spy's labyrinthine catacombs. But in westerns the enclosed world of plot and behavior faces the wide sky and the wide prairie beyond. As in a science-fiction film like *The Thing* (Christian Nyby, 1951) or a seemingly more realistic film like *Jaws* (Steven Spielberg, 1975), the skies, the water, the open spaces, may be the home of monsters. In defense, an inner architecture appears and a new motif: the small, often ugly, little town amid the beautiful mountains, the dark scientists' camp amid the snowy wastes, the defensive island community. Once again, the themes involve the combat of enclosure and openness, man's limitations and his potential. As the audience enters the conventions of the form, a character enters the space of the film: the stranger who rides into the western town at the beginning of the film and then finally rides out again, the couple who inherit an old house at the beginning of a horror film and then finally bid it goodbye, the travelers who find a mythical kingdom and then must lose it. Like such characters, the audience should not remain unchanged by the experience. Such different films as *Shane* (George Stevens, 1953), *Brigadoon* (Vincente Minnelli, 1954), and *Dr. Terror's House of Horrors* (Freddie Francis, 1965) fit into the basic movement of genre films. In a more self-conscious genre film, like *Bad Day at Black Rock* (John Sturges, 1954), the form is even clearer. At the beginning, the transcontinental express stops at a town it hasn't stopped at for four years and a one-armed Spencer Tracy gets off. He leaves at the end of the film, having changed the town and himself in the process. The audience has changed as well, specifically in its appreciation of the way Sturges and his scriptwriter have modernized the traditional western's exposition of this situation to express more explicit political problems (like racial prejudice) and implicit ones (like the Hollywood black list). Frank Capra, Alfred Hitchcock, and Preston Sturges are examples of directors whose affinity with the small-town setting shows a continuity between their films and those of genre directors. Is the enclosed world an Eden or a limitation? Not only does the studio set dictate the movement inward typical of genre films, but the convention of movie credits themselves offers a kind of borderland the viewer passes over into the world of the film. The tendency in the last few years to begin without credits, even though the film itself, like Antonioni's *Passenger,* may be involved in genre themes, illustrates again the intermingling of open and closed form after the late 1950s.

To the extent that "genre" implies a characteristic set of motifs and world view, every great filmmaker is his own genre, and it has been the closed directors who have been most attracted to genre films. Claude Chabrol has used Hitchcock as if he were a genre, not so much as an influence as a field for variation, just as Andrew V. McLaglen or Burt Kennedy might use the western. Hitchcock's Mount Rushmore (*North by Northwest*) or Covent Garden (*Frenzy*) and Ford's Monument Valley frame nominally open spaces, establishing limits within which to build the films. The frame of genre convention—the journey into the past, into the future, to small town or special geographic space—frees the closed director to experiment with received truth. Since open directors are less interested in limit than in the ragged ends of continuity, they rarely make genre films. When Renoir makes a cops-and-robbers film in *La Nuit du Carrefour* (1932), he concentrates on a character, Inspector Maigret, whose own career extends beyond the confines of the individual film. In *The Testament of Dr. Cordelier* (1959), a Jekyll and Hyde film, the demands of form make Renoir uncharacteristically didactic, and he even uses a voice-over commentary with himself as narrator to underscore the moral. In the same way, there is very little violence in the open film, because the lack of a frame allows the violence to spill too easily onto the audience. One act, one killing, will be enough to carry the resonance, whereas in the genre film, whose conventions help distance emotional impact, the violence is usually much more intense. The closed film has generally been the container for violence of all sorts: the historical film distances the great battles and atrocities; the documentary holds its truth at a distance with commentary; the horror film establishes an eerie world within which to elaborate its terror. But the pressure on the frame continues to grow. Just as the amount of violence within genre films has increased over the years, so it has come closer to home. From the upper-class parties and haunted castles of *Dracula,* from the Victorian backstreets of *Dr. Jekyll and Mr. Hyde,* from the Romantic villages of *Frankenstein,* we have come to *Night of the Living Dead* (George A. Romero, 1968), domesticated horror, experienced by people not unlike the audience— a recapitulation of the progress of literary horror from the Spanish castles and medieval settings of Horace Walpole's *The Castle of Otranto* to Stevenson's Jekyll and Hyde and Bram

Stoker's Dracula—horror just around the corner. The aesthetic distance of the genre film may translate into a psychic detachment for the audience: titillation without responsibility. As the pleasures of responsibility get duller, so the distance from the film must get thinner and thinner to supply the necessary effect. The escalation of violence may indicate the need to find more effective forms for the aesthetic expression and purgation of whatever cultural needs that violence serves. Violence in genre films has often been attacked for its excesses, while "serious" films are praised for their more sparing use of violence (and sex). But the offense seems to be more in the minds of those critics, parents, and censors of all sorts who never grant the audience any ability to be sensitive to the artifices of form, since they assume that convention makes no intellectual demands on the viewer. However, as Paul Krassner once wrote, "A violent film has failed if the audience leaves unhurt." In the films of Alfred Hitchcock, Arthur Penn, Don Siegel, Robert Aldrich, and Sam Peckinpah, to name only a few, the themes of irresponsible and socially compensatory violence call an uneasy truce. But that truce is itself an important part of their meaning.‡

All the great genre directors, like Lang and Hitchcock, refuse to let the audience emerge unscathed and unaffected. Like the closed film in general, the genre film is basically psychological in its appeal, no matter what its subject. It uses the inside only to examine the dynamics of its own tradition. Did medieval audiences "believe" that life was actually a case of Everyman being attacked by temptations named Gluttony and Sloth until Religion and Knowledge saved him? They probably believed it as much as modern audiences believe in the paradigm of the western or the musical as visions of society: certainly not to make any one-to-one equations between what they see on stage or screen and what they experience in their normal lives, no matter how the stage presentation might have influenced their categories for understanding their

---

‡ In *Bandits* Eric Hobsbawn has pointed out that "the very familiarity of killing and violence makes men extremely sensitive to moral distinctions which escape more pacific societies." Viewing the Vietnam War on the evening news created antiwar sentiment instead of cloying the audience (as the argument against film violence might assume would happen). Westerns, of course, project the process of moral distinction on an even broader canvas.

normal lives. The happy endings of Hitchcock's *Suspicion* and Lang's *The Woman in the Window* allow the audience to heave a sigh of formal relief ("he's not guilty; no more anxiety") in order to set up a certain ambivalence ("he's not guilty this time, but who knows what his real nature is like, since he could seem so strongly to be guilty"). The audience's knowledge of what generally happens in a genre film can be used to yield some more complex feeling, even while the expectation of formal closure is fulfilled. The expectation that a closed film will finally be closed, fulfilling itself and wrapping up its world in a few simple statements, thereby plays against the actual content of the film. Form, in other words, can be fulfilled, while the psychology of situations is left ambivalent. Genre enclosure enforces the happy ending as both a formal necessity and a false thematic summary. The genre goes on and the problem will be restated. Shane leaves town, like the classic drifters, after giving encouragement and solving problems. But the tensions between the wife and husband, the ideals of the boy, the conflicts within himself—all the psychological themes that have been awakened—are only put into abeyance, not resolved, by the formal completeness. To be satisfied or dissatisfied with the rescue at the end of *The Poseidon Adventure* without asking who has been saved and why their salvation *specifically* is a relief ignores most of the content of the film and the basis of its appeal. To claim that the film is unrealistic, say, because Stella Stevens wears silver high-heels throughout the disaster, evades the question of why the film uses such conventions of dress (a typical genre method). We emerge from the hull of the *Poseidon* as we emerge from every genre film, relieved by inwardly knowing that the anxieties, both psychological and social, released by the film have hardly been purged at all. Such anxieties almost always involve the kind of accommodation made between the individual and the world around him. Genre cycles, like the present one of the disaster film (or the survival film, as I would prefer to call it), engage the feelings of the audience at their deepest level. When they don't, no one goes to see them and they cease to be made.

The problems of class and society in an open film like Renoir's *The Rules of the Game* are understood by the characters and are an explicit theme. But society in closed films is iconographic and allegorical, uninterested in history or change. The genre film, like the enclosed film in general, defines both society and history as psychological projections. In the enclosed world of silent films such as Lang's *Metropolis,* Eisenstein's *Potemkin,* or Griffith's *The Birth of a Nation,* the audience has been deprived of any personal possibility of influencing history. Whatever his individual political beliefs, the closed silent film director aligns himself aesthetically with the general forces that move masses of people. As King Vidor has said, "I would rather direct five thousand people than two." But the genre film, as a product of the sound era, balances the equation by imaging the individual's relation to general forces in the director's relation to past films. When we watch the Rockettes or some other precise rendition of a symmetrical form, we may think that we are appreciating the formal perfection. But in fact we appreciate the tension between the individual dancer and the deindividualizing form. The slightly different dancer always stands out—and may be fired next week. But when the human element is eliminated entirely (when, for example, the Rockettes are all dressed in bunny costumes, including huge heads, for the Easter show) the result is only boredom. The dancer has to resist the dance, the detective has to resist the police as much as the gangsters, the violence must not be so stylized as to be abstract and undisruptive. Genre films concentrate not on the reality of a society or the reality of the past, but on the individual's perception of those superhuman orders and what they mean. The facts of the case are therefore only a diversion from the solution. The detective film is an enclosed, self-contained world because so often at its heart is a mystery which seems to have limits; at the end of the film no strings will be left dangling, in the same way that at the end of a gangster film the gang must be destroyed. But the problem of the enclosure itself, the society in which the detective works, can never be solved, only superceded. In Nicholas Ray's *On Dangerous Ground* (1951), the detective who has been brutalized by his belief that the police are the dregs of society goes out from the dark, rainy city into the bright, snowy countryside only to discover that social pressures can exist outside the urban world that he views with such loathing. The escape from formal restraint is into characterization and feeling, the problem of the emotions that seemed to demand social order to begin with. The western, with its open panorama, gets at the conflict in a different way. In contrast to the detective who tries to *solve* something, discover a pre-existing pattern, the cowboy hero generally tries to *create* something—a life, a town, a myth—from a world of openness and raw materials. Like the detective trying to make sense of the city, the western hero feels pulled by enclosure—either the cabins that keep out the harsh potential and confusion of the world outside (as in Ford's *The Searchers,* 1956) or the beckoning community that will purge the sins of individuality—the theme of so many 1950s films with western settings, as disparate as *Bend of the River* and *Seven Brides for Seven Brothers* (Stanley Donen, 1954). In westerns the rhythm exists between the confinements of social relationship, often expressed as marriage, and the open potential of the range; in detective and gangster films—both variations of the city film—the contrast is usually between the corruption of all groups, whether criminal or official, and the purer spirit of the individual. The musical usually expresses individual energy within a protected part of the city, the world of social style and dance. Between them can be arranged the many other kinds and variations of these basic forms: the reporter-newspaper films of the 1930s and 1940s, the circus films of the 1940s, the prison films of the 1950s, the science-fiction films of the 1950s, and many others. The issues I will isolate in the westerns and musicals are issues in most other genre film as well. They are often basic film issues, at least issues central to how the film has developed in the United States, perhaps because films here, unlike films in Europe, were largely created for a mass society and therefore had to deal with mass problems.

Genre films, more clearly than other types, deal directly with the problem of the individual's psychic relationship to a society, a community, a world of others. Although I have sketched the aesthetic relation of genre films to closed films in general, I would like to consider in more detail the development of the inner history of these forms until the 1950s, when American film critics and audiences were being forced to take a new look at their native products, and the way was being prepared for the new American attitude toward genre films (and films in general) in the 1960s and 1970s. Unlike the Europeans, almost all the great

American directors have been genre directors. The western and the musical are, I think, most important for their complexity, longevity, and the different ways each emphasizes the basic genre conflict between individual and society, film and form. After describing these two genres, I will be able first to discuss more clearly the contribution of directors like Godard and Truffaut to the idea of genre and then the present state of genre film in America, both in the series films and in the more personal work of directors such as Arthur Penn, Stanley Kubrick, Robert Aldrich, Robert Altman, Don Siegel, and others—the creators of what might be called the one-of-a-kind genre film, mingling the commitments to tradition and to originality.*

WESTERNS AND THE MYTH OF THE PAST

In general the genre film half-reconstructs and half-creates a group of conventions within which to express the problems that are most pressing to most members of society, the problems that the explicit politics of that society has not solved or hardly even identified. In literature, the form that has done this work most often has been the pastoral, the casting of contemporary conflicts back to a golden age or a rural setting where the complications of urban life can be ignored and the difficulties considered more purely. The western continues this tradition by defining a special place—the nineteenth-century American West, with special standards, traditions, and conventions, within which its audience can choose what it wants from that past, what examples to follow or reject, what patterns of behavior to approve or deplore. The history of the western in America, therefore, is to a great extent the history of how the American western past has been used. It has probably been more fertile in this way than any earlier part of our history. Seventeenth- and eighteenth-century America have offered very little mythic substance to films. As the history of the western shows, the public and the filmmaker have never had an equal interest in all films about specific historical-mythic characters or periods. American films have never, for example, been

* I have already discussed the place of detective films in the previous section. The other major film genre, the horror film, will be considered in the next section, in relation to the movie definition of human character. See pp. 226–34.

as interested in the Revolution as they have been in the Civil War. Only John Ford's *Drums Along the Mohawk* (1939), *Allegheny Uprising* (William A. Seiter, 1939), Cecil B. DeMille's *Unconquered* (1947), and the Walt Disney film *Johnny Tremain* (Robert Stevenson, 1957) spring immediately to mind. The reason may be that the brother-against-brother motif of the Civil War has answered the necessary assumption of film that conflict between and within individuals best expresses the disparity between the ideal and the real America. We can distinguish roughly between those films that use a western setting to expand a general western theme (cattlemen vs. sheepherders; the gunfighter; the wagon train west; the pioneers and the Indians) and those films that attempt in some way to touch on a world of historical reality, whether in time and place (the opening of the Cherokee Strip, the Washita or Little Big Horn massacres) or in the use of at least the name of someone who actually lived (Billy the Kid, Judge Roy Bean, Jesse James, Wyatt Earp). The categories, of course, overlap, and the films that touch on historical reality can be discussed in the same myth-building terms as the more thematic films. But the effort to touch the world of documented history is still a bright thread in the former kind of film, and both try to apply the conventions of the western to the life of the audience by setting them in a quasi-historical context.

The American past as used by the western has, therefore, a double nature: it is both distant in time and yet intimate in our knowledge of its conventions and morality. Its visual space is open and alluring; with widescreen it seems to be able to include as many stories as are possible: epic, comedy, tragedy, farce, history, in whatever combinations. Once the conventions are learned, the western past becomes a special place and the audience, like all genre audiences, becomes more emotionally involved in the issues and themes of that past even while they seem most distant and fanciful. As John Cawelti points out in *The Six-Gun Mystique,* the open setting is enough to arouse in the audience all the expectations of a western situation and western themes. The open setting also helps us to believe that the past is real, since the locations and the space are real. This is true of historical films in general: *The Lion in Winter* (Anthony Harvey, 1968) is even more convincing than *El Cid* (Anthony Mann, 1961), not merely because of its script or acting, but primarily because the locations of the one carry more conviction than the sets of the other. Tableaus in historical films may recall great paintings, but westerns have caused us to associate the past with space and movement, not confinement and stasis. The introduction of historical figures into fictional narrative is also enhanced by the open setting, especially if the film does not directly concern them. In *How the West Was Won* (Civil War sequence directed by John Ford, 1963) Grant and Sherman make uncomfortably stagy conversation within a film that is otherwise open and expansive in visual treatment and subject matter. But in *Skin Game* (Paul Bogart, 1971) the sudden appearance of John Brown and his men raiding a town gives one an interesting aesthetic jolt—not because it fits into the plot but because the film has somehow opened up to allow a more documented history to enter. Within the frame of the past, the sense of possibility has been preserved. Cawelti says that the western "takes place on or near a frontier." But that frontier is less often physical than it is the audience's sense of what is and what is not historically true. The acceptance of the frame of western conventions allows a freedom to experiment in crossing boundaries that might be impossible in a more contemporary genre, like the city film or the musical.

An essential part of the lure of the western is therefore not merely the closed preserve of the past, but a past that can potentially contain an incredibly concentrated history of social change, a mythic social anthropology in which the variety of social relations from the beginning of human settlements can be imaged. The wandering gunslinger who settles down; the band of outlaws preying on small towns; the conflict between cattlemen and sheepherders, or farmers ("nesters") and ranchers, for control of the open range, or between lawmen and outlaws for control of the town—combinations and variations of these elements all evoke such mythic images. The interactions of society in the western are not political and sociological, they are personal and archetypal. So often set in the past, westerns are characteristically preoccupied with the way the individual aims himself toward the future. Thus many westerns deal with dynasties. *Duel in the Sun* (King Vidor, 1947) or *The Baron of Arizona* (Samuel Fuller, 1950) depict the decay of a dynasty, through the rebellion of a son or someone who should have shown gratitude to the founders. *Red River, Giant* (George Stevens, 1956), and *Cimarron* (Anthony Mann, 1961) examine the growth of a dynasty, the change from one kind of society to another, the way in which the old, individualistic values no longer work in the new, more organized town. Movies can never take the abstract view of society possible in fiction. When Nunnally Johnson writes and John Ford directs the film version of Steinbeck's *The Grapes of Wrath* (1940), the focus is entirely on the Joads; the sections that deal with the national effects of the Dust Bowl are left out. But Ford's experience with the western and his ability to tell a visual story in genre terms infuses the family's specific problems with a general significance. In the beginning of the film Tom Joad returns home to his family and near the end he leaves them. But they also have moved, blown by the winds of change that have dried up their farm. Nominally a conservative, Ford can take a left-wing position in *The Grapes of Wrath* because it is in accord with his genre director's attitude toward society as a personal myth. In elite art the relation between the artist and his audience establishes a special group that shares values opposed to general taste. In popular art, the artist attempts to assert the wholeness of his audience, creating a community rather than a coterie, attempting to bind together the isolated individuals in his dark audience. Much critical hostility to the western seems to come therefore from a hostility to the "nonrealistic" treatment of social themes, the rooting of the critique of society in populist folk relationships rather than Marxist analysis. But the lack of any specific reference to class, other than haves and have-nots, is part of the nature of the form: the true appeal of genre films must be unrelated to class distinction because the issues are egalitarian and psychic, relevant to every American no matter from what class—dreams of power and nightmares of powerlessness. The early westerns of the 1920s and 1930s formed a continuity with the past through such former cowboys as Tom Mix or western heroes like Wyatt Earp (an occasional technical advisor until his death in 1929) and satisfied a rapidly industrializing and urbanizing America with glimpses of the open spaces of the past. But the genre showed a continued vitality and impact when it began to discover within the early simple stories of personal and social conflict the power to reveal, like a medieval dream vision, the new problems that were troubling the society outside the theater. One element that helped was the appearance of great directors like John Ford, William A. Wellman, Howard Hawks, and later Budd Boetticher, John Sturges, and Anthony Mann—who saw the potential of the form to assimilate even more complex themes.

In the hands of John Ford, the western began to achieve its greatest potential as social allegory, and the later flexibility of the western in the 1950s and 1960s is due in great part to the ability of Ford and Howard Hawks to find richer and richer ways to use its resources. Ford's westerns, like his Irish films, specifically test the values of the past in terms of community and tradition. His great theme is the family, the forces that create it and the forces that disintegrate it. Ford's family is not necessarily a family of blood, but it is definitely one whose cohesion is opposed to the artificial institutions of the society around it. The true America for Ford is an enlarged community, and the true community is a large family. The stock company of actors and technicians Ford so often calls on to make his films creates on the periphery of the film a family of strangers tied by feelings that parallel those inside the story itself and may hopefully redeem the isolated community of the audience. The community of the stagecoach in *Stagecoach* and its ability to withstand hazard, even though the passengers never met before, express a prophetic optimism about the way American society will respond to the threat of World War Two. The world is a stage, says Ford, and our ability to survive the Indians outside and the corrupt bankers within depends on our willingness to establish a community of feeling.†

Ford's West is therefore a place of possibility where people of goodwill have a chance to create a new community away from the repressive presence of organized American and European society, with their personal fastidiousness and corrupt institutional values. The creators of community are often considered misfits by

† Two other directors who use stock companies are Renoir in the 1930s and Bergman in the 1950s, 1960s, and 1970s. Each gets something different out of it. Renoir, closer to Ford, reflects through the continuity of actors and technicians his search for an integration of aesthetics and politics fueled by the contemporary reality of the Popular Front; Bergman, more like Kazan or a stage director, creates psychological complexity by overlaying our experience of the actor in the film with the experiences of that same actor in other films. See pp. 201–12.

the official society. In *Stagecoach,* the seemingly respectable people turn out to be weak and immoral, while Ringo Kid (John Wayne), arrested for the murder of a man who killed his brother, becomes the hero, an appropriate parallel to the ex-convict Tom Joad (Henry Fonda) in *The Grapes of Wrath,* a film that also systematically turns our conventional notions of respectability inside out. In the present, unlike the past, the rural world has been overrun by the forces of official society, the farms bulldozed by men who have betrayed the community so that their families can eat. Official society deprives nature of its naturalness. *The Grapes of Wrath* politically analyzes the western myth even as it absorbs its values and believes they can be perpetuated. Its inner hero is not Karl Marx, but it may be Woody Guthrie, and, like *Stagecoach,* it similarly celebrates the indomitable family that survives death and disaster not individually so much as collectively. In such postwar films as *Fort Apache* (1948) and *She Wore a Yellow Ribbon* (1949), the cavalry appears to be an institution that can combine the virtues of a family with a personal relationship between men and leaders—and wives and children nearby—while it also ideally links itself with a national government, lending its moral energy to the otherwise abstract world of the cities to the east. The emotional binder, like that in *The Grapes of Wrath* or the Irish films, is usually the folk song and the communal folk dance.

Ford's values are rooted in the emotional and timeless relations of family rather than in the pragmatic and historical relations of society. Unlike the corrupt present, the open past of the west allows those values to become social as well. But the empty dance floor that Tom Joad crosses to leave his mother and family to become an organizer is never far from Ford's mind. By the time of *The Man Who Shot Liberty Valance* (1962) the conflict has become too intense. As the modern newspaper editor in the film says, "When the facts and the legend conflict, print the legend." Admirers of Ford's style have praised *Liberty Valance* for its purity and mythic qualities. But it lacks the interaction between enclosure and openness that marks his greatest films, and its stylized sets and situations, the obvious makeup and the clichéd lines, indicate that Ford has come to see the world of the western as a theatrical retreat from the corrupt society around the films

rather than as a source of potentially energizing values. The sense
of being able to make one's own boundaries, the sense of potential,
has been lost from Ford's vision of American society. The vivid
historical imagination in *Young Mr. Lincoln* (1939) and *Drums
Along the Mohawk* has dwindled into the perfunctory human-
izing of the Grant-Sherman conversation in *How the West Was
Won*. The world of Ford's West ends in *Cheyenne Autumn*
(1964), his next-to-last completed film. The story of *Cheyenne
Autumn* deals with the efforts of a group of Cheyenne men,
women, and children to return to their Yellowstone territory
homeland from a bare and infertile Oklahoma reservation. In
his filmmaking practice, Ford has always been sympathetic to
the Indians, but the sympathy rarely entered his pictures, where
Indians were generally cast as aliens against whom the western-
ers defined their community. *The Searchers* had qualified that
relationship somewhat by presenting John Wayne as the obsessed
Indian-hater Ethan Edwards, who searches for his kidnapped
niece until he finds her many years later living with an Indian
tribe. He tries to force her to leave with him, but she has made
a home with the Indians and considers them her family. The
individual, no matter what his values, cannot fight the cohesion
of the community, and Wayne must fail, strangely dividing our
sympathies. The situation of the Indians in *Cheyenne Autumn*
is like that of the Joads; organized society has deprived both
groups of the fruits of the earth. The fort, which in Ford's
cavalry films was a home amid a hostile world, is for the Indians
a prison, presided over by a crazed Indian-hater, Captain Wessels
(Karl Malden). The final resolution comes about through the
firm humanistic hand of the central government, acting, however, through the individualistic, rule-breaking, nonbureaucratic
figure of Carl Schurz, the Secretary of the Interior (Edward G.
Robinson). Schurz, a good German to balance the bad German
Wessels, gathers his strength from his memory of Abraham Lincoln, Ford's symbol of the personal morality possible in American
politics. Because Ford believes that the individual can create a
new society based on traditional values, he can accept the situation
of Tom Joad in *The Grapes of Wrath* and implicitly defend the
Communist associations of Casey the preacher because their
beliefs are essentially non-ideological, rooted in a desire for in-

dividual satisfaction that is unambiguously continuous with the values of family and community. In his last film, *7 Women* (1966), Ford once again affirms that the best an individual can do is to insure the continuation and survival of the group through self-sacrifice. But both *7 Women* and *Cheyenne Autumn* imply that even this sacrifice will only hold out the cold a little bit longer.

The attack against destructive individualism seems to have developed in the films of Ford and Hawks as a result of World War Two. The war theme is the theme of the group; when the individual appears, he either leads the group or sacrifices himself for it. Hawks's often-noted interest in professionalism expands this group theme, and, in general contrast to Ford, Hawks usually considers women to be as much a threat to male community as any outside enemy, unless, of course, the woman can adopt the male point of view and its value system. The counterparts to these films are Hawks's comedies, which are characterized by sexual role reversal (*His Girl Friday*), the humiliation of weak and silly men by clever women (*Bringing Up Baby,* 1938; and partly *Ball of Fire,* 1941), and even the punishment of wearing women's clothes for a man who has been previously characterized as a womanizer (*I Was a Male War Bride,* 1949). In general, Hawks has less of a commitment to time, history, and the past than does Ford; his sensibility is less epic than comic epic. His heroes view themselves with too much irony to ever attain the potentially tragic tones of Ford's defenders of outmoded virtues. In *Red River,* the one Hawks western in which such tragic tones are apparent—and perhaps great because of that—the moral righteousness of Tom Dunson (John Wayne), the dynasty founder, becomes an inefficient and tyrannic weight on the next generation. Matthew Garth (Montgomery Clift), Dunson's adopted son, faces down Dunson when the tyranny threatens to destroy the community of Dunson's cowhands by forcing the trail drive to take a slow, clearly dangerous way to Missouri instead of trying a new, potentially dangerous but much faster route to a rumored railhead at Abilene. Both Dunson and Garth are western individualists who don't like to be pushed around. The difference is that Garth has an empathy with the weakness of others whereas Dunson considers everyone lacking by the standard of his own strength. As Peter Biskind has pointed out, the film implies that the old individualism could create and innovate, found a dynasty and start a herd. But the new individualism needs a community of buyers and sellers, a less openly competitive situation. Blind self-righteousness has to give way to circumspect self-righteousness, and, at the end of the film, in the final fight between Dunson and Garth, there is no conclusion. The woman who loves them both stops the fight by firing a gun at them. Like little boys puzzled by the ways of women, they make up and Dunson gives his blessing to Garth's marriage. All Dunson needs is a good beating to show him that his kind of individualism doesn't work. His old-time aggressiveness, perhaps useful for winning the West (and World War Two), can be made to fit in with the new society.

Hawks's definition of the interplay between the values represented by Wayne and Clift in *Red River* relies in great part on their different acting styles, Wayne's sincere bluster and Clift's sincere fumbling. Acting is generally irrelevant to the meaning of Ford's films, and the presence of the actor is more iconographic than ironic, viewed more from the outside than within. Ford therefore is the closed genre director, whereas Hawks is more open; Ford's open spaces are potentials upon which to impose a vision (the set made from Monument Valley), while Hawks explores the conventions of many different genres—gangster films, screwball comedy, detective film, musical, western—to frame the actually elusive nature of his central figures. In visual terms, Ford leans more toward composition, while Hawks attempts to embody motion. In the course of his films Ford's communities become more and more designed to be contemplated as ideals than participated in, more myths of western Eden than real worlds. Hawks, by his greater emphasis on the individual and the outcast, and the irony about forms that experimenting with different genres implies, offers a more inhabitable world, a world that in fact can accommodate the concerns of the audience, specifically those 1950s problems of forgetting the violence of the past and assimilating the individual to society. Hawks's humor in such late films as *Rio Bravo* (1959) and *El Dorado* (1967) emphasizes his orientation toward the individual perspective of the characters rather than the director, while Ford's reliance on his stock company shows his own effort to treat character typologically rather than individually, so that he can concentrate more definitely on the question of community. Unlike Ford's Indians in *Cheyenne Autumn* or even his Joads in *The Grapes of Wrath,* Hawks's misfits actually do clean up the town and actively teach a moral lesson to the official world.

In terms of American history, the new, softer individualism of Matthew Garth must defeat the old aggressive individualism of Tom Dunson because after World War Two the economy itself changed from production to consumption, and the hard-shelled entrepreneur had to turn into the organization man. Now the previously independent individual hungers to be accepted by the group. Glenn Ford in *The Fastest Gun Alive* (Russell Rouse, 1956) and Gregory Peck in *The Gunfighter* (Henry King, 1950) (a role originally meant for Wayne) try to settle down in the face of the "punk kids" who want to prove themselves against the great man (also a theme of Japanese samurai films of the same period). The western of the 1950s considered the 1940s to be a time of no longer relevant social dislocation that has to give way to settling down and building a family. In Anthony Mann's *Bend of the River* (1952), for example, James Stewart plays a former Missouri border raider now leading a wagon train. As a good badman, he is opposed by Arthur Kennedy, the bad badman, who willingly gives his own guerrilla-bred talents to the traveling pioneers as long as it serves him, but becomes the bouncer in a boomtown saloon when it seems more lucrative. Kennedy is out for himself no matter what, while Stewart desires acceptance by the pioneers to cleanse himself of his past actions and is haunted by the belief of the head of the pioneers that badmen can never change. Kennedy, on the other hand, like a character from a Lang film of the 1930s and 1940s—such as *You Only Live Once* (1937)—believes that society never lets you change. The film, however, rejects any individualism not in the service of social stability. As I mentioned before, the same speech that is meant negatively when John Wayne shouts it in *Red River,* where he promises to follow Clift and the other men to revenge himself on them, becomes positive in *Bend of the River,* when Stewart makes it to Kennedy and his band of pickup renegades. In *Red River,* inhumane tyranny is reasserting its rights to judge all by its own standards, but in *Bend of the River* Stewart speaks with the moral authority of the pioneer community whose food Kennedy is stealing to sell for more money. Violence sanctioned by the community in the name of community values is fine, but personal violence is not. Kennedy cannot be assimilated like Wayne; he must somehow be killed. The one positive place for such flamboyant individualism in the 1950s was in historical costume dramas. In *His Majesty O'Keefe* (Byron Haskin, 1953), for example, Burt Lancaster plays a sea captain who persuades the natives of a Pacific island, through single combat, tricks, and shrewdness, that their destinies lie with helping him to develop the copra trade. Also written by Borden Chase, a figure who deserves some attention for his role in creating American values in this period, this film attempts to define the origins of capitalist expansion in high personal adventure. Individualism in the service of trade, rather than the freelance theft of Kennedy (which could destroy the new world of the pioneers), is the only kind that 1950s society can consciously approve.

But the answer is never so pure. Since westerns and costume dramas deal with the past most effectively in terms of myths and images, the personal and anarchic energy of Lancaster in *His Majesty O'Keefe* occupies equal place in our hearts with the more socially channeled individualism of Stewart in *Bend of the River*. Finally there is no chronology beyond the images of human nature. *Bend of the River,* like every great genre film, preserves the tradition at the same time that it expresses a deep ambivalence about its relevance. The 1950s are the last American decade before the internationalization of film that marks the 1960s. With such intimacy and enclosure, genres still work. But the enclosure, like the Cold War itself, is pressing too hard, even to the point of paranoia. The resolution is often ambivalent. In *Bend of the River,* Stewart does not finally kill Arthur Kennedy. He merely wounds him enough for Kennedy to be swept away and drowned—or at least submerged—by the raging river. Kennedy is the more frantic counterpart of Stewart's icy control, the past he wishes to forget, the distrust of society and its norms that he wishes to purge. Kennedy is like a revenger whom society has left unsatisfied, the rebel who refuses to be reconciled. Stewart's vision of his place in the new pioneer community succeeds (in the film) because the traditional values embodied in the western genre—the values of pastoral and community—have succeeded in submerging individual assertion and self-expression. But the western tradition includes the loner as well, the character who wants to build a world or understand one, the director who wants to make personal sense of a set of forms and conventions handed down to him.

The ambivalence of films about the conflict between social stability and individual desires obviously derives aesthetically from the conflict between actor and director, or, in genre films, between actor and director on the one hand and the pressure of tradition on the other. When westerns are discussed, the focus tends naturally to be on stars (John Wayne) or characters (Wyatt Earp) rather than on stories. The past may provide the necessary frame, but the audience carries the individuals, real and fictional, out with them, just as the memory of Zapata in Kazan's *Viva Zapata!* (1952) will persist and energize his people long after his death. In movies, therefore, psychology is not a deviation from politics; it *is* politics. Class conflict is almost always presented as psychic conflict. The "adult" western of the 1950s was also called the "psychological" western. But usually, as in *High Noon* (Fred Zinnemann, 1952), the psychological situation of the hero (is he brave or a coward?) was parallel to a political situation (are the townspeople willing to stand up for justice?). The subject of most American films had always been the individual rather than the class, the sensibility rather than the situation. In earlier westerns, while the basics of the form were being worked out, the issues were more patterned and the individual played a more stereotyped role. Ford's emphasis on family and community is the finest expression of that possibility. The pre-World War Two period saw not only Ford's first great western, *Stagecoach,* but also several other films that emphasized the psychological side of westerns, a potential as implicit in the form as are the stories of communities and societies in conflict and disruption. The first energies for such an exploration may have come from the Depression film's glorification of the energetic entrepreneur and the personally attractive criminal (both often played by James Cagney). But the most intriguing such figure in the western is Jesse James.

Jesse James was not always a fascinating figure to film audiences. The first Jesse James film was made in 1920. Called *Under the Black Flag,* it was partially financed by the James family and starred James Edward James as his father. But, after opening in

March 1921 in Plattsburg, Missouri, near the James family home-stead, it failed to become either a financial or a critical success, except perhaps in western Missouri. Only later, with Henry King's *Jesse James* (1940), starring Tyrone Power, and Fritz Lang's *The Return of Frank James* (1940), starring Henry Fonda, did Jesse James capture the imagination of film audiences. Many excellent westerns have been made about other popular figures, including John Ford's *My Darling Clementine* (1946) and John Sturges' *Gunfight at the O.K. Corral* (1957) (Wyatt Earp and Doc Holliday), and Arthur Penn's *The Left-Handed Gun* (1958) (Billy the Kid). But the Jesse James story contains all the compelling motifs of those stories—the final betrayal of Billy the Kid, the two strong complementary men in Earp and Holliday—and much more.‡

The motifs of the King and Lang films have found their way into all the later James films and into other films about the heroes of the west as well. The basic appeal of Jesse James seems to be that of the double life: the many fake names and disguises he used, especially the combination of hell-raising, anti-establishment bandit and respectable banker and businessman with a fine house in the best section of St. Joseph, Missouri. The most familiar lines from the folk song about Jesse James memorialize the double identity: "The dirty little coward who shot Mr. Howard/ Has laid poor Jesse in his grave." This was a common motif of the dime novels about Jesse James, and the appeal to the Victorian urban reader seems obvious. Less certain is the reason why in 1939 the same appeal should be so strong, unless it was the western's special affirmation of the split vision of individual and society that the reality of the Depression and the myths of the 1930s gangster films had bred in the audience. A further reason for the continued popularity of the James story is the context of World War Two: a time when every man might be two people—the man of peace and the man of war, the respectable man and the murdering man (like Jesse, with a cause to back up his violence), the family man and the man on a dangerous mission. World War Two emphasized on an international scale the fact that

‡ The material about the early James films comes from an excellent his-torical study of the James myth that unfortunately glosses over the other film versions: William A. Settle, Jr.'s *Jesse James Was His Name* (University of Missouri Press, Columbia, Missouri, 1966).

there were many moral problems that could be solved only with guns and violence. In *The Return of Frank James* Frank's home-town firmly supports him in the revenge he has taken on the mur-dering Ford brothers, despite the governor's pardon of them. But Frank is less alluring as a character than Jesse and the many sub-sequent Jesse films attempt to penetrate both the mystery of Jesse's character as a socially acceptable outlaw and his own self-con-scious manipulation of that double role. Homilists of the nineteenth and early twentieth century could extract compelling lessons from the lives of Washington and Lincoln. But the example of great men is another nineteenth-century assumption about human behavior that has fallen by our psychic wayside. Stories about Washington or Lincoln in film, with rare exceptions, are basically costume drama now, even though such figures might appear or intervene peripherally in other works. Jesse James, like Humphrey Bogart, is a more appealing figure because he bridges what to the "normal" American might be incompatibles in his nature. Instead of em-bodying an impossible ideal, Jesse embodies a national ambiv-alence. He is the positive version of the Jekyll and Hyde figure or the Jack the Ripper figure—another favorite 1940s character—in which murder and crime wear the cloak of respectability.*

The theme of the double character parallels a growing awareness of the western itself as a vehicle for creating myth. Jesse's exploita-tion of his double nature reappears in postwar films like King's *The Gunfighter* through the outlaw's effort to return to the family once the era of violence has ended. Constantly surfacing in these films is the theme of fame that had wound its way through film since the beginnings of Hollywood, from the first Mack Sennett come-dies about the studio itself and the early spoofs of the Hollywood setting like *Bombshell* (Victor Fleming, 1933) or *What Price Hol-lywood?* (George Cukor, 1933). But those earlier films with their

---

* In *The Detective in Film* William K. Everson has pointed out that there was a strong revival of previously defunct genres in 1939, including Walsh's *The Roaring Twenties,* Rowland V. Lee's *Son of Frankenstein,* and Sidney Lanfield's *The Hound of the Baskervilles,* as well as *Stagecoach* and King's *Jesse James.* A possible forebear of the film Jesse James is Zorro, as played by Douglas Fairbanks in *The Mark of Zorro* (1920) and *Don Q, Son of Zorro* (1925), whose double identity is presented more comically. For further discussion of these themes from the perspective of character rather than society see pp. 226–34.

interest in movie-star fame were more gentle and mocking. The sense of fame explored by the late 1930s was the fame that kills by absorbing the real individual into a reduced and artificial public self. Jesse James's identity as a businessman is a diminishment of his real self, a frame he puts around his naturalness. (Jesse is of course shot in the back while he is adjusting a picture frame.) The dime-novel vision of Jesse James that is so often alluded to in these films diminishes him as well, even though he often explicitly considers it to make him more real. Here is the trap of fame: to accept a limited and warped sense of self because it makes you known, puts your name in the paper. Arthur Penn's elaboration of this theme in *Bonnie and Clyde* is only the most complex version of a motif that is inherent in almost all post-1940 westerns that deal with a specific historical character: what does my life mean beyond the fact that I have lived it?

The implied answer in so many of these films is that the story means something because art has chosen to embody it—the self-conscious theme of a director who has discovered the resources of the form in which he works. "This song was made/ by Billy Gashade/As soon as the news did arrive" is a less familiar part of the ballad of Jesse James. But it emphasizes that Jesse's story means something because someone has decided to tell it. The songs that are in the background of so many good and bad westerns of the 1940s and 1950s mirror the desire in the traditional Jesse James story to embody both story and storyteller's point of view in the same form. The songs may be effective or ludicrous, but the reason they are used (and the irrelevance of realist objections to such usages) should be explored further. The chorus of voices in *Red River,* the introductory songs of *Rancho Notorious* (Fritz Lang, 1952) and *Johnny Guitar* (Nicholas Ray, 1954) all attempt to evoke the power of the Jesse James song and its implication of disinterested involvement. By placing himself in the position of celebrating the fame of the hero, the director separates himself from those like the murderer of Jesse James, who seek to win fame by their untalented actions. "Me, Robert Ford, I killed him," yells Bob Ford (Frank Gorshin) to everyone in the street who will listen in Nicholas Ray's *The True Story of Jesse James* (1957), while Arthur Penn includes in his films a character who serves as chronicler, for the purpose of either romanticization (*The Left-Handed Gun*) or historical research (*Little Big Man*). In Lang's *The Return of Frank James,* the Ford brothers are performing in a mining-town vaudeville show a one-act play called *The Death of Jesse James,* in which Jesse is killed while supposedly robbing a widow. In the midst of their play-acting in the broad accents of the Victorian stage, they glimpse a movement in a box above the stage. Frank James himself is standing there watching them. They shoot and flee. Frank James never did seek the revenge on the Fords depicted in the film. But they did appear in just that way on the stage, willing to play distorted and inaccurate versions of their real-life selves. The James story expresses the split between the normal, peaceful self and the dark marauding self as well as the split between the private self and the play-acting self, underlining both the assumption of the genre films that reality may need stylization to be fully realized and the fear that excessive style and excessive obeisance to tradition may hide a dark ambivalent world beneath. Before discussing how the western in the 1960s and 1970s deals with these issues of society and individuality, it is necessary to enter the inner history of the musical as well.

MUSICALS AND THE ENERGY FROM WITHIN

A great part of the positive appreciation of private energy, whether criminal or not, that appears in the westerns of the 1940s comes from the musicals of the 1930s, with their celebration of the energy of dance and its opposition to the artifices of tradition, social formality, and high art of all kinds. The attractiveness of Jesse James, the outlaw beneath the banker's respectability, parallels the attractiveness of Fred Astaire, the musical-comedy exuberance beneath the fashionable dinner-jacketed cool of the social surface. James Cagney as both eccentric crook and George M. Cohan again brings the two images together in a single visual personality. Both westerns and musicals are fascinated by the hidden self. But while in westerns that hidden self is often criminal and antisocial, in musicals it is a force that can reinvigorate and reform the stodgy society against which its rebellion had first taken shape. The western places the individual within a setting of either community or nature and observes the interaction of those forces until one seems to win. Most often the "winner" can be identified with history—the coming of civilization, the establishment of community and social virtues, which, no matter how boring, represent the future. The individual can be a catalyst for those changes or rebel against them. But the western always has a double consciousness of the potential refuge of the past— when ideals and actions were pure and seamless—and the equally necessary process by which the past has become the present. In essence the western inclines to tragedy and the musical to comedy, since tragedy deals with the necessities of style and form and the need to take them seriously, while comedy views form ironically and always tries to puncture pretension. The western tends to consider society to be a repressive force on the individual; the musical considers society to be a joke. The western looks back to a purer presocial world; the musical looks ahead to a utopian world born of individual energy. In the musical, success is achieved through the assertion of personal force; in the western, by the assertion of personal morality. Whereas energy in the western is often inimical to the good community and yields ambivalent villains whose attractiveness conflicts with their obvious moral unsuitability, morality is an irrelevant issue in the musical and appears only as a comic pretext (are Fred Astaire and Ginger Rogers actually married in *Shall We Dance?* has Gene Kelly actually seduced Judy Garland in *The Pirate?*).

The essence of the musical is the potential of the individual to free himself from inhibition at the same time that he retains a sense of limit and propriety in the very form of the liberating dance. In a musical there is no need for Shane to wander off, left out of the world he has united by his actions; instead the energy of the central character or couple can potentially bring the community together in an array around them. Musicals have two primary themes: first, the self-consciousness of the form and of style in general and the effort to relate that style to everyday life; and second, the consciousness of the self, the search for the perfect partner, and the effort to define the perfect community. Although the themes obviously do not exist in isolation (nor do the methods that express them), one can trace the changes in these themes through what could almost be called a periodization of musicals, not unlike the periodization of westerns I noted earlier.

The epic sweep of the early westerns could be conveyed by the silent screen, but musicals necessarily begin their real film career with sound (and sound films begin, appropriately enough, with *The Jazz Singer*). The Charleston sequences of the silent *Our Dancing Daughters* (Harry Beaumont, 1928) look oddly impersonal and detached today, hardly more real than the bunny-costumed Rockettes. Sound not only individualizes the performer, but also provides a bridge of music between otherwise separate visual moments, a continuity against which the image can play, potentially freeing the film from a strict adherence to a one-to-one relation between sight and sound. Once sound frees image from the necessity to appear logical and casual, the director can experiment with different kinds of nonlogical, noncausal narrative. But, after the first years of sound and such experiments with the new form as René Clair's *Under the Roofs of Paris* (1929), Lang's *M* (1931), Renoir's *Boudu Saved from Drowning* (1932), and Ernst Lubitsch's *Trouble in Paradise* (1932), primarily musicals explored its possibilities. The western may be self-conscious about its myths, but the musical is self-conscious about its stylization, the heightened reality that is its norm. The games with continuous narrative that Busby Berkeley plays in the musical numbers of *Footlight Parade* (1933), *42nd Street* (1933), or *Gold Diggers of 1935* are hardly attempted by nonmusical directors until the jumpcutting achronicity of the New Wave.

Berkeley's films show how the stylistic self-consciousness of musicals directly concerns the relation of their art to the everyday world outside the confines of the film. His camera presses relentlessly forward, through impossible stages that open up endlessly, expanding the inner space of film and affirming the capacity of the world of style to mock the narrowness of the "real" world outside the theater walls, populated by bland tenors, greedy producers, and harried directors. Ford uses theater in *Liberty Valance* to purify his genre vision. But Berkeley uses theater, the impossible theater available to film artifice, to give a sense of exuberance and potential. Playing with space, Berkeley in *Footlight Parade* creates an incredible extravaganza supposedly taking place in miniature within a waterfall, with pyramids of swimming girls, diving cameras, and fifty-foot fountains.

Berkeley's real problem, however, is his concentration on the production number and the spectacle. The sense of play and opulence he brought to the musical, his effort to make its stage artifice a source of strength, was, if we look back upon the direction the musical took, a minor stream in its history. His influence appears in the show business biography (*A Star Is Born,* 1937; *The Jolson Story,* 1946; *Funny Girl,* 1968), the production story (*Summer Stock,* 1950; *The Band Wagon,* 1953), and that great amalgam of realized style and stylized realism, *Singin' in the Rain* (1952). There is also a darker side apparent in a film like *All About Eve* (1950), in which the urge to theater is considered to be manipulative, a reduction of the self rather than an expansion. The dark side may be the truer side of Berkeley's inheritance, because his musicals lack any sense of the individual. The strange melancholy of the "Lullaby of Broadway" number from *Gold Diggers of 1935,* in which, after some elaborately uplifting production numbers, an unsuccessful showgirl commits suicide, combines comedy and the tragedy of sentimental realism in a way that only penetrated serious films in the late 1940s. It presages the urbane tragedies of fatality in a theatrical setting that mark the late films of Julien Duvivier (*Flesh and Fantasy,* 1943) and Max Ophuls (*La Ronde,* 1950; *Lola Montès,* 1955). The showgirl commits suicide in "Lullaby of Broadway" in part because the Berkeley ensemble of faceless dancers holds no place for her at all, perhaps because of her lack of talent, but more clearly because her individuality is contrary to the demands of the uniform musical group. Like Eisenstein or the Lang of *Metropolis,* Berkeley magisterially juxtaposes sequences and articulates crowds with ritual symmetry. Berkeley's attitude toward individuals is that of a silent film director, iconographic and symmetric. The community of the Berkeley girls is cold and anonymous, like Lang's workers, a community created by a nonparticipating choreographer-director. But the kind of musical that had the greatest popular strength, spawned the largest number of descendants, and historically defined the American musical film, is the musical in which the dancer-choreographer himself was a participant, in which an individual man danced with an individual woman, and in which the theme of the individual energy of the dance, the relation of the dancer to his own body, became the main theme of the film. Obviously I am referring to the films of Fred Astaire and Ginger Rogers.†

Shall We Dance (1937, songs by George and Ira Gershwin), the last film of the basic Astaire-Rogers series, is a model of their films, perhaps not least because it contains a final sequence that seems to be an implicit attack against the Berkeley emphasis on anonymous spectacle. Astaire plays the Great Petrov, star of the Russian ballet, who is in reality Peter P. Peters, from Philadelphia. The basic conflict of the film is established in the first scene, when Petrov's manager Jeff (Edward Everett Horton) comes into his rehearsal room to find Petrov improvising a dance to a jazz record. "The Great Petrov doesn't dance for fun," he tells him, emphasizing that ballet is a serious business to which the artist must devote his full time. "But I do," responds Astaire. "Remember me? Pete Peters from Philadelphia, P.A.?" Horton points to the taps on Astaire's ballet shoes and continues his insistence that whatever Astaire is doing, it's not art. "Maybe it's just the Philadelphia in me," says Astaire, and begins dancing again. The forces have been set in motion: the dancing that Astaire likes to do when he is alone directly expresses his personal emotions as well as his real identity—the American tap dancer under the high-culture disguise of the Russian ballet dancer. Horton, as he usually does in these films, comically combines a commitment to high culture (and high society) with a definite antagonism to emotion and feeling. When Astaire falls in love with Linda Keene (Ginger Rogers), a nightclub dancer, after seeing a series of movie-like flip cards of her dancing, Horton speaks darkly of the danger to Astaire's "serious" career and the need to be personally pure (i.e., nonsexual and nonemotional) for art. Like so many musicals, *Shall We Dance* contrasts the emotionally de-

† Rouben Mamoulian in *Love Me Tonight* (1932, songs by Rodgers and Hart) focuses on individuals (Jeanette MacDonald and Maurice Chevalier), but the style of the film is still one of directional control rather than a performer's energy. The most impressive song settings are those in which parts of the song are sung and played by people in isolated places, visually linked by the director's wit and style (for example, "Isn't It Romantic?").

tached and formal patterns of high art with the involved and
spontaneous forms of popular art. (Vincente Minnelli's *Meet
Me in St. Louis,* 1944, for example, establishes the same relationship between serious music and popular music, and many
musicals include parodies of serious theater by vaudevillians.)
The 1930s musical may have its historical roots in the silent-film
urge to the respectability of theater, the importation of theatrical
performers both to give the young industry tone and to banish the
generally lower-class associations that film had from its vaudeville
beginnings. But the sound musical—like so many genres of the
1930s, comedies and horror films included—begins to mock this
respect for older forms just as it parodies the upper class in
general. Tap dancing is superior to ballet as movies are superior to
drama, not merely because they are more popular, but because
they contain more life and possibility. The flip-card stills that turn
into a sequence of Rogers dancing present her as a creature of the
film, not the stage. Like Astaire in the film, Rogers is also an
American, but more proudly: she doesn't like the "hand-kissing
heel-clickers of Paris" and rejects Peters when he attempts to impress her by coming on as the formal Petrov. Berkeley attacks
theater in favor of film and dance by destroying the limits of
theatrical space. But Astaire and Rogers (and their directors,
especially Mark Sandrich and choreographer Hermes Pan) attack
all high art in favor of the new dancing forms of spontaneity,
American style. The Berkeleyan world spawns the myth of show-
business biography that success on stage buys only unhappiness
in one's personal life. But the silvery world of Astaire and
Rogers celebrates the ability of individual energy to break away
from the dead hand of society, class, and art as well. The open
space of the western that offers a chance to build becomes in the
musical the endless inner energy released in dance.

Shall We Dance is defined by the collision between the forces
of inertia and stasis and the forces of vitality, between Astaire as
Petrov—the commitment to high art and personal repression—
and Astaire as Peters—the commitment to an art that attempts
to structure individual energy instead of excluding it. Musical
comedy therefore also attacks any theories of acting in which
character comes from the past. Character in musical comedy is
physiological and external: the ability to dance and the way

dancing functions in specific situations becomes a direct expression of the tensions within the self. In the first scene Astaire dances along at the proper speed; and then, when the machine needs to be wound up again, he slows down as the record itself slows down. On the ship that takes him and Rogers back to America, he descends into the engine room and dances there in time to the pistons while black members of the crew who are taking a musical break play for him. In both sequences the energy of the dance —the personal emphasis in the first, the relation to jazz and black music in the second ("Slap That Bass")—draws upon the analogy between body and machine. But here, unlike literary attacks against the machine, the film, true to its mechanical and technological origins, celebrates the machine as a possible element in the liberation of the individual rather than in his enslavement (similar to the ambivalence about machines that characterizes *Metropolis*). Machines are outside class, purifiers of movement. The real threat to individual energy and exuberance is not the machine, but the forces of society and respectability —the impresario Jeff, the rich suitor Jim with the weak chin (William Brisbane), who wants to take Rogers away from show business, and the punctilious hotel manager Cecil Flintridge (Eric Blore). Here they are comic, but they nevertheless play the same repressive roles as they would in the more melodramatic world of the western.‡

At the end of *Shall We Dance,* the comically hostile forces (including an outside world of publicity and gossip) are reconciled by Astaire's typical process of self-realization—the search for the perfect partner. The perfect partner is always a dancing partner, since it is within the world of dance that true communication and complementarity can be achieved: the male-female dance duo is a model of male-female relationship in general. Dancing isn't a euphemism for sex; in Astaire-Rogers films at least, dancing is much better. Two sequences in *Shall We Dance* constitute the dance of courtship and they appear after the first dancing sequences, which establish the separate personalities of

‡ The positive interpretation of the machine analogy to the body is a constant theme in musicals, most recently expressed in the Ken Russell film of *Tommy* (1975, words and music by Peter Townshend and The Who), in which the deaf, dumb, and blind boy first discovers his real nature through his symbiotic relation with pinball machines.

Astaire and Rogers. In the first, "They All Laughed," Astaire begins with ballet-like steps while Rogers stands still. Then she begins to tap, and he responds, first with a ballet version of the tapping, then a straight tap. In the second such number, "Let's Call the Whole Thing Off," the importance of the dancing situation to their relationship is further underlined. They are taking a walk in a stage-set Central Park and decide to go skating, even though neither of them has skated in a long time. They begin very haltingly, with frequent stumbles. But, as soon as the music starts, they skate perfectly together. Then, at the end of the song, as the music ends, they hit the grass outside the skating rink and fall down. Once the magic world of dance and its ability to idealize personal energy into a model of relationship has vanished, Astaire and Rogers again become separate and even bickering individuals. "Let's Call the Whole Thing Off" memorializes their differences, even while it provides a context for their relationship. The next musical number, "They Can't Take That Away from Me," contains no dancing. It takes place at night on a ferry between New Jersey and New York and emphasizes the problems of their relationship, especially the seeming conflict between their real feelings, which can be expressed at night, and the public and social demands on them that the daylight world of the rest of the film exerts. Like Astaire and Rogers themselves, who feel the pressure to continue their successful film partnership despite their own wishes, Peter Peters and Linda Keene have been forced into marriage primarily so they can get divorced. The publicity generated by their managers is meant to connect them, but it succeeds only in driving them apart, as aesthetic as well as emotional partners.

Astaire solves the conflict and rejoins Rogers in the remarkable final sequence. In a theatrical setting reminiscent of the roof of the Winter Garden, an open space within the city, Astaire stages a show that summarizes the main elements of the film. In the early sequences Astaire plays a Russian ballet dancer; Rogers appears; he loses her. Meanwhile, the real Rogers, the comic Claudius in this mousetrap, sits in a box, part of the audience, but separate from it. Astaire reprises "You Can't Take That Away from Me" to lead into a sequence in which a whole group of dancing partners appear—all wearing a mask with Rogers' face on it. The song then becomes ironic, since the memory of her uniqueness that it celebrates has been confused in the many Rogers of the present. Ruby Keeler is obviously pleased to be multiplied into many images for the adoration of Dick Powell in Berkeley's *Dames* (1934), but the Ginger Rogers in the audience of *Shall We Dance* cannot take this anonymous crowd of Busby Berkeley chorus girls all wearing her face. Astaire's message makes the same plea: deliver me from the life of a single man amid innumerable faceless girls by asserting the perfection of our relationship. Rogers goes backstage and puts on one of the masks. She comes onstage, briefly reveals herself to Astaire, and then glides back into the anonymity of the many Rogers. Which is the real Rogers among the false, the reality and energy of the individual beneath the generalized artifice of the image? Astaire finds her and together they sing and dance the final song, "Shall We Dance," an invitation to let the dancing, emotional energetic self out, to reject depression and the forms of society, and to accept the frame of theater that allows one, through the exuberance of dance, to be free.

The figure of Fred Astaire implies that dance is the perfect form, the articulation of motion that allows the self the most freedom at the same time that it includes the most energy. The figure of Gene Kelly implies that the true end of dance is to destroy excess and attack the pretensions of all forms in order to achieve some new synthesis. Kelly the sailor teaching Jerry the Mouse to dance in *Anchors Aweigh* (George Sidney, 1945) stands next to Bill Robinson teaching Shirley Temple to dance in *The Little Colonel* (David Butler, 1935). Astaire may move dance away from the more formal orders of the ballet, but Kelly emphasizes its appeal to the somewhat recalcitrant, not quite socialized part of the self, where the emotions are hidden. Astaire and Kelly are part of the same continuum of themes and motifs in musicals (an interesting study could be done of the interaction of their images in the 1940s and 1950s). There are many contrasts that can be made between the way they use dance and the way they appear in their films, but the basic fact of their continuity should be remembered. The question of personal energy, which I have characterized as the musical's basic theme, once again appears centrally. The social world against which Astaire defined himself in the 1930s no longer had the same attraction to movie audiences in the 1940s; it was a hangover from the early days of film and their simultaneous fascination with 1920s high life and the higher seriousness of theater, in a double effort both to imitate and to mock. Astaire is the consummate theatrical dancer, while Kelly is more interested in the life outside the proscenium. The energy that Astaire defines within a theatrical and socially formal framework Kelly takes outside, into a world somewhat more "real" (that is, similar to the world of the audience) and therefore more recalcitrant. Kelly's whole presence is therefore more rugged and less ethereal than Astaire's. Both Astaire and Kelly resemble Buster Keaton, their prime ancestor in dancing's paean to the freedom and confinement of the body. But Astaire is the spiritual Keaton while Kelly is the combative, energetic Keaton, compounded with the glee of Douglas Fairbanks. Kelly has more obvious physical presence than Astaire, who hides his well-trained body in clothes that give the impression he has nothing so disruptive as muscles, so that the form of his dancing is even more an ideal and a mystery. Astaire often wears suits and tuxedos, while Kelly generally wears open-collared shirts, slacks, white socks, and loafers—a studied picture of informality as opposed to Astaire's generally more formal dress. Astaire wears the purified Art Deco makeup of the 1930s, but Kelly keeps the scar on his cheek visible —an emblem of the interplay between formal style and disruptive realism in his definition of the movie musical.*

Astaire may mock social forms for their rigidity, but Kelly tries to explode them. Astaire purifies the relation between individual energy and stylized form, whereas Kelly tries to find a new form that will give his energy more play. Astaire dances onstage or in a room, expanding but still maintaining the idea of enclosure and theater; Kelly dances on streets, on the roofs of cars, on tables, in general bringing the power of dance to bear on a

* I have been using Astaire and Kelly to represent the change in the movie musical as much as I have been describing what they do themselves. A full account would also have to include a close consideration of Eleanor Powell, whose fantastic exuberance and bodily freedom often threatened to destroy the generally theatrical plots in which she was encased. The most important film for these purposes might be *Broadway Melody of 1940* (Norman Taurog), in which she and Astaire dance together with an equality of feeling and ability that presages the teaming of Kelly and Judy Garland.

world that would ordinarily seem to exclude it. (Astaire absorbs this ability of Kelly's to reorganize normal space and integrates it with his own lighter-than-air quality in the dancing on the walls sequence in *Royal Wedding,* 1951, directed by Kelly's favorite collaborator Stanley Donen.) Astaire usually plays a professional dancer; Kelly sometimes does and sometimes does not, although he is usually an artist of some kind, often, as in *The Pirate,* a popular artist, or, as in *Summer Stock,* a director, associated with the stage but not totally inside it. Kelly therefore merges the director emphasis of Berkeley with the performer emphasis of Astaire. To complement the distance from theatrical form Kelly maintains, his whole style of acting is self-mocking, while Astaire's is almost always serious and heartfelt, as far as comedy will allow. Because the film attitude toward serious art is less defensive in the 1940s than in the 1930s, Kelly can include ballet and modern dance in his films, although always in a specifically theatrical setting (the pirate dream ballet in *The Pirate,* the gangster ballet in *Les Girls*). Theater and style in Astaire's films reconcile the conflict between personal life and social pressures, and allow the self to repair and renovate its energy. Many of his films have more or less autobiographical elements in them, not the autobiography of Astaire's private life, but the autobiography of Astaire's professional life: the effect to get a new partner after Ginger Rogers decided to do dramatic films instead (*Easter Parade,* Charles Walters, 1948, with Judy Garland), the celebration of Rogers' return to dance after several "serious" films (*The Barkleys of Broadway,* Charles Walters, 1949). Kelly, however, far from taking refuge in theater, wants to make theater take over daily life. His films are hardly ever autobiographical; unlike Astaire's, they have stories in which Kelly plays a role. Astaire may dance by himself, with a partner, or with a company of dancers. Kelly wants to galvanize a community of nondancers as well. Astaire and his partner are professionals; Kelly and his partner are often amateurs, but everyone they meet knows the steps to their dances and the words to their songs.†

---

† It is worth mentioning that Astaire and Kelly are appropriately enough the two supreme examples of Hollywood stars who never really gave their private lives in any way over to the fan magazines or the mechanism of offscreen publicity, since their screen presences are personal enough.

A Kelly film that highlights the differences and similarities between the two great definers of the American musical comedy is Vincente Minnelli's *The Pirate* (1948, songs by Cole Porter, story by Frances Goodrich and Albert Hackett). In the beginning of *The Pirate*, Manuela (Judy Garland), the poor niece of a wealthy family on an eighteenth-century Caribbean island, is leafing through a book detailing the highly romanticized adventures of the pirate Macoco. She dreamily desires the embraces of Macoco but is realistically resigned to marrying the unromantic, fat town mayor (Walter Slezak), who courts her with propriety and respect. One of her companions tells her that the life of Macoco is pure fantasy and she responds by expressing the sense of separate worlds she feels within her: "I realize there's a practical world and a dream world. I won't mix them."‡ Enter Serafin (Gene Kelly), the head of a traveling company of players. He flirts with Manuela, and falls in love with her. By accidental hypnosis the reserved Manuela changes into a manic performer, and she and Serafin dance and sing together in a funny scene in which Serafin thinks he's tricked this pretty girl into dancing with him, while the exuberance released in Manuela by the hypnosis threatens to knock him off the stage. Horrified at what she's done, Manuela leaves for her hometown away from the big city to prepare for her marriage to the mayor. Serafin follows her and recognizes the mayor as the real Macoco. He threatens to expose him unless the mayor allows Serafin to pretend that he is Macoco, since Serafin knows of Manuela's hero-worship. The mayor agrees, until he sees that Manuela's attraction to Serafin is increased by the impersonation. The mayor then arrests Serafin and is about to hang him when Serafin, asking for the opportunity to do a last act on stage, plays a scene with Manuela that reveals to the mayor her actual love for Macoco the Pirate. Unaware of the game, the mayor announces that he is the real Macoco and therefore Manuela should love him. He is arrested, and the united Kelly

‡ Observers of Vincente Minnelli have often pointed out the constant interest in the clash of reality and dream in his films. Here, of course, I am considering these themes in terms of the larger issue of the history of musicals as a genre. The way specific directors, with their own thematic and stylistic preoccupations, interact with pre-existing conventions to change those conventions and clarify their own interests at the same time is a topic that requires much more minute examination than I can give it here.

and Garland appear in the last scene as stage partners singing "Be a Clown" to the audience.

Through the personalities of Garland and Kelly, *The Pirate* explores the theme of identity I have discussed in Astaire's films in a very different way. Serafin's courtship of Manuela reveals that her desire for Macoco is a desire for a romantic individualism outside society—a theme made especially strong by setting the film in an eighteenth-century Spanish Roman Catholic country with all its elaborate social forms and ceremonies. Kelly hypnotizes her with a spinning mirror—an image of the many possible selves. The Manuela that is released, the self below the social surface, is a singing, dancing self. Her exuberance indicates that Serafin has in fact released more than he expects or may want. He is a professional artist. But she gets her art directly from her inner life, untamed by society or by learned craft. Garland is perfect for this kind of role because she projects so clearly the image of a restrained, almost mouse-like person until she begins to sing and dance. (Her first important film, *The Wizard of Oz,* Victor Fleming, 1939, solidified this tension in Garland between the acceptance of daily life in a world of drabness and moral boredom, and the possibility of escape to an exuberant singing, dancing world of dream. It appeared as well in *Meet Me in St. Louis,* 1944, another Minnelli film, where the pattern of stability and release is more parallel to that of *The Pirate.*)

Serafin is the alternative to Macoco in more ways than one. The real pirate has changed from an antisocial adventurer to a socially dictatorial mayor, thus rejecting the Macoco side of himself to become almost the opposite. But Kelly instead tries to mediate individuality and community. His first song in the film is "Niña," a typical Kelly dance in a street fair, where he sings and dances with half the surprised people there to weave together a kind of community of otherwise isolated individuals and objects through the catalyst of his own personality and artistic ability. The song relates how he calls every girl he meets "niña," that is, little girl. At the end of the song Garland appears and the amazed Kelly asks her what her name is. Like Rogers at the end of *Shall We Dance,* she stands apart from communal anonymity. Serafin is the articulate adventurer, the popular artist, who sees his art to be part of a creation of community; she is the individual artist, whose art is less craft than a swelling sense of herself from within. We admire and feel friendly to him because he includes us in his dance. But we identify with her, for she, like us, is not professional, even in the loose sense in which Serafin is professional. Serafin realizes this and therefore pretends to be Macoco to win her. In the climactic moment, when he is plotting to get the real Macoco to reveal himself and brings out the mirror to rehypnotize Garland, Slezak breaks the mirror. But it doesn't matter. Manuela is willing to go along with Serafin's plot, as Garland accepts Kelly's choreography and control. Her energy, once released, can be controlled, especially within the context of love and theater. *The Pirate* is therefore a next step from the themes of the Astaire-Rogers films. Kelly makes the perfect couple the center of an ideal community created by dance, a world of harmony where everyone on the street not only sympathizes with the exuberance you feel because you're in love, but also knows all the words and dance steps that express your feelings.

The context of the ideal, the place where the true self can be revealed, is still theatrical space. The final song, "Be a Clown," emphasizes the responsible escape of art, especially popular art, in a way very reminiscent of the title song at the end of *Shall We Dance*. But the inclusion of the Garland figure—the nonprofessional dancer from the heart—indicates the direction that Kelly has taken the musical, as does the fact that Kelly and Garland are not elegant in their world of theater, but clownish and self-mocking, more willing than Astaire and Rogers to include the potential disruptiveness of the world outside them and the world within. Astaire and Rogers dance for us, looking at each other primarily to integrate their dancing. Kelly and Garland convey a much friendlier and more personal relationship. We may watch Astaire and Rogers. But we empathize with Kelly and Garland.*

* The strength of Minnelli's own vision obviously has its place in understanding *The Pirate* (1948), although the comparative visual stasis and the commitment to the values of stability that characterize *Meet Me in St. Louis* (1944) indicate the importance of Kelly in changing his style and his ideas. Minnelli's musicals may try to celebrate the triumph of the individual through art, but just as often (for example, in *The Band Wagon*, 1953) they catch a tint of gloom from his more melancholic nonmusical films, which often deal with artistic compromise and disintegration, either in the context of the world of film (*The Bad and the Beautiful*, 1952; *Two Weeks in Another Town*, 1962) or the other arts (*Lust for Life*, 1956; *Some*

Kelly in *The Pirate* is an entertainer. But the emphasis of the film is less on his dancing and singing than on the world that dance and theater can create together. The stylization and historical setting of *The Pirate* emphasize the release from the stultifying social self dance allows; the contemporary setting of most other Kelly films further highlights Kelly's effort to bring his dancing out of the enclosed world of theater and make the whole world a theater, responsive to and changed by his energy. Astaire's dances define a world of perfect form, while Kelly's often reach out to include improvisation, spontaneity, and happenstance. The scene that contrasts best with Astaire's imitation of the record player and the machines in *Shall We Dance* is Kelly's marvelous interweaving of a creaky board and a piece of paper left on the stage in *Summer Stock* (1950). Kelly's self-mocking smile reflects the way most of his films continue the attack of Astaire's films against artistic pretension. Embodying the catalytic possibilities of dance to create a new coherence for the nontheatrical world, Kelly journeys through parody and realism, attacking formal excesses on the one hand and transforming everyday reality on the other.

Singin' in the Rain (Kelly and Stanley Donen, 1952), is one aspect of his effort and *On the Town* (Kelly and Stanley Donen, 1949) is the other. The frame of *Singin' in the Rain* is a full-scale parody of the early days of sound film (an appropriate subject for the musical), complete with an attack on artistic high seriousness in favor of the comic exuberance of popular art. The essential scene is Donald O'Connor's incredible acrobatic dance "Make 'Em Laugh" (unfortunately often cut for television), like "Be a Clown" a description of the popular artist's relation to his audience. But this time, instead of being on a stage, the number is done amid a welter of different film sets depicting different worlds, with stagehands moving through the scene. O'Connor's partner for a while is a featureless, uncostumed dummy that he makes seem alive (a reminiscence of the Ginger Rogers dummy in *Shall We Dance*), and for a finale he starts walking up the set walls and finally jumps right through them. In the early scenes of the film, Kelly, the phony silent-screen lover, needs to set up a

---

Came Running, 1958). Only in the pure world of the musical can art and individuality succeed without compromise.

sound stage and props before he can tell Debbie Reynolds he loves her and sings "You Were Meant for Me." But the declaration becomes acceptable as real emotion only when, in the next scene, he and Donald O'Connor parody the demands of their diction coach in "Moses Supposes." By this time, to parallel his change from form to substance, Kelly has left his suits and tuxedoes behind and dresses in the more familiar open-collared shirt and loafers. Once again, the scar on his cheek is an emblem of the reality that will emerge. In *Singin' in the Rain* silent films are artificial in their stylized actions and hoked-up emotions; only sound is real. The discovery of communication with an audience changes clearly from "Shall We Dance" to "Be a Clown" to "Make 'Em Laugh," with an increasing emphasis on the place of informality and personal style. The solution of the plot of *Singin' in the Rain* is to make the bad serious film into the parodic musical; almost all the dances in the film contain parodies of earlier dances and dancers, in the same somewhat mocking homage that characterizes the attitude to Impressionism in *An American in Paris* (Minnelli, 1951). This is the essence of the kind of energy Kelly's film embodies: theater, like the ability to dance, is a manner of inner perspective on the world outside. The reality of sound film that Kelly discovers follows his own curve of increased dancing in the film until the great set piece of "Gotta Dance," another statement of Kelly's belief that dancing is a compulsion from within more authentic than the forms imposed from without. The final scene, in which Debbie Reynolds is revealed as the voice of Jean Hagen from behind the curtain, repeats on still another level the basic theme of outer form and inner reality. Music and dance are the real spirit of film in the same way they are the real soul and energy of New York in *On the Town*, or Paris in *An American in Paris*.

Kelly's dancing tries not to be the aesthetic escape of Astaire's. It is more utopian because it aims to bring the world together. Astaire's films often imply that dance and therefore energy itself can be a refuge from a stuffy world of social forms; Kelly's films imply that dance and the individual can change the world. The three sailors on leave in *On the Town*—Kelly, Frank Sinatra, and Jules Munshin—are searching for the perfect partner and all find their girls, not in a purified world of dance, but in a real New York (the first musical made on location) that embraces both their dancing and their search. The women—Vera-Ellen, Ann Miller, and Betty Garrett—are all at least the equals of the men in exuberance, energy, and wit. They make their own space in a public world, like Kelly in the "Singin' in the Rain" sequence, splashing through puddles of chance and nature. The great pretenders in *On the Town* are Kelly and Vera-Ellen, the small-town kids who come on to each other as sophisticates. The moral is that of almost all Kelly films: don't worry about the true self; it will turn out to be better than the one you're pretending to be. Kelly's kind of musical doesn't retreat from reality. It tries to subvert reality through its new energy, an energy available to everyone in the audience through Kelly's insistence on the nonprofessional character, the musical self that wells from inside instead of being imposed from without, whether by training, tradition, or society.

Formal self-consciousness, the shapes of individual energy, and the definition of the ideal community are the basic themes of musicals. Social utopia especially has always been an attractive theme for musicals, on screen and on stage as well. Astaire's attitude toward dance in the 1930s could be a refuge from the tangled Depression world outside films, and Kelly's common man getting in touch with his feelings through dance in the 1940s seems in accord with the optimism of going to war in camaraderie and then coming home to build a new society. William Goldman in *The Season* points out that all the most important writers of musical comedies, with the notable exception of Cole Porter, are Jewish. I would rather take this observation in a more social sense. If the western is the epic of the unassimilated individual in his constant tug of war with the demands of society, history, and the future, the musical memorializes the effort to remake society so that individual energy need not be left out or defined as archaic. The assimilationist desires of the early Jewish producers and the social radicalism of many of the later Jewish writers creates a world in which the power and beauty of individual energy can assert itself against the externals of class or profession, find its ideal partner, and create its ideal world. The Jewish feeling of alienation from American life, the desire to assimilate, the fear of the loss of special identity by that assimilation, and the vision of a society in which exclusion or deindividualization has no part— as such feelings have been expressed in film—are therefore not alien to American life, nor are they only left wing. In fact, they touch on anxieties about social acceptance and rejection, tensions between individual assertion and repression, dreams of communal order and individual release that are fundamentally American, at least since De Tocqueville commented on their place in American life in the early nineteenth century. The nineteenth-century popular answer to such ambivalences was too often the English model of the importation of more and more forms, of institutions and etiquettes multiplied so that no moment should be left unguarded. The genre film returns America to the basic problems of its founding and growth; it allows an aesthetic acting out that may finally be more fruitful than the nineteenth-century desire either to ignore popular culture or to consider it to be totally an opiate and a diversion.

As musicals move into the 1950s we see more and more films dedicated to the definition of the perfect group: the backstage world of *Singin' in the Rain* (1952), *The Band Wagon* (Minnelli, 1953), and *Les Girls* (George Cukor, 1957); the good fellows together in *On the Town* (1949), *An American in Paris* (1951), and *It's Always Fair Weather* (1955); and the communities, dreamlike and real, of *Brigadoon* (Minnelli, 1954), *Seven Brides for Seven Brothers* (Donen, 1954), and *The Pajama Game* (George Abbott, 1957). But the shadow is beginning to fall as the middle 1950s are reached. That sense of openness and possibility in the immediate postwar films—we won the war abroad and now let's win the war at home—has soured, and the potential for personal and social utopia is embarrassingly and harshly rejected. *Jolson Sings Again* was the top grosser of 1949; in 1951 its star, Larry Parks, told the House Committee on Un-American Activities that "I am probably the most completely ruined man you have ever seen." Of the three ideal couples in *On the Town*, Betty Garrett (Parks's wife) and Jules Munshin were blacklisted, Sinatra and Kelly were almost blacklisted, and only Ann Miller and Vera-Ellen were personally untouched. Musical idealism had collided with cold-war paranoia. The electrocution of the monster in *The Thing* (1951) might be a covert plea to do the same to the Rosenbergs, while films like *Ivanhoe* (Richard Thorpe, 1952), starring Robert Taylor, (a "friendly" witness) showed that Jews could be patriots, too, especially when the ruler was the cowardly King John. *An American in Paris* ironically compounds the relation between musical urges to the ideal community and the left wing politics that might nourish such beliefs. The story deals with an artist who goes to Paris to make his fortune because he is artistically unrecognized in America. In fact, in a reversal of *Shall We Dance,* Kelly had gone to Paris more because of his politics than his art—and *An American in Paris* was part of his passport back to Hollywood and a special Academy Award in 1951. But his wife, Betsy Blair, seemed to remain unemployable until *Marty* (Delbert Mann, 1955), a film whose success inspired Hollywood producers to employ the generally more liberal New York television directors.†

The dream of the future that the musical could embody was being suffocated by the harshness of the present. The cop who stops Kelly's exuberant dance in *Singin' in the Rain* asserts the reality of the streets and the rain and the lamppost Kelly is holding on to—a reality that is in opposition to what dance would like to make of the world. Throughout the sequence our point of view is with Kelly, but at the end we stand behind the cop's shoulder and watch Kelly walk away. Acting out, exuberance, energy all seem suspect, both psychologically and politically. There is a definite historical line from Chaplin's roller-skating sequence in *Modern Times* (1936) and that of Astaire and Rogers in *Shall We Dance* (1937) to Kelly's in *It's Always Fair Weather* (1955) to Barbra Streisand's in *Funny Girl* (William Wyler, 1968). Chaplin balances on the edge of disaster in blithe (and blinded) elegance. Transfigured by music, dance, and love, Astaire and Rogers turn their inability to roller-skate into a timeless image of perfect form. But when Kelly roller-skates on the street, for basically the same reasons, he is looked at strangely and even somewhat hostilely by the crowd—the same resistance to eccentric individuality represented by the cop in *Singin' in the Rain*. With Streisand's roller-skating, we are back on a real stage.

† For further discussion of the period of the blacklist and its effect on actors, see pp. 238–40.

The artist is no longer assertive about the ability of art to change the world or even himself. Streisand as Fanny Brice is a comic figure on stage, fumbling and uncertain, parodying the formal and the stylish not by opposing an alternate definition of style, but by affirming her own lack of style. Astaire and Kelly could reasonably be considered ideals for the audience; Streisand in *Funny Girl* assures the audience it doesn't have to be anything but what it already is. In the typical mode of show business autobiography, even the assertion of being a star is ridiculed in *Funny Girl* by the depiction of Fanny Brice's unfulfilled and pathetic offstage life: no more Gershwinesque lyrics about the life and camaraderie of show business. Astaire and Kelly try to establish myths of development; Streisand and the musicals of the late 1950s and 1960s establish myths of comfort and stasis. The essential change has been the growing hostility within the musical form to the power of individual energy, coupled with a belief that circumstances, the world outside, are too much for any one person to understand, let alone cope with. The sense of individual style so celebrated in the musicals of the 1930s and 1940s rings hollow in the Eisenhower years. *It's Always Fair Weather* proclaims the collapse of the transforming power of theater and style that will undermine *West Side Story* (1961). In both films the city is a mere set: the viewer wonders about dirt when Kelly, Dan Dailey, and Michael Kidd dance with garbage cans in *Fair Weather;* the viewer wonders if the Jets are all gay when they dance down the street in *West Side Story*. It is hard too decide between the defects of particular movies (which definitely have other pleasures) and the degeneration of the form. The clash between dance and reality could still be thematic and funny in *Singin' in the Rain,* but in a few years it becomes a conflict and a disruption in tone. The transforming power of genre convention has been lost.

Stanley Donen's *Seven Brides for Seven Brothers* (1954) memorializes the process in some detail. Howard Keel, the eldest of seven brothers who live and trap in the backwoods, comes to town to get a wife. He woos and brings back Jane Powell, who is appalled to discover the squalor in which the brothers live, and the fact that she is expected to be a servant more than a partner. She refuses him her bed, but decides she will clean up their lives anyhow. In the process she reverses all the musical values I have described above. The socialization she institutes is a domestication of their eccentricities: first washing their faces, and then teaching them table manners and proper etiquette. The first *dance* in the film is called "Goin' Courtin'." Instead of the celebration of the values of individual energy that dance so often stands for in Astaire's and Kelly's films, *Seven Brides* makes dance into another way of bringing the eccentric into society, forcing him to mind his manners and accept society's values, with very little feeling for the importance either to himself or to society of his individual nature. James Stewart's desire to become one of the pioneers after his Missouri border raids in *Bend of the River* is perfectly paralleled by Jane Powell's gurgling injunctions to the seven brothers to respect women, religion, the family, and society. Even though *Seven Brides for Seven Brothers* could be considered the search for the perfect partner times seven, the end of that search here is not greater freedom but greater confinement. The best dancing sequence in the film is the barn-raising, in which the brothers compete for the girls with their town boyfriends—once again a dance domesticated to the vision of family, Thanksgiving dinners, and children. This is not the family as an alternative to a corrupt society that marked *The Grapes of Wrath,* but a vision of the family as the bulwark of society, ready to defend itself with ferocity against any outsiders or aliens. When the brothers all marry at the end, they marry as a group, not as individuals, and, except for Keel and Powell, the viewer is unclear about their separate identities. *Seven Brides* has also revised the musical definition of male-female relations. In Astaire's films, his generally more formal nature was tempered and his real energy brought out by Rogers; in Kelly's films, he could awaken the same sources of energy in Garland or, in *On the Town,* for example, the women could match the men in dancing power. But with *Seven Brides* and the era of togetherness, women are expected to help domesticate men, supplying the forms for their energy. Any aggressive women that inhabit these films are always presented as unhappy.‡ Individuality must retreat, if it survives

‡ The varieties of this theme may be observed in *Gigi* (Minnelli, 1958) and *My Fair Lady* (George Cukor, 1964; stage, 1956), both written by Alan Jay Lerner and Frederick Loewe. Social forms must be learned to control emotion and thereby achieve success. But even when the truth of emotion

at all, into an actual theater. Gene Kelly becomes the Noel Air-
man of *Marjorie Morningstar* (Irving Rapper, 1957), the self-
indulgent manipulative smalltime artist (who incidentally is also
guilty of rejecting his Jewish heritage). The unassimilatable person
must be left off the showboat, like the mulatto Julie (Ava Gard-
ner) in George Sidney's *Show Boat* (1951), or be condescendingly
assigned to a world of his own, as in Otto Preminger's all-
black *Carmen Jones* (1954) and *Porgy and Bess* (1959).

One musical of this period that preserves some of the subver-
sive individualism of the past is *The Music Man* (Morton Da
Costa, 1962), written by Meredith Willson (stage version, 1958)
to celebrate his own past in early twentieth-century Iowa. Like
Spencer Tracy in *Bad Day at Black Rock* or William Holden
in *Picnic* (Joshua Logan, 1956), Robert Preston (Professor Harold Hill) enters the hostile small town and changes it, only to
change himself in the process. The town, he believes, has
music in its heart that need only be released. But the practical
people think he's a fraud and has taken their money for instruments that no one knows how to play. Spellbinders, shapers of
audience energy, don't have credentials; suspiciously enough, they
only make people happy. Like the librarian with whom he falls in
love, Harold Hill is a threat to smalltown values, he for his
feeling, she for her intelligence. But he has created a new community within the town, a band of eccentrics in which the town
bad boy is the most sincere musician. They stand up for him—
like the villagers stand up for Zapata (Kazan, 1952) or the slaves
stand up for Spartacus (Kubrick, 1960)—and from their untrained
instruments comes the music of ideal community energy. The only
trouble with the myth is that we don't quite believe it. Preston as
an actor tries to make up in physical energy what he cannot convey
spiritually. Kelly and Astaire make us feel good, but Preston makes
us admire him as a great performer, a stage actor whose self-con-

asserts itself, it appears in a social context. In these later films, it is the man
who raises the woman socially, but, unlike in *Seven Brides for Seven Brothers,* both men and women are English or European. The presence of so many
European and English performers in musicals of the 1950s (Maurice
Chevalier, Julie Andrews, Rex Harrison, Georges Guétary, and Stanley
Holloway, to name a few) argues a search for respectability that might also
explain the presence of Oscar Levant and his classical piano interludes.

sciousness of his role stands between us and the community created onscreen.

The most important musical star to emerge in the 1960s was Barbra Streisand (Julie Andrews never quite worked out), and her stock in trade, true to the direction the musical has taken, is self-indulgence. She extends and elaborates the potential for narcissism in Kelly's dance with himself in *Cover Girl* (Charles Vidor, 1944). With Judy Garland we feel that the song and dance allow her to transcend her personal problems in a real liberation. With Streisand we feel that the song and dance merely project an essential egotism. Streisand is the center of things. The world stops for her—and her offscreen reputation for willfulness completes the picture. Far from avoiding publicity, as did Astaire and Kelly, she courts it. To identify with Astaire and Kelly was to identify with potentials of one's nature; to identify with Streisand is to identify with the complacencies and self-indulgences of one's nature: "Don't Rain on My Parade." As far as musicals go, she affirms, with brilliance and talent to be sure, the decline and perhaps the final disappearance of the attempt of the musical to mediate the individual and society, to offer saving myths for that potential union. *Hello, Dolly!* (1969) embodies the loss by being a boneyard of old musical talent: directed by Gene Kelly, directed on stage by Gower Champion (who with his wife Marge had been a mechanistic and athletic 1950s version of Astaire and Rogers), and choreographed by Michael Kidd, who had choreographed *Seven Brides* and starred in *It's Always Fair Weather*. Streisand's Dolly stands with the mother-replacement stars of musicals like *Gypsy* and *Mame*. The Fanny Brice of *Funny Girl* used jokes to break moods and distance herself from hurt; sentiment and relationship were threats. The Dolly Levi of *Hello, Dolly!* continues Streisand's patterns of hostile insecurity. Her first song is "Just Ask Me" and her role in the film is teaching, manipulating, and socializing. But her world is without even the warmth of *Seven Brides*. In the dances we can hardly distinguish the principals from the chorus. There is no transformation, only pattern and repetition. The chorus is professional, the principals amateur; but nothing flows between them. The songs do not come organically from the emotional situations that precede them. There is only a slight pause for the audience to steel itself for an obvious extravaganza, the projected feeling of "now, a production number." Instead of the singer and dancer galvanizing the group, the group focuses solely on her. The central scene of *Hello, Dolly!* as William Goldman has pointed out, is patently ridiculous: a smalltown dressmaker comes to a big New York restaurant she has visited once or twice before and is greeted by the staff and all the diners as if her visit were their only reason for life. Ridiculous certainly. But in what way? Instead of the dream of a perfect society that Kelly's dances could express in his films of the 1940s and early 1950s, a society created by the artist's sense of energy and style, this scene embodies a pure fantasy of self-importance: no society, no energy, just me.*

In the same year that *Hello, Dolly!* seemed to announce that a limit had been reached in the movie musical's fascination with the individual, Francis Ford Coppola's version of *Finian's Rainbow* brought musical formal self-consciousness to a level it might never reach again without falling into problems of false nostalgia and camp. *Finian's Rainbow* is clearly a musical made in a time when musical values are collapsing under the pressure of greater and greater social conflict. Too long by half, *Finian's Rainbow* still has a sweetness about it that must attract anyone who has been touched by musicals and their themes. It is first of all an exercise in creative nostalgia, the self-conscious employment of a genre that was already self-conscious in its origins. Fred Astaire, aging and grizzled, plays Finian, the elf who travels the world with his daughter (Petula Clark, whose Englishness may be a comment as well on the bankruptcy of the American musical and the rise of the Beatles) until he comes to a small utopian community in the South where blacks and whites live and work together threatened by a bigotted Senator who lives nearby. Hermes Pan did the choreography, as he did for Astaire in the 1930s, and Coppola added lines to the script taken from Astaire's old films and songs. Through the magic of an elf (played by Tommy Steele, another English entertainer) the Senator becomes black, is abused for his blackness, and finally becomes a member of a black singing group. One member of the community is accused of being the

---

* Streisand continues this image in *Funny Lady* (Herbert Ross, 1975), whose main song is "Let's Hear It for Me."

witch who caused the transformation and is almost burned to death by the police. The comic reversals of the ending are so abrupt—the bigots become helpful, the elf becomes human, the Senator becomes white again—that it is hard to believe in it as a myth of community, except in the most distant and longing way. In the midst of political utopia, Coppola has complicated his theme by focusing on the breakdown of the musical form as well. Within the film he emphasizes the clash of styles: the dancers in the community dance across real fields in a ragged "natural" form; but the wood the elf lives in is obviously a studio set and he speaks in a high style, not the slang and informality of the other characters. In a certain sense the film holds together only because it includes all within it—artifice and reality, individual and community. The true refuge for the musical has become the film itself. When Astaire leaves at the end of *Finian's Rainbow,* doing several of his most familiar turns, we feel both his ideal virtuosity and his age, just as the beginning of the film, with its panorama of American places through which Finian and his daughter walk, reminds us simultaneously of the ideal and the real visions of America and American life, which for so long the musical had precariously attempted to hold together. The necessary next step would seem to be the Fred Astaire-Ginger Rogers retrospective of today—the final retreat into an irrelevant but comforting world of beauty and personal style.

TRUFFAUT, GODARD, AND THE GENRE FILM
AS SELF-CONSCIOUS ART

In the western the new community is corrupted by history, as individual values are left behind; the musical is optimistic about the ability of the community to grow out of individual energy because the refuge of theater and the show business community always seems possible. The musical is therefore a more self-enclosed form than the western, less interested in the pressures of society than in its ideal form. By the middle 1950s musicals show a growing inability either to extend or to transform their old conventions. What is disturbing and ambivalent in *Bend of the River* is happily embraced in *Seven Brides for Seven Brothers.* In the best musicals there is a casting about for new forms, with no authoritative line of development. Traditional assumptions may be reversed (*Seven Brides*), shown to be naïve (*It's Always Fair Weather*), reduced to their most extreme narcissistic statement (*Hello, Dolly!*), turned self-consciously campy (*Cat Ballou*), or employed without realizing their incompatibility (*West Side Story*). *Finian's Rainbow* is different because in it Coppola combines a self-consciousness about the history of the musical with a realization that the conventions may no longer work—a western-like pessimism about history. When the meaning of the musical passes from implicit to explicit self-consciousness, it requires a director with a critical as well as a creative sense. After the 1950s the various genres of film no longer inhabit the same isolated worlds they had before. Instead of being relegated to the periphery, genre films in the 1960s enter the mainstream of film history. And the main influence on directors like Coppola are the early films of François Truffaut, Jean-Luc Godard, and the French New Wave.

Truffaut and Godard considered film to be a total aesthetic world—with a definite influence on the experiential reality of the audience—rather than a world with artistic parts (the "serious" films similar to other types of great art) and unartistic parts (the genre films). The locus classicus of the New Wave interest in genre is Godard's dedication of *Breathless* to Monogram Pictures, an act meant both to outrage the highbrow critics and to assert the one source of film craft—the self-consciously conventional—that the New Wave believed was the most neglected aspect of the art and the history of film. The power of these early films rested not only in their ability to pay wry homage to a purely cinematic tradition of genre narrative and convention, but also to express the way these fables had influenced and shaped what the audience considered reality to be. Realism was only another set of conventions, irrelevant as an absolute standard because of the actual interplay between the world of normally unorganized experience and the world of genre fairytale, the paranoid hyperorganization of art. Europeans were less surprised than most "cultured" Americans, and the reaction to Truffaut's *Shoot the Piano Player* (1960) is indicative of the disruptive effect the New Wave attitude had on the understanding of film in the United States. The greatest producer and developer of genre films in the world—the United States—which for years and years had looked down on its native products and looked up to European film as the only serious expression of the art, suddenly was being told that its most neglected and critically patronized movies were its greatest contribution to the art of film, perhaps greater than the classics that had been revered in the art houses for so many years. Critics as disparate as Bosley Crowther and Stanley Kauffmann complained about the seeming haphazardness and incoherence of *Shoot the Piano Player*. But what actually is so disruptive about the film? It begins with a man running down a street, being chased by someone we don't see—the kind of *in medias res* beginning that had been a staple of American action films in the late 1940s—the way, for example, we first see Burt Lancaster in *Kiss the Blood Off My Hands* (Norman Foster, 1948) or Cloris Leachman in Robert Aldrich's *Kiss Me Deadly* (1955). The question for the audience is "Why is this person running?" and what better way to draw an audience into a film? Truffaut's abrupt beginning to *Shoot the Piano Player* attacks the elaborate narrative exposition (derived from the novel), which had been the hallmark of serious films from Griffith and Eisenstein through Welles, and replaces it with a more oblique, allusive narrative. Renoir, Rossellini, and many of the more open-form directors had also used such a juxtapositional, rather than causal, narrative in their various films (compare the beginning of *Piano Player* with, for example, the beginning of *The Rules of the Game*). But Truffaut's story didn't seem to be serious enough to hold together the fragmented and associative narrative. It was a crime film, with murders, greed, petty gangsters, and bantering dialogue. Instead of being economical in the fashion of the enclosed urban crime film, it focused on the variety of the city, a long opening dialogue with a character who never reappears, comic turns, and songs. Inspired by the American film noir in tone and convention, it, like *The 400 Blows* and Godard's *Breathless,* was held together by character as much as by style. As Truffaut said in an interview at the time, "Because spectators see the same scenario in so many films, they have become good scenarists and can always foretell what's coming and how it's going to end. With *Piano Player* I would like them to go from surprise to surprise." Truffaut defined the genre conventions as a frame within which he was free to do as he pleased, at the same time that he could ironically reflect on the reasons the conventions existed.

The critics who were upset at his film had either, like Crowther, grown up in a tradition where popular and serious films occupied different compartments in their heads, or, like Kauffmann, considered film to be aesthetically interesting primarily when it was thematically interesting. Those who appreciated it, like Pauline Kael, had no rigid line to draw between varieties of film seriousness, and no inherent prejudice against American films for their mass appeal. That an audience could respond to *Shoot the Piano Player* or *Breathless* in a way that critics often could not indicated that not all film aesthetics were defined by the great tradition of "classic" films. The film audience's experience of all films was aesthetically continuous; films by Renoir, Nicholas Ray, and Stanley Donen could all be alluded to in *Shoot the Piano Player* because all had contributed to Truffaut's sense of the possibilities of film.†

The genre film, most markedly in the New Wave's use of it, asserts that there is a *normal* film aesthetic that is unobtrusive and yet complicated, hardly visible if one looks for technical flash on the screen and yet perfectly understandable to the audience. Genre art, they implied, is the art we learn when we are unaware we are learning it. It is no less important than the art we learn at the height of our intellectual awareness, and it may be more influential, since its power is frequently unmediated by the detachments enforced by the "art"-perceiving mind. The old distinction between the serious and the genre film could never be the same. If what the New Wave brought into film can be described in one word, that word might be "self-consciousness" at all levels; a self-consciousness about film history and tradition, a self-consciousness about the act of making a film, a self-consciousness in the audience that approaches the film more as a cultural artifact than as an entertainment for which the mind was turned off, and, perhaps the most important aspect, a self-consciousness about the role of the director, matched with the audi-

† I have discussed *Shoot the Piano Player* in more detail in *Focus on Shoot the Piano Player* (Prentice-Hall: Englewood Cliffs, N.J., 1972), an anthology that includes interviews with Truffaut as well as contemporary reviews of the film. The American film audience had already been prepared for the New Wave self-consciousness about film history by television reruns. Truffaut and Godard may have spent their days in the Cinémathèque, but the average American filmgoer was being exposed to the growing film repository of television.

ence's increased awareness that the director is a "star" too. Inspired by the sense of tradition and formal self-awareness that marks genre films, the New Wave at its best treated convention seriously, as it treated technical devices seriously. Some of the effects of the self-consciousness have been negative, or have had negative aspects, as interest was displaced from the film to allusion, director, or anything but the experience of the film itself. As we see in *Finian's Rainbow,* when formal self-consciousness does not stay inside the form, it frequently heralds the end of the effectiveness of the conventions that are its subject. Many directors tried for easy brilliance by self-reference and self-mockery. The seeds are already there in *Breathless* and *Shoot the Piano Player*—the allusions to friends, to other films, the awareness of being inside a film, the role of the director in putting the film together—a centrifugal allusiveness that threatened to make the audience forget the main point of being there, a film story and its characters. While the New Wave shed much light on the previous history of genre films and exposed their aesthetic tenets, its polemic therefore often produced films that were less interesting or moving than the old "classics." The self-consciousness that existed within genre film found it hard to retain its innocence in the face of the self-consciousness that referred to the act of filming itself. Every young director out to make his name in the 1960s believed that his work was automatically intellectually and artistically respectable if he included a camera or a scene from the production of the film. A director like Fellini, who added fuel to the trend toward directorial self-consciousness with his film *8 ½* (1963), could, because of the theatrical roots of his realistic method, move between literal exposition to dream exposition without obvious halts and stops. But when realistic directors whose roots were in documentary, like Lindsay Anderson, attempted such external references, the result was more often incoherence than extension of the possibilities of film. *If . . .* (1969) and *O Lucky Man* (1973) try to use frame-breaking, illusion-shattering devices to convey a Brechtian thematic seriousness. But, without genre, or some other implied order, the breaking of the frame has no context and becomes merely fragmentary and disruptive. Particular sequences may work, but the film as a whole is too easily dismissible as an arch and unnecessarily allusive joke. An effort to go beyond the inherent aesthetic

bounds of film comes off as a self-consciously "arty" playing
with those bounds, with little enrichment in the play.

Complexity for the New Wave was not only a matter of themes
and visual style, but also an effort to treat film conventions in an
explicitly self-conscious manner. Playing on the mythic interactions of the implicitly self-conscious genre films, they told stories
in which the moral judgments implied by the aesthetic pattern
were inadequate to judge the actual events and characters. Instead
of calling on dramatic irony or the bathetic happy ending, they
trusted the audience's ability to know the conventions of various
form and the openness that results when forms collide. This active manipulation of film tradition and the new star status of the
director as self-conscious artist might recall the relation between
Lang and Rotwang in *Metropolis* or between Renoir and Octave
in *The Rules of the Game*. At the same time that, outside the film,
the creative strength and power of the filmmaker is being celebrated, within the film the main character, usually a man, often
an artist of some sort, is presented as a basically weak, self-
involved, often impotent figure. Charlie Kohler in *Piano Player*
thinks of taking a course in daring, falls in love, kills, but finally
withdraws again; Michel in *Breathless,* living as he imagines
Bogart would, dies because his girlfriend wants to play Bogart
as well. Sandro in *L'Avventura,* a failure as an architect, continually fails in all his human relations; David in *Through a Glass
Darkly* and Elisabet in *Persona* use and almost cannibalize others
for the purposes of their art. Charlie Kohler, in flight from his
celebrity as a concert pianist and what it has cost him personally,
stands in contrast to his creator Truffaut, able to distance his own
confusion about the virtues of fame and anonymity by embodying
them in a character, Michel, who tries to escape his problems by
fitting into Bogart's image, stands in contrast to Godard his
creator, who in the film appears as a bystander who recognizes
Michel and turns him in to the police. The failures of Sandro,
David, and Elisabet as well are the material for the successes of
Antonioni and Bergman.

In the period of the 1960s and 1970s, therefore, the exploration
of genre structure necessarily intersects the exploration of character. The old genre forms are no longer substantial enough to express fully and satisfactorily the themes that now most attract the

film audience. Without tradition, the directors must create their own forms, hopefully with more success than their characters explore their own psyches and shape their lives. The New Wave helps mark the way in which films, with their mixed art and their ability to manipulate and transform conventions, have helped free us from the outworn aesthetic distinctions of the past. The end of the 1950s begins the first new era since the introduction of sound in the late 1920s and early 1930s, coinciding with the decline of studio power and the rise of a more independent kind of director in Hollywood itself. The characteristics of that era are not yet fixed, even in the mingling of earlier characteristics of open and closed form I have already described. The essential element that concerns me here is the refusal of the new filmmakers to make any absolute or even partial distinction between the methods and techniques of "serious" films and the methods and techniques of popular, genre films. Like the Elizabethans who could take high tragedy and low comedy, often in the same play, the same film audience can appreciate both serious and popular films and find within them explorations of the issues that equally animate their feelings and their intellects.

THE TRANSFORMATION OF GENRE: FILM AND SOCIETY IN THE 1970s

What happens to genre films after they attempt to include the theme of their own nature? Despite the New Wave contributions to the understanding of genre, European directors were never noted for their interest in conventional form and did not get any more involved after genre films were beginning to be considered so self-consciously.‡ But in America and England genre films were greatly affected, both in style and content. The New Wave had shown how the combination of an open visual style with enclosed or even fatalistic situations and characters could express an attitude toward society and its traditions. The tension in 1950s

‡ When I speak of European films, I generally mean those films that have a place in the international market. Many films made primarily or solely for national markets have a good deal of genre flavor to them, for example, the French "Gendarme" series starring Louis de Funès.

genre films between the ordered society and the disruptive individual, previously resolved conservatively by the demands of a formal and economic narrative, could now become more complicated. Within the genre conventions, characters became more psychological and personal: the individual was once again an issue and the self-consciousness of genre conventions allowed a new distance from the forces that had previously controlled him. In this new genre world, which often valued a concentration on the episodic adventures of individual characters, the musical, with its formal narrative balance, seemed less able to absorb the changes. Richard Lester in his Beatles films, *A Hard Day's Night* (1964) and *Help!* (1965), used a disjointed narrative and a mélange of styles (two New Wave hallmarks) to present with imitative clarity the music of a group whose own greatest strength was in their understanding and artistic manipulation of their musical influences. But such experiments could really be done only once. Bob Fosse's *Cabaret* (1973) visually alternated inner and outer space, theater and nature, to present the satiric cabaret songs and dances as both a criticism of Hitler's Germany as well as an irresponsible refuge from it. The real danger must be faced outside. Fosse's next film, *Lenny* (1974), although not technically a musical, extended his ambivalent attitude toward theater by both praising Lenny Bruce's satire and attacking the messed-up psyche through which Bruce's tormentors brought him down. As the Nazis finally invaded the cabaret, the American establishment of the 1950s invaded the coffee houses and nightclubs to quench Lenny's cauterizing energy. But theater, Fosse implies, has traditions richer than those of official society, and the values Lenny represents will make their way after his death. Lenny, like Bonnie and Clyde, was warped because he defined himself against a warped society. But within the protective frame of theater he could still nurture and create.

The major musical trend of the late 1960s was the effort to record communal musical events, making stage musicians into agents of audience release and galvanization, along the lines of the rock movies of the 1950s and 1960s. On film were the documentaries *Monterey Pop* (1968) and *Woodstock* (1970); on stage were *Hair* (1967) and *Godspell* (1971). The stage musicals had no stars, and the stars of the films seemed to be the audience, until the fragmented world the new musical technology had brought with it exploded in *Gimme Shelter* (David and Albert Maysles, Charlotte Zwerin, 1971). As Fosse's films implied, the only refuge for music did seem to be the structured film and the stage. After a career of exploring musical community, Stanley Donen made *The Little Prince* (1973), a musical in the desert, with only five characters (including Bob Fosse as a snake). Newer and more compelling genres were the caper film and the Bond spy film, with their exotic locales, gadgets, and sex strung together by a cartoon story. Many younger directors, like Peter Bogdanovich (previously a film critic) and William Friedkin, seemed to become victims of auteurist Romanticism, using the New Wave attitude toward genre to relieve themselves from making the social criticism that attitude could imply. Bogdanovich especially retreated into a black-and-white genre past (*The Last Picture Show,* 1972; *Paper Moon,* 1974) or used color with a much stronger genre frame (horror in *Targets,* 1968, screwball comedy in *What's Up, Doc?,* 1972, historical romance in *Daisy Miller,* 1974). Sidney J. Furie even more extremely combined a commitment to genre films with an emphasis on directorial self-consciousness in *The Ipcress File* (1965), *The Appaloosa* (1966), and *Lady Sings the Blues* (1972), in which stylistic irrelevancies either juice up a bad plot or drown a good one. The flashy self-display of directors such as Bogdanovich, Furie, and Friedkin, sits uneasily with their plots. They imitate New Wave style without the content and formal self-awareness its style at its best implied. They have learned only to assert the director, not his problematic relation to his story and his characters, but his self-congratulation and his desire for fame. Their films have some place, according to their grosses, in an analysis of social myths. But they are finally only mechanical exercises, whose display of directorial virtuosity vainly attempts to make up for an inability to understand the dynamics of form. The best new genre works of the 1960s and 1970s, however, did progress in two directions that intermingled form and content: first, the strong narratives of social allegory typified by the films of Don Siegel and Robert Aldrich; and second, the more episodic, stylistic meditations on the relationship between genre and social forms typified by the work of Arthur Penn and Robert Altman. Francis Ford Coppola, because of his interest in the theme of family and its moral relation to society (in such disparate films as *Finian's Rainbow,* 1968; *The Rain People,* 1969; *The Godfather,* 1972; and *The Godfather II,* 1974), may be the one young director whose understanding of the possibilities of playing with genre conventions is comparable to that of Truffaut or Godard. Like Siegel, Aldrich, Penn, and Altman, he understands genre from the inside.

Siegel especially has played subtly between the realistic and the stylized potentials of genre. All genre films must maintain some kind of balance between style and normality, and the trend in the 1960s and 1970s has been to try to introduce as much normal and familiar local color as possible. In *Madigan* (1968), Siegel shows us a real New York City in which Detective Madigan (Richard Widmark) must make his compromises and be corrupted at the same time that he believes in his job; a parallel subplot involves the adultery of the Police Commissioner (Henry Fonda) with a woman he has met as part of his public relations work with the wealthier members of the Manhattan community. The settings are solid and evocative, perhaps the best use of New York since Jules Dassin introduced New York location shooting in *The Naked City* (1948). But the tone of the story is fatalistic, an encircling corruption that brings the ultimate death of Madigan. Siegel has set in an actual New York a story whose confines are closed. This could not have been just another case for Madigan; it had to be his last. In Siegel's next film, *Coogan's Bluff* (1968), he took a star, Clint Eastwood, who made his reputation in the Italian westerns of Sergio Leone (*A Fistful of Dollars,* 1967; *For a Few Dollars More,* 1968; and *The Good, the Bad, and the Ugly,* 1969), and cast him as a country sheriff who has to go to New York to extradite a criminal. The dynamic of the film rises from the contrast between the open, straightforward moral world of nature and the closed, ironic world of the city. Accordingly, the New York of *Coogan's Bluff* is hardly realistic at all. If one followed the geography, Greenwich Village, for example, would be in northern Manhattan. While in *Madigan* there is never any sense of distortion, in *Coogan's Bluff* the distortions are obvious, even for the viewer unfamiliar with New York. In *Coogan's Bluff,* New York is a city of the mind, created from conventions, a mythic city to match the mythic country sheriff who enters it.

When Eastwood leaves the city at the end, he leaves by helicopter, straight up.

Siegel continues this dialectic between the closed mythic and the open realistic in two later films, *Dirty Harry* (1971) and *Charley Varrick* (1973). Eastwood, playing Detective Harry Callahan, is again the moral avenger, but now he is on the police force itself. Like the older detective hero, he is also repressed, in 1971, not by a corrupt or lax bureaucracy (as, say, in Lang's *The Big Heat,* 1953) but by the liberal courts and district attorney's office. (It is interesting to see how the aesthetic forms retain their strength by picking up contemporary issues that fit into their paradigms.) Like Robert Ryan in Ray's *On Dangerous Ground* (1951), Eastwood is more like the maniacal killer he seeks than he is like anyone else in the official world of the film; both feel that the shape of society has to yield to their dreams. *Charley Varrick,* on the other hand, stars Walter Matthau, an actor associated with cities and even with the kind of ironic comedy typical of the New York sensibility. But in the plot of this film, Matthau plays a kind of archaic bankrobber ("the last of the independents" is lettered on the paint truck that serves him as a front) who by accident robs a bank that is being used as a Mafia drop point. But Matthau outwits all the organizations, both official and criminal, and gets away with the money, drawing, appropriately enough, on his ability as a stunt pilot to fly away from the final trap. Siegel, more self-conscious about his form than about his own directorial sensibility, has cast and plotted to mix his conventions —cowboy in the closed city, ironist in the open country—in a way that only the resources of genre allow.

Siegel's cowboy-turned-urban-detective is another step toward the transformation of western themes in the 1960s and 1970s out of their past world and into more contemporary settings. In the westerns of the post-New Wave period the past cannot be recaptured. The main theme is that of the loss of a time in which the individual could make moral choices that were clear and distinct. The violence of such films as Sam Peckinpah's *The Wild Bunch* (1969) or *Straw Dogs* (1972) expresses an impotent rage against the possibility of making one shot count: blood bath has drowned out the professional pride of the single gunfighter. The compromises and the accommodations necessary in the city film have invaded the purer world of the western past. *The Wild Bunch* and *Butch Cassidy and the Sundance Kid* (George Roy Hill, 1969) both deal with the same gang and the same theme of loss. The first is tragic and elegiac; its fall is within the film. The second is more comic; it preserves the western Eden by the freeze frame derived from *The 400 Blows:* "here we are with nowhere to go." The New Wave focus on a passive or impotent central character is therefore paralleled in the American genre film by a focus on either fantasies of escape from impotence in the present or dreams of the end of innocence in the past.

Whether their specific orientation is toward the left or the right, the genre films of the late 1960s and early 1970s generally indict an incoherent institutional structure and praise heroes whose solutions are only personal, with no general relevance and therefore no solace for the audience supposedly finding "escape" in such films. Genre films such as *Hello, Dolly!, The Wild Bunch, Easy Rider, McCabe and Mrs. Miller,* and *Dirty Harry*—at different levels of intensity and for different segments of the population—make the same social points: true individualism is either dead or impotent; true friendship cannot help; true feeling is possible only in dreams, whether the self-indulgent dreams of art in *Hello, Dolly!* or *Funny Girl;* the self-indulgent dreams of the old West in any John Wayne film; the dreams of individual urban power in any Charles Bronson film; the dreams of male friendship (*Scarecrow, The Sting, Papillon, California Split, Thunderbolt and Lightfoot*); the dreams of rebel communities (*The Wild Bunch, Bonnie and Clyde, The Godfather*); or the just plain dope dreams of *Easy Rider* and *McCabe and Mrs. Miller.* The shift of emphasis from the frame of the genre film to the creator of the genre film mirrors and accelerates a cultural shift from placing the weight of responsibility on society to placing it on the individual. The anxieties about impotence and failure reflect the search for myths of individual responsibility that can survive the collapse of the social forms outside the films.

Nineteen sixty-eight seems crucial as the year when American society felt truly for the first time the impact that the Vietnam War had made in its coalition and concentration of the forces of ferment and change that had existed potentially in America since the beginning of the 1950s. For genre films to exist and develop, the society that gives them birth needs to be coherent, at least in the commonality of its basic assumptions about its values. The most pervasive criticism that the outgroups of the 1960s and 1970s made of American society was that the gap between ideals and realities had gotten too wide. How could works that depend for their power on the congruity between ideals and reality survive such a fragmentation? A musical that celebrates the energy of the individual dancer to become a catalyst for an ideal community sounds hollow in a country where the consensus has become divided and hostile. The western might still preserve some compelling force by presenting a past world where conflicts were simple and solvable. A horror film might help to explain and satisfy those fears about the curability of uncontrollable forces from within. A James Bond film could assert that urbanity and personal style would triumph over the hordes of (usually) slavic or oriental forces that might otherwise overwhelm a civilization defined by the knowledge of martini-mixing. A jewel heist film could siphon off a growing hostility among the left and the right toward the rich and powerful.

For individualism to thrive and grow, at least in movies, it needs a frame that controls without compelling and defines without determining. Siegel's *Dirty Harry* and Sidney Lumet's *Serpico* (1972) are essentially the same film. Whether in one the hero rights wrong or in the other the hero lefts wrong, the search is still for the one just man whose individual moral nature can recreate the values of the past. Unlike the films of the 1940s and 1950s, the films of the 1960s and 1970s do not tell us that society preserves individualism, but that it warps and distorts it. The gang families in *Bonnie and Clyde* and *The Godfather* are attractive in spite of their violence. Inside society the family is breaking up, but outside, extralegally, it seems to survive in feeling and affection. Both *Dirty Harry* and *Serpico* celebrate a professionalism and personal integrity that is necessarily opposed to institutions and bureaucracies. The progression in attitude can be traced as well from the figure of Custer in *They Died with Their Boots On* (Raoul Walsh, 1940) to Custer in *Little Big Man* (Arthur Penn, 1971). In the first film Custer (Errol Flynn) is the noble, glory-seeking individualist opposed by a venal and greedy individualist named Sharp (Arthur Kennedy) with es-

tablishment connections. Like Sergeant York, Custer can allow
his individual nature full play only within the Army. In civilian
life he doesn't know what to do with himself. His death at Little
Big Horn is an act of self-sacrifice to save his men from the Indians who have been stirred up by evil entrepreneurs, destroying
the wonderful relation of trust Custer had previously built with
them. In *Little Big Man,* on the other hand, Custer is a crazy,
glory-seeking individualist who is willing to sacrifice anything and
anyone to his dreams of personal fame. He is opposed by Jack
Crabb (Dustin Hoffman), the hero and narrator, who is interested
only in his own survival. Walsh's Custer will not work outside
the system; he feels sure evil will ultimately be punished. Penn's
(and Thomas Berger's) Custer represents the irrationality of institutions: individual desire masquerading as abstract public
policy. In 1940 society could absorb individual energy and make
it work. In 1971 society warps and maims individual energy when
it doesn't crush it entirely. It inspires heroic ideals and then
tramples on them. The old institutional eccentric is no longer
trusted; he has betrayed us too many times. Like Custer, the
heroic Jesse James of the 1940s and 1950s has declined into
the religious psychopath of *The Great Northfield Raid* (Philip
Kaufman, 1971). The significance of the heroic actor has
changed as well. Charlton Heston, for example, is primarily a
western hero, but he also carries with him the extra self-righteousness of his biblical roles. *Planet of the Apes* (Franklin Schaffner,
script by Michael Wilson, 1968) turns this image around to
criticize that aggressiveness, the adventure hero's version of
American imperialism. At the end of the film Heston is no longer
an exuberant civilizer but a destroyer, and the wrecked Statue of
Liberty he sees affirms his role in bringing about the final catas-
trophe. All institutions finally are suspect. The sequel to *Dirty
Harry,* called *Magnum Force* (Ted Post, 1974, script by John
Milius), carries Harry's character a little further. He discovers a
death squad working in the police department, who expect him to
approve because of his reputation for violence and self-righteousness. But the distinction is clear: they are another organization.
They are photographed usually in their rookie patrolman leather
jackets and white helmets to underline their uniformity, while
Harry himself wears a tweed jacket with patches on the elbows.

Patriotism is also an irrelevant trap. The death squad leader wears a business suit and an American flag pin. But any ideology beyond himself is anathema to Harry. *Magnum Force* implies that the desire for individual moral solutions lives inside a measured and tentative acceptance of whatever system exists. Without the confinement to react against, it might not exist at all or it may turn into the fatal self-centeredness of the return to *Chinatown* (Roman Polanski, 1974) or the fruitlessly circling boat in *Night Moves* (Arthur Penn, 1975).

Individualism becomes problematic in the genre films of the 1960s because the previous genre types have become more individual themselves, with things going on in their minds behind the conventions of plot and situation—lineal descendants of Bogart's visit to the bookstore in *The Big Sleep*. The stars with sex appeal, with the old iconographic flatness, are few, like Steve McQueen and Paul Newman, both of whom have been in films—like *Bullitt* or *Sometimes a Great Notion*—that tend to emphasize the fantasies of freedom rather than the realities of enclosure and impotence. McQueen's screen character, perhaps in its derivation from that of Richard Widmark, still preserves some of the divided, almost schizophrenic force it had in such early films as *Hell Is for Heroes* (Don Siegel, 1962), *Love with the Proper Stranger* (Robert Mulligan, 1963), and *Baby, the Rain Must Fall* (Mulligan, 1965). But the idealizing tendency that earlier had swallowed up Newman has by now overtaken McQueen as well. Even in a cultural moment when the great bulk of films emphasize the loss of power, there have to be some stars who represent the solace of success. But stars like Newman, McQueen, and Streisand are exceptions; they are objects for the audience to admire rather than fellow conspirators with whom to identify. Robert Redford and Eastwood, on the other hand, seem to have more inside themselves than they can express and enrich their films with a mysterious presence.

The decline of the star has frequently been noticed throughout the 1960s and 1970s. In part it occurs because the audience no longer identifies with the sexual and psychic energy of the figure on the screen so much as it identifies with his impotence or failure in one kind of film or his self-indulgence and self-centeredness in another. The use of violence is ultimately futile if its point is to make up for the sense of loss of personal importance and centrality in the individual character and the individual filmgoer. The increasingly obvious phallic use of guns in films from *Bonnie and Clyde* to the John Wayne film *McQ* (Andrew McLaglen, 1973) should not be a source of ridicule by undergraduate Freudians. Obvious symbols have aesthetic functions different from those of hidden symbols. Once everyone knows what they mean—like a cross or a gun—they have not lost their meaning. Like genre conventions themselves, once understood, they can achieve a different kind of meaning. The phallic guns function in the films of the 1960s and 1970s precisely as penis substitutes. They don't *mean* penis, they *are* penises: Clyde's caressable gun, Dirty Harry's Magnum, James Bond's custom-made Beretta, Wayne's six-shooter. In all such films the assertion of violence through the gun is linked to a desexualized masculine image: Clyde's impotence, Bond's promiscuity, Dirty Harry's voyeurism, and Wayne's farce of politeness and age. Sex and violence have become so explicit in popular films today because the theme of such films, the feeling they appeal to in the audience, is impotent rage. Whether in the genre films or in those films that draw on genre conventions for their strength—like *Fat City, Deliverance,* or *J. W. Coop*—the situation is that of masculine testing. Set in a world of the decay of the city and the hostility of nature, the outcome is generally failure, whether outside you in society or within your body. Musicals may be gone, but the musical problems are still with us.

The genre films of the 1960s and 1970s mix the two basic visual styles of open and closed film as well as the social implications of the two forms: the closed film belief that society is repressive but necessary with the open film desire to find a new community. One line of development has been what I might call the paranoid pastoral. Related to male camaraderie films such as *Deliverance* and *Butch Cassidy,* it draws strength from *Bonnie and Clyde* as well: the social outcasts in the midst of a seemingly benevolent nature. Three examples from 1974 are Terrence Malick's *Badlands,* Steven Spielberg's *Sugarland Express,* and Robert Altman's *Thieves Like Us*. Appropriately enough, Malick and Spielberg are just beginning their careers, while Altman has made his reputation as the first genre/art or popular/serious director who explores conventionalized forms without committing himself to any particular genre mode, a kind of self-conscious Howard Hawks.

Like Robert Aldrich, Altman draws on genre energy but considers each of his films as a meditation on form as well as an exploitation of it. The old genre director, who "just made westerns" or horror films or musicals seems to have virtually disappeared, except for such perennials as Andrew McLaglen, Richard Fleischer, and Burt Kennedy. Albert LaValley has said that the present period is marked by an "exhaustion of genres." But such recent types as the survival film show an effort to move beyond the problems of individualism into a greater interest in possible community in the face of disaster.

Conventionality in popular art is the emblem of a unified culture, with a generally acceptable system of gestures, themes, characters, situations, and motifs. Until the 1960s the existence of pure genre films seemed to imply that America had such a unified culture, at least on the surface. In fact, the history of convention in American film has always been the history of successive exhaustions of convention. The exposure and elaboration of certain actors and actions pleases and solaces the audience but then finally leaves it cold. When the genre conventions can no longer evoke and shape either the emotions or the intelligence of the audience, they must be discarded and new ones tried out. Genre films essentially ask the audience, "Do you still want to believe this?" Popularity is the audience answering, "Yes." Change in genres occurs when the audience says, "That's too infantile a form of what we believe. Show us something more complicated." And genres turn to self-parody to say, "Well, at least if we make fun of it for being infantile, it will show how far we've come." Films (and television) have in this way speeded up cultural history. The western and the musical have been fairly long-lived forms because they were flexible enough to contain an increasing variety of changes. Other kinds of genre film occupy more time-bound points in cultural history. Our sense of the history of American culture comes from looking back on such films and perceiving their strangeness in a way that would have been difficult at the time—a strangeness that is a direct function of our emergence from the conventions they dealt in and thereby exposed and purged. In our understanding of the relationships possible between men and women, for example, we cannot go back to *The Bride Came C.O.D.* (William Keighley, 1941) or *Westward the Women* (William A. Wellman, 1951), except to see them with anthropological eyes as an important expression of a particular time. Condemning "escapism" is less fruitful than considering the terms of the escape and thereby discovering what is being escaped from. The paranoia about outside forces that sapped individual will in the films of the 1950s can by the 1970s turn into a valid mode of activist social criticism. Within the history of the detective form, James Bond, the civil service employee with a license to kill, tells us that Bogartian detachment has become only nostalgia.

Allowing us to know the way we see and have seen ourselves has been one of the greatest contributions of films to culture. The way so many great directors have loved the collectivity of the film enterprise enough to make it part of their subject matter (Renoir, Ford, Bergman, Fellini) illustrates their effort to get in touch with the community that gives them energy. The model of the isolated Romantic artist does not fit the film director because one of the greatest achievements of film is its ability to open itself to cultural influences so directly. Genre films may therefore contain a more accurate description and a more radical critique of the values of the society that produced them than can the serious film, which is so self-contemplative, so obsessed with its own aesthetic status, that it neglects its connection to the audience. The only barrier to the appreciation of genre films is a prejudgment that the genre emphasis on feeling and sentiment in their various forms automatically makes the films mere escape. Genre conventions are a vocabulary by which films try to deal with issues that are continually pressing to their audiences. The vocabulary may date, the issues may fade, the answers may be meretricious, but the possibilities are also there for a rich reflection of the concerns of a society, expressed in a way that can lead as much as follow. Genre conventions allow filmmakers to express themes too painful or confusing to talk about directly. Like psychotherapy, the successive eras of genre film do not just purge or distance emotions; they work through the problems to reach another, more complex stage. If the history of genre films and the history of American culture are investigated with any thoroughness, in a way I can only begin to suggest here, we might conclude that we have been more influenced and molded by films that we have previously dismissed than we have by films that we praise as classics. Classics set up a distance between themselves and their audience, compounded of awe and emotional disdain, but genre films in their unpretentious and often ambivalent way can be more effectively didactic. Appreciating the terms of their art may make our own reactions to them more complex.

The success of genre films argues a community of feeling about the world and the self that must be understood before it can be changed. To deplore or to condescend, the usual responses of reviewers who are marketing their superior sensibilities, are useless confusions. The thematic and aesthetic crisis of genre films in the 1960s and 1970s reflects a period of redefinition in the society outside films. The old distinctions of visual mode (open and closed) and aesthetic level (popular and serious) have broken down. Highly self-conscious directors like Altman and Penn are freely using popular forms, while successful genre directors like Siegel and Aldrich have become increasingly ironic. What will emerge? What new forms will be taken by the genre film's urge to explore the relationship between individual and society? The material of many films now may be frustration and impotence, but in the light of the history of genre films, we have entered a period of great possibility. The old ways cannot be restored without a debilitating cynicism (like that in Altman's *The Long Goodbye*). One new direction seems to be toward the building of community from the individual, an exploration of psychology within the system that is potentially liberating. The new forms are still unclear. But the direction is one of synthesis, a search for new ways to mediate the relation between the individual and society in culture, and new ways to mediate the relation of form, content, and character within the individual film. In their explorations, genre films attempt to define not the separations but the connections of individuals. The voyeurism of the individual may be culpable, but the communal voyeurism of the audience of a genre film can be responsible because it is ultimately a self-examination that is under way. Even more than other films, genre films draw upon the odd ambivalences of the situation of the filmgoer, part isolated and part communal, a member of a society in the dark.

Acting and Characterization: The Aesthetics of Omission

Don't waste your time in the so-called real life. You belong to us—the actors, acrobats, mimes, clowns, mountebanks. Your only way to find happiness is on any stage, any platform, any public place, during those two little hours when you become another person, your true self.

Jean Renoir,
The Golden Coach

The ordinary way of picturing a person is by picturing the human face or the human body . . . But once one has the idea that a person is something logically distinct from his body, this way of picturing a person no longer seems to do. It is, among other things, the apparent lack of a philosophically suitable way of picturing a person that makes persons seem a mysterious sort of object.

Sidney Shoemaker,
Self-Knowledge and Self-Identity

The one aspect of serious art that has been firmly denied to films is the ability to create a complex character. In the literature-into-film courses that are too quickly becoming traditional in many universities, movies generally turn out to be deficient versions of novels. Characters that are rich in works of fiction, it is argued, become "flattened out" in films. Fiction permits psychological intensity, while film must stop at the surface, unable to peer into the supposedly far richer interior. Some have even complained that a fictional character transferred into film can never be thought of again without substituting the face of the actor or actress who played the role, even though the screen version, for example, Susannah York in *Tom Jones* (Tony Richardson, 1963), looks nothing at all like Fielding's original description of Sophia Western. The visual imperatives of film therefore tyrannize and reduce our sense of character. When films do attempt to be psychological, they are called "clinical" (Polanski's *Repulsion*) or "simplistically Freudian" (Hitchcock's *Spellbound, Vertigo,* or *Marnie*). At best, continues this view, film can add only a panoramic perspective to the adapted novel. "The omnipresent eye which surveys the scene is like the lens of the film camera," says W. J. Harvey of *Bleak House* in *Character and the Novel,* and many directors have implied similar assumptions about the relative perception available to films and fiction by "opening" their novel or stage adaptations with a few exterior scenes.

When critics say film allows no psychological complexity, they are drawing their standards from the nineteenth-century French and English novel, with its omniscient look into the inner thoughts of its characters, its decision to place the reader in a detached position about those thoughts, and its didacticism about the right kind of character and understanding one should have. Character in omniscient psychological fiction purports to be totally explainable because to a great extent it is totally explained by that narrator who is the mouthpiece of the author within the work. When the narrator is himself a character and the narration is a world viewed from the outside, we have a different kind of complexity—that of the character who cannot be totally explained. With a disembodied narrator, the

film must present character from the outside, like the picaresque
novel and all fictional forms that try to mirror the way we
actually see other people. Mystery replaces articulation; the
ability to convey feelings replaces the refinement of ambiguities;
contradiction and inconsistency become a more important process
than intricate elaboration. In paintings and films character is
ultimately elusive because its core and connectives are hidden
within the visible body one sees on the screen. No matter how
much we know, there is always something more, something
analysis can never quite totally encompass, something that
stretches beyond or between the immediate contexts of plot
and circumstance. The characters of most nineteenth-century
fiction exist fully in their own works, whereas film characters
can leave their plots and inhabit our dreams, so free because
they are so elusive. When all the mysteries are solved, when
all the facts are brought together and the plot explained, one
mystery remains—the actor, the continuing human being, whose
body has existed before us in all those separate moments. The
closest that fiction gets to the effects possible on film is in pseudo-
autobiographical novels—Defoe's *Moll Flanders,* Dickens' *Great
Expectations,* Ford Madox Ford's *The Good Soldier,* Mailer's
An American Dream—in which the seeming openness and
honesty of the narrator serves only to alert the reader to what
has been left unsaid.

The basic nature of character in film is omission—the omission of connective between appearances, of reference to the actor's
existence in other films, of inner meditation, in short, of all
possible other worlds and selves except the one we see before
us. Directors omit in different ways and actors establish continuity in different ways. But film character achieves complexity
by its emphasis on incomplete knowledge, by its conscious
play with the limits a physical, external medium imposes upon
it. The visible body is our only evidence for the invisible mind.
But the tyranny of the visible turned inside out can discover
a freedom based on nuance and allusion. The muted emphasis
on gesture, makeup, intonation, and bodily movement possible
in film can enrich a character with details that would intrude
blatantly if they were separately verbalized in a novel. Instead
of giving us any insight into a character's inner life, film accepts
the necessity of defining problems of character primarily in

terms of a character's actions and statements—the only avenue of knowledge we ourselves usually have. In plays and in fiction central characters are often surrounded by peripheral characters who act as foils to help us understand them more fully. But in films we tend to see characters alone, separate bodies before our eyes, neither playing parts nor caught in the uniform pattern of the printed page. By their ability to concentrate on a single person, movies can give us a more palpable feeling of isolation than many of the greatest novels. In Nicholas Ray's *On Dangerous Ground* (1951), for example, our perspective in one scene is limited to that of a blind woman (Ida Lupino). Because the camera follows her so closely, we both see her blindness and are limited ourselves. We stumble with her, and, when a mysterious hand comes at her from outside the frame, we are frightened with her. In fiction a narrator may give us a perspective on the main character, but in film all characters share the same mystery: Nick Carraway is as elusive as Jay Gatsby, and when we are reminded that the character Peter Ustinov plays in *Topkapi* (Jules Dassin, 1964) is the narrator of the original Eric Ambler novel, the revelation is oddly irrelevant to our experience of the film. The necessity of films is to deal with exteriors, in objects and people; to separate and objectify, and pause in wonder at what is hidden. Mr. Hyde in Stevenson's story is "small and very plainly dressed . . . pale and dwarfish . . . giving an impression of deformity without any nameable malformation." But all the great Jekyll and Hyde films make him undergo a physical transformation, exercising makeup and camera artistry. This change is not a diminution; it does not exemplify the lower artistic status of films compared to novels. It means that films discover a different message in the Jekyll and Hyde story. Rather than Stevenson's verbal play with the social distinctions between Jekyll and Hyde, movies, with their greater commitment to the physical, transform the story into an examination of the relation between scientific and sexual curiosity, between the realms of laboratory and brothel, the separation and interconnection of mind and body.*

* A recent imaginative recasting of the Jekyll and Hyde theme is *Dr. Jekyll and Sister Hyde* (Roy Ward Baker, 1972, script by Brian Clemens) in which the sexual element has become even more apparent (including a

Aside from the odd necessity to sit with such concentrated attention, we are held to films by the human face. Fiction films work most immediately through their characters. To attack Stanley Kramer for his film *Ship of Fools* (1965) because he expresses the conflict of historical forces through individuals ignores the necessities of the film medium. The particular way Kramer does it may be wrong or inadequate, but the fact that he does it is not a choice; it is an essence of the nature of the way film presents the world to us. One could make the same objection to Renoir's *La Grande Illusion*. The film focuses on representatives of all branches of French society: the Jew, the workingman, the intellectual, the aristocrat, etc. The difference, of course, is between the styles of Kramer (and Katherine Anne Porter) and Renoir, not between a false or a true understanding of history. Whatever films cannot achieve through the methods of psychological complexity available to fiction or the immediate physical presence of theater, they gain from the sense of extension beyond the film, which allows actors the same dimension of added significance it gives to objects. We are more likely to sit through a badly directed, badly scripted film with attractive actors (like *A Touch of Class,* 1973, directed by Melvin Frank, with George Segal and Glenda Jackson) than we are to accept good scripting and good direction in compensation for bad acting (unless we have a special commitment to the writer or director). The worst, most confused plot, the most inept style, will usually not prevent the audience from the pleasure of being in the celluloid presence of a favorite actor or actress with whom it feels comfortable (and I mean sinister and disturbing presences as well as soothing or congenial ones). In Richard Lester's *Petulia* (1968), for example, the direction is so flamboyant and the plot so intricate that we may forget (as Lester seems to) that what holds us to the film is really

---

brother and sister respectively in love with the appropriate elements in the Jekyll/Hyde personality). Here is the point where cultural history and aesthetics meet: is this barely veiled exposition of the possibilities of bisexuality an expression of cultural fears, or is it an effort to talk about forbidden topics within the conventions of a popular form that allows their displaced expression? In other words, is the film an unself-conscious or a self-conscious use of genre? For further discussion of the Jekyll and Hyde theme, see pp. 226–34.

Julie Christie, George C. Scott, Shirley Knight, Richard Chamberlain, and Joseph Cotten.

Faces in film are like faces in life; they can be familiar and mysterious at the same time. The face is also a fact, and, just as films find some part of their essential nature in the intense search for facts and the simultaneous awareness of their actual elusiveness, they are also obsessed by the human face, yet constantly collide with its final inscrutableness. Novelists can go beyond this ultimate blankness if they choose, or at least they can sit back and allow the reader to analyze the nuances of interaction. But in a film such interaction must come subliminally or at the edge of perception, for nothing exposes the literary crutches of a film more than explained action or heavily wielded chunks of exposition.

The physical image of the film actor can frame and connect more disparate elements than the series of words that defines novelistic character or the three-dimensional body that anchors one dramatic character. Silent film especially emphasized the possibilities of solely visual character. In a famous experiment, Lev Kuleshov juxtaposed the same actor's face and expression with a variety of objects and discovered that the audience would impute different emotions to the actor, depending on what the object was. He concluded that the montage juxtaposition was more important than any expressive technique of the actor's. Soviet film theory therefore tended to downgrade the individualism of the actor. Eisenstein and Pudovkin considered the typological use of actors to be the most important function of the cinema, because in films a "type" is defined more by the person who plays the role than by the role itself. Characters in silent films could be iconographic because they were like moving statues, with a solidity and visual continuity that somehow raised them out of their individuality into some timeless image of human nature, a force the Soviet filmmakers considered to be akin to the abstract forces of destiny and history. But the practical necessity in silent films to establish a continuity that could bridge the gaps made by the intertitles existed whether the director had an explicit ideology or not. Expressionist acting, with its commitment to the moments of extreme emotion and its general lack of interest in the less intense moments in between, was especially suited to a visual world in which the audience's attention had to be regained after each interposition of the printed word. Like the characters in Paul Leni's *Waxworks* (1924), actors were statues that moved. Iconography at one extreme shaded into idealized images and at the other into caricature— the vamp and the virgin, Valentino and Ford Sterling. The passionate narcissism of the actor drew the audience into hypnotic complicity. Silent films played especially on the visual resources of stage drama—the importance of clothes and costume, the emphasis on social groupings within one frame, the closeup on characteristic facial expression and gesture.

Considering the formalist film aesthetics that dominated discussion in the 1920s and 1930s, one would expect a silent film without subtitles to be a pure exercise in the attraction of the film image. But Murnau's *The Last Laugh* (1924), one of the greatest of the films that attempted to do away with intertitles entirely, is, unparadoxically, a study of personality. Kuleshov was not observing an invariable method of film style, but a primitive definition of the film sense of character. Formal continuities may counterpoint a film, may even support a film for a limited amount of time (as in many avant-garde and underground films), but a concentrated and continuous attention is possible only through the link with an actor. When the story itself—like *The Last Laugh*—is about the interplay between character and role (the doorkeeper at the Great Hotel who loses his impressive uniform and is demoted to men's-room attendant because of his age), the continuity of audience fascination with the actor is heightened even further. In silent films especially, great weight is placed on the continuity of an actor's image, whether in the more melodramatic forms of Valentino or Garbo or the stability in a world of comic chaos projected by Chaplin and Keaton. Versatility in a silent-film actor, like that of Emil Jannings, seems less a professional talent than an ability to play characters with divided natures, like the doorman in *The Last Laugh* or the Professor in von Sternberg's *The Blue Angel*.

The history of theater from the medieval period until the nineteenth century has been in large part a history of further and further separations of the scene of dramatic action from the physical situation of the audience. Even as the subject matter—in the plays of Ibsen, Chekhov, and Strindberg—became more and more continuous with the life of the audience, the stage itself pulled in its apron, emphasized its proscenium, and became a room with an invisible fourth wall, allowing the audience to look in, while keeping it more definitely outside. The progress of film was the reverse. From the stylized and theatrical settings of the early dramas, silent films moved into greater and greater involvement with the actors. Previously the audience saw actors from a distance, with a sense of tableau and formal separation. Although they seemed to be like us, they were not: silent, hieratic, caught in heightened frenzies of comedy, tragedy, and melodrama. The silent image and the piano kept the audience out of the film and enhanced its feeling that silent-film space and occasion were extensions of their theatrical counterparts.

But the insistence on soundless dialogue, the miming of an aural reality, had always implied in silent films some urge toward the nonvisual continuity sound and language allows. Light may create objects in film, but sound created people. Sound allowed more audience involvement because the interplay of sound and image implied that an actor could be present when we did not see him. It gave a roundness to the previously flat film image that the best lighting and the best deep-focus lens could not have supplied. If an actor could speak offscreen, the audience might be inside the film instead of only watching it; it could be implicated in the action instead of being merely passive observers or voyeurs. The separation of piano player from silent screen could in sound film be an integration, with each playing hide-and-seek with the other; sometimes attuned, sometimes obliquely related, sometimes not related at all. Before sound, films could reasonably be considered an amalgam of theatrical and visual art. Only with sound could films really achieve an aesthetic status of their own—no longer a stepchild of the other arts, but a new synthesis.

Because in sound film there were two continuities of character for the audience to consider—face and voice—the actor and the director could be freer to experiment with seeming inconsistency in characterization and the image of the actor became less fixed. Silent films could be a tribute to humanity in general: silent characters were detached from the audience, whether Russian sailors, American Southerners, or French peasants. But sound admitted the less resounding emotions and paid its tribute to individuality, bringing films a little closer to the life of the audience, even in the most grandiose subject. Silent-film fascination with the power of destiny and general historical forces turned into sound-film fascination with populism and the nation as defined by its "little men"; Eisenstein gave way to Capra. Sound had become another dimension possible for character, a coherence beyond the visual. In silent films, passion was intensified and released in discreet moments. In sound films, the continuity of the ear could allow a lowering of intensity and a greater modulation in characterization. Sound made possible nuances and ironies of voice that were impossible in prose, unless spelled out in dialect and commentary, and difficult on stage, unless heightened to sarcasm or pathos. With sound the actor could better internalize the discontinuities and juxtapositions of montage, just as he later learned to internalize the gestures previously underlined by "reaction" shots. Since it was no longer necessary to overcome the discontinuity caused by intertitles, the style of expressionist acting became the style of sound-film insanity—the discontinuous, disruptive gestures of the mad.†

Perhaps the closest approximation to the old aesthetic of silent-film acting we have with us now is television acting. As the silent actor (and director) had to develop a dynamic visual intensity to bridge the intertitles, so the actor, director, and scriptwriter now have to overcome the commercials and logos. Television comedy therefore often resembles vaudeville in the discontinuous intensity of its skits, while television drama tends toward melodrama. The most common television settings are, as I have argued above, familiar and familial—talk shows, soap operas, sports events, news

---

† The superiority of subtitling to dubbing rests on just such a sensitivity to the intermingling of face and voice in film acting. The attack on subtitles is usually made in the name of an integration of image and sound, a desire to see the film purely, as it was made, whatever the sacrifice of understanding. The defense of subtitles ideally stands for a belief in the primary need to preserve the integrity of the actor's projected personality, even at the expense of distracting somewhat from the purity of the visual image. It emphasizes instead the real life that has momentarily been poured into the character by an actor whose continuity from scene to scene, from film to film, offers an extra dimension that the silent icons, whether tragic or comic, could not.

shows—and the extent to which the one-shot dramatic shows and television movies preserve that domestic feeling is usually an indication of their success in the medium. The television emphasis on closeup (which returns to films primarily in the 1950s with the advent of television-turned-film directors) is aesthetically the descendant of silent-film closeups, with many of the same problems and pleasures. In the stars made by television— such as Milton Berle or Lucille Ball—there is no relationship whatsoever between the admiration or connection one feels with them and the quality of their work in the traditional terms of acting. (Often their ability is assumed to be nonexistent and its inadequacy becomes part of the format.) We connect instead with indomitability and survival. If Lucy can last for twenty-three years, doing exactly the same kind of thing through divorce and age and all the changes of life, perhaps we can do it as well. Family shows, continuity shows—whether *All in the Family; Bonanza; Upstairs, Downstairs;* or *Ozzie and Harriet*—satisfy our hunger for private continuity in the midst of public chaos and bring us out of ourselves into a purer, more controllable world in the same way that we could once transcend our natures through the voiceless images of the silent films.

ACTING: STAGE VS. SCREEN

Acting in Europe and America has been historically defined by the varying interplay of the heightened and the normal, the theatrical and the nonchalant, in the conception of the role. Until the Renaissance, there was little attempt to place any special value on the absorption of the rhythm, themes, and gestures of everyday life into drama or acting style. Aristotle had taught that the most intense feelings possible in drama were those in tragedy, when the characters and the acting style were on a much higher plane than the normal life of the audience. Everyday life, where the characters and the way they behave tend to be on the same or lower social levels than the audience, was primarily a source of stylized comedy. The stage was raised above the audience in part because the characters and their impersonators were not to be considered as individually as the audience might assess each other. In Greek, Roman, and medieval society, actors therefore tended to portray beings purer than the audience, the somber figures of myth and the caricatures of comedy—a division of acting labor not unlike that of the silent screen.

Shakespeare helped make an enormous change in this relation between the audience and the actors by elaborating the analogies possible between the world and the stage. He began the European theater's effort to absorb and reflect the life of the audience as much as to bring the audience out of itself into another world. Comedy could therefore become more serious because it was no longer necessary to involve emotions lower than the grand style of tragedy. More intimate theaters and better lighting permitted a more nuanced acting style. By the mid-eighteenth century David Garrick had become the first to attempt historical authenticity in costuming, once again asserting the need to ground the play and the style of acting in some possible and plausible setting rather than a special world of theater. The "fourth wall" theories of the latter nineteenth century further defined theatrical space and dramatic acting as an extension of the world of the audience. Stylized acting did not disappear, of course. The broader styles remained in opera, ballet, and popular comedy, as well as re- vivals of classics, symbolic and proletarian drama, and the ex- periments with ritual theater from the end of World War Two to the present.

Acting on stage had necessarily developed a tradition of natural- ness as well. In the eighteenth century Diderot had argued that the paradox of acting is that an actor must be cold and tranquil in order to project emotion. Actors who play from the soul, he said, are mediocre and uneven. We are not moved by the man of violence, but by the man who possesses himself. In the early twentieth century, Konstantin Stanislavsky turned Diderot's view of the actor self-possessed in passion into a whole style. He rejected theories of acting based on imitation and emphasized in- stead an actor's inner life as the source of energy and authenticity for his characterizations. More "mechanical" and expressionist styles of stage acting implicitly attacked Stanislavsky's methods by their emphasis on the intensity of emotion and the visual coherence of the stage ensemble. Minglings of the two traditions produced such hybrids as the Group Theater, in which the inter- play between ensemble and individual produced a thematic tension often missing from Eisenstein's productions, whether on stage or in film. Elia Kazan's film style, for example, with its mixture of expressionistic, closed directorial style and open, naturalistic acting, is a direct descendant of this tradition.‡

Our ability to learn what films can tell us about human character has suffered not only from preconceptions derived from the novel of psychological realism, but also from assumptions about acting that are drawn from the stage. We know much better what our attitude should be toward characters in fiction and drama. Unlike those forms, films emphasize acting and character, often at the expense of forms and language. Films add what is impossible in the group situation of the stage or the omniscient world of the novel: a sense of the mystery inside character, the strange core of connection with the face and body the audience comes to know so well, the sense of an individuality that can never be totally expressed in words or action. The stage cannot have this effect because the audience is constantly aware of the actor's impersonation. Character in film generally is more like character as we perceive it everyday than it is in any other representational art. The heightened style of silentfilm acting could be considered an extension of stage acting, but the more personal style allowed by sound film paradoxically both increased the appeal of films and lowered their intellectual status. The artistic was the timeless, Garbo not Dietrich, Valentino not Gable.

But character in sound film especially was not so much deficient as it was elusive. Films can be less didactic about character because the film frame is less confining than the fictional narrative or the theatrical proscenium. Sound films especially can explore the tension between the "real person" playing the role and the image projected on the screen. The line between film actor and part is much more difficult to draw than that between stage actor and role, and the social dimension of "role" contrasts appropriately with the personal dimension of "part." Film acting is less impersonation than personation, part of personality but not identifiable with it. "Can Ingrid Bergman commit murder?" ask the advertisements for

‡ Diderot's *Paradoxe sur le comédien* was not published until 1830, although it was written in the late 1760s. A later printing in 1902 may have had an influence on Stanislavsky's theories.

Murder on the Orient Express (Sidney Lumet, 1975); the casual substitution of actress for character crudely makes an assertion that better films explore more subtly. Unlike the stage actor, the film actor cannot get over the footlights. Although this technical necessity may seem to make him less "real" than the stage actor, it makes his relation to the character he plays much more real. Audiences demand to hear more about the private life of the film actor than the stage actor because film creates character by tantalizing the audience with the promise of the secret self, always just out of the grasp of final articulation and meaning. The other life of a stage character is the real life of the person who plays him. But the other life of a film character is the continuity in other films of the career of the actor who plays him. In plays the unrevealed self tends to be a reduced, meaner version of the displayed self; in films it is almost always a complex enhancement. Within the film a character may have a limited meaning. But the actor who plays him can potentially be a presence larger than that one part, at once more intimate and more distant than is ever possible on stage.*

Film preserves a performance that is superior to the script, whereas stage performances and plays are separate realities, with the performance often considered second best. The stage actor is performing a role: he may be the best, one of the best, the only, or one of many to play that role. But the role and its potentials will exist long after he has ceased to play it, to be interested in it, to be alive. The film actor does not so much perform a role as he creates a kind of life, playing between his characterization in a particular film and his potential escape from that character, outside the film and perhaps into other films. The stage actor memorizes an entire role in proper order, putting it on like a costume, while the film actor learns his part in pieces, often out of chronological order, using his personality as a kind of armature, or as painters will let canvas show through to become part of the total effect. If the movie is remade and another actor plays the part, there is little sense of the competition between actors that

---

* In these remarks and in most of the section to follow, I am obviously talking not so much about the craft of acting as about the effects of acting on the audience. I would hope, however, that what I say has implications for craft and method as well, at least in terms of a test of effectiveness beyond the pleasures of theory.

characterizes revivals on stage. "Revival" is a stage word and "remake" is a film word. Hamlet remains beyond Booth's or Olivier's or Gielgud's performance, but Alan Ladd as Gatsby and Robert Redford as Gatsby exist in different worlds.

Filmmaking is a discontinuous process, in which the order of filming is influenced more by economics than by aesthetics. Film actors must therefore either have stronger personalities than stage actors or draw upon the resources of personality much more than stage actors do. Strong film actors can never do anything out of character. Their presence defines their character and the audience is always ready for them to reveal more. Even though studio heads like Louis Mayer forced actors and actresses to appear "in character" offscreen as well, we sense and accept potential and variety from the greatest movie actors, while we may reject less flamboyant fictional characters as "unreal" or refer to the woodenness of stage characterization. Continuity in stage acting is thematic continuity: "Watch in happiness someone whom you will soon see in sorrow" is one of the fatalistic possibilities. But the discontinuities of film acting allow the actor to concentrate on every moment as if it were the only reality that existed. No matter how conventionalized the plot, the film actor can disregard its clichés and trust instead to the force and continuity of his projected personality to satisfy beyond the more obvious forms of theme and incident. Because he must present his play in straightforward time, a stage director will work with the actor to get a "line" or a "concept" of the character that will permeate every scene. But movie acting, bound in time to the shooting schedule and the editing table, must use what is left out as well as what is expressed. The greatest difference between a film and a stage version of the same work is less in the "opening" of space that films usually emphasize than in the different sense of the inner life of the characters we get.

Going to the theater is a social occasion in a way that going to films is not. Stage characters always exist in a society, and the great plays are almost all plays about the problems of living within a social context. Any bad film brings the audience more directly in touch with human presence than the actually present human beings of the stage because on stage there is so much emphasis on the correct filling of the role, parallel to the correct filling of the social role. The Shakespearean metaphor of the world as a stage expresses the new Renaissance awareness of self-presentation as a process of social interaction in which one defined oneself by social roles, the ones rejected as much as the ones accepted. On the stage we appreciate character generally as part of an ensemble of actors or in brief individual moments, and our understanding of those characters comes from our understanding of the relations between characters—how the stage looks—much more than from the revelations of an inner life. Olivier's *Hamlet* (1948), for example, with its Oedipal interpretation, is less forceful than the play because Hamlet's secrets are not the problems of interpretation—what's really stopping him?—but problems of decision *in front of other people*. Plays, and therefore theatrical acting, emphasize acting out, being seen, being overheard, or being spied upon. A common theme of all drama from the Renaissance on is the problem of honor, fame, and reputation—in short, all the ways in which the individual is known socially. But this theme appears only rarely in films. In its place is the problem of personal identity: who is Charles Foster Kane? who is Charlie Kohler? When a film is set in the context of a mannered society (like *The Awful Truth,* Leo McCarey, 1937, or *Blume in Love,* Paul Mazursky, 1972), the question of the film involves the benevolent discovery of the "real" nature of the characters, not the satiric exposure of that real nature, which would be the theatrical way of organizing the action. The faults of hypocrisy and insincerity—two other traditional themes of drama—also appear very rarely in films. The hypocrite on stage, or the audience's awareness of a character who says one thing and does another, becomes in films the character who deceives himself as well. In films, the theatrical emphasis on the importance of the role is replaced by the authenticity of feelings, the preserved human being with whom we have come into contact. Film acting expands the ability of art to explore the varieties of the intimate self, apart from social awareness, outside of ceremonial or semi-ceremonial occasions, with a few others or even alone.

Movies therefore stand between the strongly social emphasis of theater and the strongly individual emphasis of novels, incorporating elements of both. At a play we are always outside the group, at the footlights. But at a film we move between inside and outside, individual and social perspectives. Movie acting can therefore include stage acting better than stage acting can include movie acting. George C. Scott, for example, is essentially a stage actor who also can come across very well in films. When he was making *Patton* (Franklin Schaffner, 1970), he insisted that he repeat his entire first speech eight times to allow for the different camera angles; he refused to repeat only the sections that corresponded to the rephotographing. His sense of the character was therefore what I have been describing as a stage sense of character, in which the continuity is linear and spelled out. The performance is excellent and effective, but Scott's way of doing it tells us nothing of the differences in stage and film acting. It may have a touch of the New York stage actor's almost traditional hostility to films. At best, it is only another example of the way a newer art can more comfortably embrace the methods of an older art than the other way around. In fact, virtuosity in films tends to be a characteristic of second leads or medium minor characters, not stars, and the Academy Awards perpetuate the stage-derived standards by giving so many awards to actors and actresses cast against type, that is, for stage-style "virtuosity."

The film actor emphasizes display, while the stage actor explores disguise. But stage acting is still popularly considered to be superior to film acting. An actor who does a good job disappears into his role, while the bad (read "film") actor is only playing himself. The true actor, the professional craftsman, may use his own experience to strengthen his interpretation. But the audience should always feel that he has properly distanced and understood that experience; it is another tool in his professional workchest. The false actor, the amateur actor, the film actor, on the other hand, works on his self-image, carries it from part to part, constantly projecting the same thing—"himself." Such a belief is rooted in an accurate perception; but it is a false interpretation of that perception. The stage actor does project a sense of holding back, of discipline and understanding, the influence of head over feelings, while the film actor projects effortlessness, nonchalance, immediacy, the seemingly unpremeditated response. Thus, when stage actors attack film actors, they attack in some puritanical way the lack of perceptible hard work, obvious professional craft, in the film actor's performance. Like many nonprofessionals in their audience, such stage actors assume that naïveté, spontaneity, "being yourself," are self-images that anyone in front of a camera can achieve. A frequent Actors Studio exercise, for example, is "Private Moment," in which the student is asked to act out before the group something he or she ordinarily does alone that would be very embarrassing if someone happened to see. Private self-indulgences and private games are thereby mined for their exposable, group potential. But the concentration of film, its ability to isolate the individual, makes every moment that way, and so the problem of the film actor may be to scale down intimacy rather than discover and exaggerate it.

How do we know the "themselves" film actors play except through the residue of their playing? How much do film actors, as opposed to stage actors, model their offscreen selves to continue or contrast with their screen images? To accuse an actor of "playing himself" implies that we have seen and compared the "real" and "false" selves of the actor and reached a conclusion. Film acting deposits a residual self that snowballs from film to film, creating an image with which the actor, the scriptwriter, and the director can play as they wish. Donald Richie has recorded that the Japanese director Yasujiro Ozu said: "I could no more write, not knowing who the actor was to be, than an artist could paint, not knowing what color he was using." Ozu's remark indicates how a director takes advantage of a previously developed image in order to create a better film. But the stage actor in a sense ceases to exist from play to play; we experience only the accumulation of his talent, his versatility. In our minds the stage actor stays within the architectures he has inhabited, while the film actor exists in between as well, forever immediate to our minds and eyes, escaping the momentary enclosures that the individual films have placed around him.

"Playing yourself" involves one's interpretation of what is most successful and appealing in one's own nature and then heightening it. Film actors play their roles the way we play ourselves in the world. Audiences may now get sustenance from films and from film acting because they no longer are so interested in the social possibilities of the self that has been the metaphysic of stage acting since Shakespeare and the Renaissance, the place of role-playing in the life of the audience. The Shakespearean films of

Laurence Olivier and Orson Welles clearly express the contrast. The tendency in stage acting is to subordinate oneself to the character, while the great film actor is generally more important than the character he plays. Our sense of Olivier in his Shakespearean roles is one of distance and disguise: the purified patriotism of Henry V, in which all the play's negative hints about his character have been removed; the blond wig he uses to play Hamlet, so that, as he has said, no one will associate him with the part; the bent back, twisted fingers, and long black hair of Richard III. But Welles assimilates the roles to himself. Costume for Welles is less a disguise than a generation from within and so he presented it in various television appearances of the 1950s, gradually making up for his part while he explained the play to the audience, until he turned full face into the camera and spoke the lines. In theater we experience the gap between actor and role as expertise; in film it may be described as a kind of self-irony. The great stage actor combats the superiority of the text, its preexistence, by choosing his roles: Olivier will play Hamlet; Olivier will play a music-hall comic. The great film actor, assured that his image absorbs and makes real the script, may allow himself to be cast in unpromising roles, if only for visibility. In the audience we feel Welles's character to be part of his role, whereas we perceive not Olivier's character but his intelligence and his ability to immerse himself in a role. Olivier is putting on a great performance, but Welles feels superior enough to the Shakespearean text to cut, reorganize, and invent. Olivier is a great interpreter; Welles is an equal combatant. For both, Shakespeare is like a genre, similar to the western, that offers materials for a contemporary statement. But Olivier sticks closely to the language and form of the play itself. We judge Olivier finally by Shakespeare, but we judge Welles by other films. Both choose those Shakespearean plays that emphasize a central character. But Olivier's willingness to allow Shakespeare the last word frees him for the more assertive political roles, whereas Welles stays with the more domestic or even isolated figures of Macbeth and Othello. Olivier began his Shakespearean film career with the heroic self-confidence of Henry V, while Welles, at least for the moment, has ended his with Falstaff—the choice of the ironic imagination of film over the theatrical assertion of social power.

These distinctions between stage acting and film acting are, of course, not absolute but points on a slippery continuum. Marlon Brando's career, for example, is a constant conflict between his desire to be versatile—to do different kinds of films, use different accents, wear different costumes—and the demand of his audience that he elaborate his residual cinematic personality. Brando tries to get into his roles, and often sinks them in the process, while Cary Grant pumps them up like a balloon and watches them float off into the sky. The main trouble that Chaplin has in *A Countess from Hong Kong* (1967) is taking two actors (Brando and Sophia Loren), whose own sense of their craft emphasizes naturalistic, historically defined character, and placing them within a film world where they would best exist as masks and stereotypes. Their efforts to ground their characters destroys the film. It may be funny if Chaplin or Cary Grant vomited out a porthole, but it's not funny when Brando does it. Brando can be funny in films only as a counterpoint to our sense of "Brando," for example in *Bedtime Story* (Ralph Levy, 1964). When he is acting someone else, the ironic sense of self-image that is natural to a film actor does not exist. We share Cary Grant's sense of distance from his roles, whether they are comic, melodramatic, or whatever, because it corresponds to our sense of personal distance from our daily roles in life. The sense of "putting it on" that we get from Brando's greatest roles—*A Streetcar Named Desire, Viva Zapata!, The Wild One, On the Waterfront*—stands in paradoxical relation to Method theories of submergence in the role. Brando's willingness to cooperate with Bernardo Bertolucci in the commentary on and mockery of his screen image that forms so much of the interest of *Last Tango in Paris* may indicate that he no longer holds to the theatrical definition of great acting. His progenitor role in *The Godfather* seems to have released him to create the paradox of the self-revealed inner life of a screen image elaborated by *Last Tango*. In the films of the 1970s, character, and therefore acting as well, has taken on the central importance in film. And the stage actor in film finds that his virtuosity is more a parlor trick than a technique of emotional and artistic power. Films make us fall in love with, admire, even hate human beings who may actually in the moment we watch them be dead and dust. But that is the grandeur of films as well:

the preservation of human transience, the significance not so much of social roles as of fragile, fleeting feelings.

ROLE-PLAYING AND TYPE-CASTING

In every film there are at least four films: the one written, the one cast, the one shot, and the one cut. Of these, the one cast receives probably the least critical attention. We decide whether the actors and actresses have done good or bad jobs, and then generally ignore the influence they have on the total effect of the film. But in fact our past knowledge of a film actor and actress feeds into our immediate experience of them in a particular film. Because stage acting emphasizes versatility and professional expertise we come on these individuals in yet another role with gratified surprise or we follow their careers with interest. But our interest in film actors constitutes an aesthetic connection with film much more thematically important than the connection of our past experience of any stage actor to our present appreciation of a particular play. We live with film actors the way we live with characters in a long novel; they are not necessarily ideals, but after a time (depending on their personal power) we assign them a place, part real and part fantasy, in our lives. Through our empathy and identification, they become bridges into the films their characters inhabit.

The character types created in films constitute a psychic landscape that is not so much concerned with psychological realism as it has been defined in the novel as it is with a heightened view of complex and pleasing types. When I say "types," I don't mean the types that theater has defined and commedia dell'arte still exploits. "Type" in movies is a much different concept than "type" in theater. It is closer to the efforts of the nineteenth-century novel to create an individualized characterization, but mixed with the heightened glow that the cinematic capturing of a transient human image can bring. The "type" character on the stage is like a generalization, isolating certain characteristics (the pedant, the lecherous widow) and creating a character from them. But "type" character on film resembles the effect of a substage light in a biopsy: all the individual structures are there, but each has somehow become a generalized statement. Stage types fulfill and interpret a pre-existing role, but film types are created in the historical interaction between character and role. Who can really say which came first? Was it the characterization, or did a particular actor define a characterization that was then elaborated and perpetuated by scriptwriters, directors, and producers who felt its lure? Frank Capra has described how, as scriptwriter and director, he helped create the screen character of Harry Langdon, whereupon Langdon, believing he alone held the key to his image, went off on his own to several failures. He may have understood the schematic image, but it took Capra and others to create a filmed embodiment of the intersection of that image with the film audience.

In the successes of different film actors and actresses we can read something of the ideals of the audience for their own self-images. Both stars and minor actors express what the audience would like to consider as possibilities for themselves. Stars are most often ideals, while minor characters can be either outmoded selves, now suitable only for laughter or derision, or new selves, being tested for their potential. The minor male characters (and stars) of one era may become the major stars of the next era, as, for example, Lee Marvin moved from supporting to central roles. The kind of person he played had become more fascinating and needed to be placed in the center of attention. (There is usually a more disjunctive relation between the female stars of different periods because women in films have historically been less individually than socially defined.) To understand an era we must understand the lure of actors and characterizations that now may seem silly or uninvolving. What did Blanche Sweet or Eugene Pallette mean to their audiences? Why did their physical and personality types appeal then and not now, except as nostalgia or conscious archaism? Why is there no longer any character actor who looks like Percy Kilbride? How does the stylized comic eccentricity of Edward Everett Horton in the 1930s and 1940s become the comic neuroses of Tony Randall in the 1950s and wind up as the pathos of Jack Lemmon in the 1960s and 1970s? What is the mutation from W. C. Fields to Paul Ford to Walter Matthau? How does Joanne Woodward gradually escape from the shadow of Barbara Stanwyck? Such questions are difficult to ask and answer in theater not only because of the self-conscious artistry of the stage actor and the inaccessibility of past performances, but also because there is a greater continuity in film images of human nature than in stage images. Stage roles exist in a kind of continuous past; all characters in the repertory are equally accessible, no matter what their antiquity. Hamlet's problems seem as immediate as Blanche Dubois'. But the seamless relation between film character and film performance allows a greater interaction between aesthetics and culture. Old films are constantly available to show us the kind of people we once admired so that we might better know our prejudices now. The cynical idealist, for example, was a basic film character type of the 1930s —the hard exterior and the soft interior. It seemed to satisfy the demand for a personality equal to the problems of the Depression and, in the hands of Humphrey Bogart and Lauren Bacall, it achieved a grandeur and permanence that in historical context could also serve as a reaction to World War Two. How long can it last? The Bogart image that might have been a life possibility to the audiences of the 1940s has become primarily a nostalgic look into what can never be again, if only because it would be too self-aware to create such an image now. The Bacall style of self-contained femininity similarly belongs to a past age, and its descendants in the Angie Dickinson of *Rio Bravo* (Howard Hawks, 1957) or the Diane Cilento of *Hombre* (Martin Ritt, 1967) tend to inhabit genre rather than realistic contemporary worlds.

The actual Bogart of *Casablanca* (Michael Curtiz, 1942) and the use of Bogart that Woody Allen makes in *Play It Again, Sam* (Herbert Ross, 1972) illustrate the disparity. The difference is that between an actor who creates a character with a specific personal image and an actor who has been given iconographic status. It is the difference basically between personality in motion, reflecting on itself, and personality frozen into an invariable mask, congratulating itself—the difference between a model for the audience and a costume for the audience. The line between the two is thin because the immobility of the Bogart image, like the immobility of all attractive film images of the past, results from the actor's success in presenting himself as a chosen and possible style of being. In *Casablanca* we are introduced to Bogart as a procession inward. First there is a documentary-like prelude; refugees are pouring into Casablanca and there is frequent violence on the street. Then we see the street life of the city and a plane carrying refugees to freedom flying over the marquee of "Rick's Café Americain." The camera enters Rick's with the viewpoint of a customer and in the snatches of conversation and glimpsed faces of the people in the restaurant—making deals, bargaining, arguing—we see all the characters who will later make more prominent figures in the body of the film. Meanwhile we hear as well the first murmurs about Rick: the way he has remained untouched by the police despite the clandestine activities going on, how he never drinks with customers. Then finally we enter Rick's office. But still we don't see Rick, only his signature, then his hand playing chess, and finally his face—Bogart talking to a pleading Peter Lorre: "You're right, Bulgatti. I am a little more impressed by you." At the center of this chaotic world of war and personal disruption is the untouchable Rick, whom everyone in the film is trying to move in some way, to get him to respond, to show some emotion: "I stick my neck out for nobody."

Released only a few weeks before the Allied invasion of North Africa, *Casablanca*, through its concentration on the character of Rick, summons up all the ambivalence in American films of the late 1930s about the turmoil in Europe, particularly the desire to take a moral stand without being personally threatened or vulnerable. Rick in the film plays against three other men, each of whom illuminates his own choice. First is Sam (Dooley Johnson), the black piano player, his friend and emotional protector; then Louis (Claude Rains), the French police chief, a conformist Vichy official with a touch of romantic wit, usually aimed at Rick: "If I were a woman and Rick were around, I'd be in love with him"; and finally Victor Lazslo (Paul Henreid), the engaged political activist, for whom the individual and his desires are unimportant next to the struggle. After many protests and complications, Rick finally helps Elsa (Ingrid Bergman), his old love, and Lazslo escape. But he has not changed from the detached individualist to the engaged activist. He has merely realized what Louis has been telling him since the first scenes: "I suspect that under that cynical shell is a sentimentalist." He doesn't give up Elsa to Lazslo; he realizes that her emotional commitment to Lazslo and his cause is not threatening to his own self-esteem and is therefore uninteresting to him. His true mate in the film is Louis and so they both walk off together into the mists of the airfield, at "the beginning of a beautiful friendship." Louis has broken through to Rick by showing that he too is a sentimentalist, where Rick is concerned, and Rick has agreed with Louis that women, even undoused old flames, are more trouble than they're worth.

I have given this account of what seems to me to be the dynamic of Bogart's character in *Casablanca* (and his choices bear a remarkable resemblance to those of American heroes from Natty Bumppo on down) because it is obviously *not* the interpretation of Bogart held by Woody Allen in *Play It Again, Sam.* For him Bogart is the consummate manager of women, who has as many as he wants at his beck and call. Allen's Bogart is not the complex figure of Rick in *Casablanca,* with Bogart's image of barely repressed violence; he is instead a static and stereotyped symbol of what Allen himself can't achieve, self-containment and cool. Barbra Streisand controls her narcissism through song and sarcasm. But Allen's screen image is more uncontrolled, victimized, and frantic. He uses the ballast of Bogart's image to indulge the kind of character that really interests him, the person unable to keep cool, constantly undermining his own control in one way or another. The self-conscious and nostalgic style of *Play It Again, Sam* (and the necessary misquotation of the title) indicates the actual insufficiency for our own culture of Bogart's answer. It works as nostalgia and even inspiration, but finally it is only "played again," not really re-created as a viable personal style.

The end of Allen's film perfectly mimics the end of Curtiz's, but in Technicolor and wide-screen: two men walking off together with not a woman in sight. In our context it evokes the male camaraderie film of the past few years, and Allen's basic comic image of the ineffectual male is therefore revealed as only the contemporary reduction of the Bogart myth of masculine self-containment. Homage necessarily turns into implicit criticism; the veneration that many writers have expressed recently for the "model" of the Bogart-Bacall screen relationship glosses over the defects of the kind of defensive self-sufficiency they always project when together on film—hostility disguised as witty banter— because it also ignores the historical context in which that hostility could have been an improvement on male-female relationships, but no longer is. The Bogart-Bacall image has caused our present situation much more than it can save it. To be self-conscious about the psychic American history embodied in films brings with it the obligation to be critical and understanding as well.†

Since characterization is so important to films, acting and the choice of actor is equally important. Long before the self-consciousness of direction and story that began to typify films in the late 1950s, casting and typing had furnished a psychological self-consciousness more akin to the novel than to drama. Audience sympathy as well as audience understanding can be manipulated by the appropriate choices. Bad acting on stage, for example, is experienced primarily as bad acting. But bad acting on film is often experienced as an aspect of character, like insincerity. It is therefore very difficult to act badly in films because acting is absorbed into our feeling for the gap between a person and his beliefs about himself in daily life. The phrase "bad actor" to designate someone whom it isn't pleasant to be around seems derived from films rather than theater. Since sympathy and identification are an important part of our response to a film, a director can therefore judiciously use bad acting to cut off our sympathy or good acting to involve it, with ensuing complications in our perception of the film. Hitchcock in *Psycho*, for example, depends on the wooden acting of John Gavin to complicate our feelings, since in moral terms Gavin, the boyfriend of the murdered Janet Leigh, should have our sympathies. As a further complication, the good acting of Tony Perkins as the psychopathic murderer attracts us while Gavin's acting repels us. (I am here as usual talking about effect. Whether Hitchcock chose Gavin because he knew he would act badly or directed him to act badly is another issue entirely.) Hitchcock's larger point awakens us to the fact that while we like to believe we judge morally, in fact we judge aesthetically, often on the basis of physical beauty, and in this case on the basis of "good" acting. Jean Renoir, in *The Golden Coach* (1956), uses wooden acting in yet another way. His "bad actor" is Felipe (Paul Campbell), who plays the only one of

---

† It is interesting to parallel Allen's critical treatment of the Bogart image and his own in *Play It Again, Sam* with the fact that it is the only one of his films that carries plot coherence beyond his more usual episodes and one-liners. Allegiance to older forms, even mock allegiance, must work on many levels to be truly effective. *Play It Again, Sam* is also the only one of his films that Allen didn't personally direct.

the lovers of Camilla (Anna Magnani), and one of the few characters in the film, who is neither an actor nor involved in a self-displaying profession (like the bullfighter and the Viceroy). Felipe's attack on the insincerity of the actors is undermined by his own ineptness. Once we are aware of his bad acting, we look on his efforts to take Magnani away from the "false" world of theater and into some real world of nature with more suspicion than the mere plot lines allow—and Renoir's interplay between the values of theater and the values of nature becomes much more complex.

The wise director, recognizing the contribution to characterization an actor brings, uses casting to create meaning inarticulately. He may elaborate the already established image of an actor, as John Ford uses John Wayne; he may play against it, as Robert Aldrich uses James Stewart in *The Flight of the Phoenix* (1968); he may even attack it, as Howard Hawks attacks Wayne's authoritarian self-sufficiency in *Red River* (1948) or Franklin Schaffner attacks Charlton Heston's self-righteous aggressiveness in *Planet of the Apes* (1968). Depending on an actor's presence, ability, and acceptance by an audience, the possibility of manipulating his image can be exploited in a very short time. By 1935, John Ford already could play on the odd mixture of toughness and intellectuality in Edward G. Robinson's screen image to make *The Whole Town's Talking,* in which Robinson plays the meek clerk Arthur Ferguson Jones and his double, the escaped gangster "Killer" Mannion. The potential malevolence of Tony Perkins was so well established by one film, Hitchcock's *Psycho* (1959), that it could be invoked in *Pretty Poison* (1968) with almost nostalgic wonder to contrast with the clean-cut American evil represented by Tuesday Weld. Peter Bogdanovich uses Boris Karloff in almost the same way in *Targets* (1968) to embody a virtually benevolent gothic horror in combat with the faceless suburban horror of the young psychopathic killer. A similar juxtaposition in another genre appears in *Prime Cut* (Michael Ritchie, 1972), in which Lee Marvin represents a world of gangsterism derived from such films as Lang's *The Big Heat* (1953) that looks with disgust at the new-style gangster evil of Gene Hackman. Perkins, Karloff, and Marvin in these films are less threatening than their antagonists because we perceive their "evil" as more comfortable and familiar. They belong to a world of self-awareness that the unthinking murderers do not inhabit, a world that knows its movies.

Playing against an actor's past film roles to enrich his present one is ultimately rooted in the self-conscious use of star personality and star autobiography. But whereas the continuity of an actor's image can supply complex filling for the gaps in his immediate characterization, the invocation of offscreen personality and autobiography is more often a source of straight or melancholic comedy. With the beginnings of sound came a much greater exploitation of the public knowledge of the life of the actor and the activity of the Hollywood studio. The detachment that comes from reading notices about oneself permeates the films of Douglas Fairbanks, Jean Harlow, and Will Rogers, the musicals of Busby Berkeley, Fred Astaire, and Ginger Rogers. With sound, films become freer to play on the double possibility of actor inside and outside a role. In *Dinner at Eight* (George Cukor, 1933), John Barrymore's personal autobiography is used to enhance his part as the unsuccessful actor. He talks about his profile and his drinking, and the audience can appreciate that a successful Barrymore is playing a Barrymore *manqué*. But a more sinister note appears as well. "You're two people really. One's magnificent and the other's very shoddy," says one character to her philandering husband. By implication the remark also refers to Barrymore, since one of the main themes of the film is the double and triple nature of the characters, their deceits and self-deceptions. Perhaps the real Barrymore is as deficient as the fictional. Barrymore will again play the ham/great actor in Hawk's *Twentieth Century* and allow his offscreen self to be drawn on by films throughout the 1930s.

The 1950s were the last great period in which films dealt thematically with acting. The change might be indicated by two films directed by Billy Wilder, *Sunset Boulevard* (1950) and *Kiss Me, Stupid* (1964). Gloria Swanson in *Sunset Boulevard* and Dean Martin in *Kiss Me, Stupid* play different versions of their film selves. They both have two faces aesthetically, in a way typical of film and no other form: each faces into the film as a fictional character—Norma Desmond and Dino—and each faces out as a star. Each as they appear in the film is a caricature of the way they might be, save for the self-consciousness involved in taking such a role and the detachment toward the screen self playing the role implies. (William Holden, who narrates *Sunset Boulevard*, even though his character is dead at the beginning of the film, similarly faces inward and outward at the same time, and we accept what would otherwise be a morbid film joke because of its relevance to such doublenesses in the rest of the picture.) Swanson, however, plays a role that is a meditation on her screen image and the relation between the old world of silent films and the new world of 1950s Hollywood. Within the film, only her former director, Cecil B. DeMille, is still working. The actors who were her contemporaries (Buster Keaton, H. B. Warner, and Anna Q. Nilsson) are embalmed with her in the past, playing an eternal bridge game. *Sunset Boulevard* thereby documents the way film stars belong to particular eras and disappear, losing their power, when their personalities are no longer relevant to the needs of their audience. *Kiss Me, Stupid,* on the other hand, plays upon the way Dean Martin has set up a tension between his straightman-singer personality and his drinking, casual personality, the one "professional" and the other hopelessly unable to do anything according to the script. Wilder's Dino is the public star as personal pig and one of the most savage accounts of the role of fame in American life that has ever been filmed. Its critical and commercial failure showed that the American public in 1964 was still not quite ready to disbelieve its own myths. Only a hustling newcomer like Anne Baxter's Eve in Joseph Mankiewicz's *All About Eve* (1950) could be really offensive; established stars were at most sarcastically gracious. But naïveté moves quickly into cynicism. Robert Aldrich's *What Ever Happened to Baby Jane?* (1962) played self-consciously with the audience's beliefs in the "truths" behind screen personalities, the rivalry between Bette Davis and Joan Crawford. Hitchcock's *Vertigo* (1958) could invoke the making of Kim Novak into a star as a backdrop for James Stewart's creation of her as a replica of his dead wife. But by the time Aldrich makes *The Legend of Lylah Clare* (1968), in which Kim Novak plays a more direct version of her own autobiography—the film star created to order from the most unpromising materials—the public had already begun to admire the artifice of personality creation, instead of being shocked at the disparity between "real" and screen self.

Without an awareness of the aesthetic weight of a film star's accumulated image, a director can easily make mistakes that destroy the unity of his film. My previous comments about the success of political films within a silent or a sound documentary format apply equally here. Good acting and a sympathetic screen image merely overweight the audience's tendency to identify with the face rather than the force. The most politically effective films are silent films, like those of Eisenstein and Pudovkin, and documentaries, where the continuities of character are never developed enough to upset the effort to define the issues. The most emotionally effective plays, whether *Hamlet* or *A Streetcar Named Desire,* usually deal with characters whose essence is in self-display and theatricality—personality with an audience. When a political documentary emphasizes individual responses and gets much of its material from interviews, like Marcel Ophuls' *Le Chagrin et la Pitié* (1969), the effect diminishes political and economic statement in favor of the complexities of sensibility and individual response to crisis, no matter what the particular political leaning. Good acting may therefore play a paradoxical role in creating audience sympathy. Jean Martin, the actor playing the paratrooper Colonel Mathieu in *The Battle of Algiers* (Gillo Pontecorvo, 1966), for example, does such a good job that he confuses our understanding of the political point of the film. In films one well-acted fascist easily overbalances mobs of politically correct people. We feel in the performance the submerged continuity of film characterization, and we begin supplying motivation, complexity, and perhaps finally exoneration. As Virgina Woolf says in *To the Lighthouse,* "But nevertheless, the fact remained, it was almost impossible to dislike anyone if one looked at them."

Martin's portrayal of Colonel Mathieu in *The Battle of Algiers* would have its aesthetic impact increased immeasurably if he were also personally recognizable. It is interesting how studio directors understand this kind of elementary aesthetics much better than some more intellectual directors. Ted Post, Terence Hill, or any of the James Bond film directors know very well that anonymous groups can be slaughtered in the hundreds without disturbing the audience excessively (especially if they have attacked the hero to begin with). But Costa-Gavras will cast Yves Montand as the AID-operative Dan Mitrione in *State of Siege* (1973) and seem to expect that the audience will still appreciate the political appropriateness of his execution. The issue of Costa-Gavras' use of Montand is further complicated by Montand's appearance as a politically sympathetic victim in *Z* (1969) and *The Confession* (1970). The many times we have seen Marlon Brando being oppressed by various kinds of power necessarily complicates our reaction to his role as William Walker in Pontecorvo's *Burn!* (1970)—at first an agitator who helps create revolution in a Caribbean country and then the colonial agent who helps destroy the revolution when England has decided it has gone too far. In film an individual victim is an object of sympathy no matter what his politics. Like the victim oppressed by his tormentors, we in the audience are being imposed on by the experience of the film, unable to escape without sacrifice. For these reasons, Leni Riefenstahl in *Triumph of the Will* (1934) never seeks to humanize Hitler because that would bring in the variables of his personality. Montand's personality has already been created by himself and his audience. When Costa-Gavras ignores it, he ignores the importance of the actor to the effect of a film and seems to accept instead a mistaken belief that the politically "correct" plot and style will be enough to involve and mold the beliefs of the audience.

Jean Paulhan has said that ". . . the most mysterious authors are generally the most literary, and the strangeness in their writings is owing precisely to the disparate elements they contain, to this yoking together of characters come from the remotest milieux—and works—who are quite astonished to encounter one another." The history of film is similarly embodied in the history of film acting and its colliding styles of the self. Literary critics may tell us that Shakespeare intends a satire on the old standards of Marlovian heroism by including Pistol in *Henry IV, Part Two* and *Henry V*. But we receive the interplay of John Wayne and Montgomery Clift in *Red River* with much more impact. Instead of making us reflect only on past plays or films, such a juxtaposition makes us reflect on our past selves as well. The Grand Hotel films of the 1930s, the war films of the 1940s, the way-west and spaceflight films of the 1950s—all draw on pre-existing stereotypes to try to create an image of cooperation and a possibly pluralistic society. When Robert Aldrich in *The Flight of the Phoenix* shows that all the traditional movie characteristics of the national types don't work anymore—the Frenchman is melancholic rather than urbane, the American is sentimental rather than resourceful, the German is the hero rather than the villain—he makes a criticism possible only in movies: society itself will not work unless the previous stereotypes of character are re-evaluated and repersonalized.

THE METAPHYSIC OF THE BODY

The people that we see in movies are both reflections and ideals, bridges by which we enter the film and extensions of parts of ourselves. Film takes what is seemingly its greatest weakness —the visual emphasis on the body, the skin sense of character —and makes it into its greatest strength, creating from two-dimensional images metaphysical bodies that live beyond the three-dimensional but fleeting appearances of actors on the stage. Plays have always been concerned with the varieties of sexuality in society. Paintings could display the body in public postures, or (in nudes) attempt to define ideal types of static beauty. But not until the appearance of movies was there any art form whose main business was the depiction of bodies in motion, whose reality was akin to that of the audience, despite the overlays of class, race, age, sex, and dramatic situation. Film idealizes the face and preserves the performance, making it more permanent and seemingly more true. Every Academy Award presentation invokes the histories of those faces, the interplay between the decaying bodies on the stage and the perpetual embodiments on the screen behind them—an escape from time through art that no previous art form has ever allowed us to accomplish so well.

Uncomplicated by the possibility of sound, the silent-film body could be a pure form, a release from time, the potentially deifying part of the self. Whether in comedy or melodrama, the silent-film body floated above the world of mundane viewers, as the stars themselves (according to the fan magazines) rose from humble beginnings to live in unimaginable luxury. The technical capabilities of silent film emphasized high-contrast makeup and purified emotion, which filmmakers would exploit even further. Gerald Mast writes in *The Comic Mind:* "Just as Chaplin thought words more limited, less communicative than mime or gesture, Keaton thought facial expression more limited than physical gesture or motion." Unlike the stage actor, the silent-film actor could not use his voice to project any of the feeling his part required. No wonder then that so many silent films now seem so primitive in their view of human relations and psychology. Of necessity they concentrated on identity defined by bodies in relation to other bodies. The intertitles may have supplied a verbal dimension, but it was irrelevant unless grounded in the motions and form of the actor and actress.

The silent-film body was therefore a moving emanation of the silent-film face. The change from silence to sound caused a change in the image of the body and a parallel change in the idea of character. No longer could the surface of the body be the only reality. Sound brought film actors closer to their audience by increasing their similarities, and thereby increasing the possible range of imitation. The change from silent film to sound was a change from Theda Bara to Harlow and from Valentino to Gable, from taking one's face and body seriously with transcendental narcissism to standing back from one's body, half in admiration and half in mockery. In silent film the body was the self; in sound films the body could be changed, mended, or discarded like any other costume.

Because the silent-film body so thoroughly defined character, sex was the great mystery, the one essential of the world of physicality that could not be shown. But sexuality in sound films, although of course still not shown directly, could be a subject of much more irony and humor. Clara Bow, for example, who in sound films might have been a great comic actress, had to be dubbed the "It" Girl to assimilate her to the silent-film mystique about sex. But in sound films, the audience could connect more readily with personalities on which it could model itself, no matter what the momentary nature of their parts. In effect, it put an even greater premium on actors and actresses who could use their bodies well, who could project personality through their skin, through their reflexive awareness of the way they looked to others. Gossip about the fact that film actors and actresses may have been prostitutes or may have performed some kind of sexual acts to get their jobs has often been used as a way of minimizing them by those who thought they were upholding the standards of professionalism associated with stage acting. But such charges show an ignorance of stage history. Many great stage actresses in the Restoration, when women were first allowed onto the English stage, often kept up their practice as prostitutes; the most successful, Nell Gwyn and Anne Barry, were simultaneously the mistresses of the rich and powerful. There is an aesthetic continuity between all the professions that display the body. Prostitution, like acting, emphasizes individual pleasure through a kind of benevolent deception, a "trick." Theater and films emphasize the pleasure—and instruction—of many more people, an instruction in the potentials of self-display. The morals that prevent us from understanding the appeal of many of the arts often express themselves with great absurdity. Sarah Bernhardt—whose stage career, like that of many of the great nineteenth-century actresses, competed for public attention with her libertine private life—appeared in films as the grande dame of the theater, in a wooden performance that belied all she was famous for, ignoring the ever greater demands for bodily awareness that the new medium made.

Film may have allowed the audience to be more aware of the possibilities of the body, but, even more than the other representational arts, it also contributed to the increasing objectification of the body. The perfect body on screen could imply that it was *only* an idealization, a manufactured image. William Everson in *The Western* remarks of Tom Mix that "his body was literally a mass of scars, while shattered bones were held together with surgical wire." The film preoccupation with the Frankenstein myth stretches from the earliest days down to films as different as Hitchcock's *Vertigo,* Frankenheimer's *Seconds,* Aldrich's *The Legend of Lylah Clare,* and

Antonioni's *The Passenger*. An old body no longer works; it must be escaped from and a new one created, often from the parts of the dead. The Invisible Man may dispense with his body, but the sense of power he gets thereby causes his downfall. Like the energetic actor or actress onstage, the character who wishes to transcend the limitations of his body must finally be punished. The normal confusion that identifies Frankenstein with the monster is comparable to the confusion between the film character and the "real" actor who plays him. (In James Whale's *Frankenstein* the cast list tells us that the monster is played by "?") The lure of the monster, the lure of the vampire, and the lure of the film actor are the same—the double identity, the simultaneous subordination to and freedom from the limits of the body.

From the first days of sound there has been a thematic preoccupation with the paradox of the actor's body—its physical presence and its metaphysical absence, its visibility and its invisibility, body and mind, action and meditation. Unless it is distanced with irony and humor, the body and its sexuality can be hostile and threatening. Robert Donat in *The Thirty-nine Steps* (Hitchcock, 1935) is first picked up by a woman who is murdered in his apartment. He spends the rest of the film simultaneously trying to discover the real murderer and convince another woman, to whom he has become handcuffed, that he is innocent. Her sexual antagonism to him (they met when he faked kissing her to mislead the police) must be translated into aid and support if he is to succeed. But she is also his proper partner because, unlike the first woman, she is not attracted to him at all. Proving his sexual innocence to her is the key to proving his criminal innocence to the world. The antagonist will finally become the spouse when the uncertainties of sexuality are transformed into maternal aid and trust. The bystander may have been sucked into the whirlpool of events because of his own inner darkness. But marriage will furnish a frame that can deal with the darkness and combat the threats of the oppressive world, even though the psychological lures of sexuality and crime may not have changed at all. Such characters want to become only their surfaces, define themselves by their naïveté, even though they thereby become the perfect victims of the paranoid worlds they are constantly fleeing, unwilling to recognize the actual appeals of what they try so desperately to put aside.

The solution to such conflict is generally the comic one of marriage, although the tones get progressively darker. In Hawks's *I Was a Male War Bride* (1949), Cary Grant is accidentally trapped in the bedroom of a sleeping Ann Sheridan and tries to go to sleep in a chair. But, whatever position he gets himself into, his hands wind up in an odd relation to the rest of him— and he looks at them quizzically as if they were some strange beast, with a life of their own. The free and glorious body of the silent films and the Astaire-Rogers musicals has become more problematic and reproachful. The rest of *I Was a Male War Bride,* after Grant and Sheridan are married, dwells primarily on their failure to consummate the marriage (again, the failure to find a place to sleep) until Grant disguises himself as a woman. Grant's undomesticated hands imply the demands of the body, the presence of erotic stimulation in an inappropriate moment, the muscles of Gene Kelly beneath the ethereal formal clothes of Fred Astaire. The theme of diverted sexuality retains its power only when the actors, such as Donat or Grant, can project intense but impersonal passion, so that we identify more with them than with the seeming object of the emotion. We could never sympathize with Donat in *The Thirty-nine Steps* or with Grant in *I Was a Male War Bride* if we thought they were as threatening as Madeleine Carroll and Ann Sheridan think they are. Instead, their self-contained passion binds us to them, separated as it is from the possibility of a threatening sexuality, striving to mediate the satisfactions of the body with its betrayals. Frankenstein's monster is ugly only in movies; in Mary Shelley's novel, it is beautiful but looks dead.

As a twentieth-century art form, the movies reflect and influence twentieth-century preoccupations, in the case of the body what Gail and Snell Putney have called "our inability to find our real selves in physical enjoyment or material activity." The more sound films satisfy the audience by revealing sexuality and the body, the more they may hold back the intangibles of personality, until the body image becomes not character but caricature. The untold mysteries of Greta Garbo's face and personality give way to Marilyn Monroe's pathetic effort to assert that she was more than a body. Instead of a costume, the body has become a trap. How much more trapped are both we and the actors when the body is displayed only for its surface. The irony that Jean Harlow and Mae West could have about their physicality has vanished by the time of Monroe.

Films after World War Two are filled with motifs that imply an effort to escape from the body—dreams, double identities, sexuality diverted into murder and demonic possession. It is difficult not to conclude that the progress of films from the 1930s to the 1960s has involved a growing repulsion from and fascination with the body, especially in its interaction with the mind. The science-fiction films of the 1950s—*The Thing* (Christian Nyby, 1951), *The Day the Earth Stood Still* (Robert Wise, 1951), *Forbidden Planet* (Fred Wilcox, 1956)—all focus on the split between the body and the mind, and the need for some kind of conscious control over the primitive sources of horror: the fear of the demons of the mind and the demons of the body. Such themes have much to do with historical changes in the method of film characterization and, as I shall discuss, suit the political atmosphere of the 1950s as well. But attitudes toward the body cut across genre and serious film and point us to the essences of film itself. Films lure us into them by their emphasis on the body. Leni Riefenstahl must make Jesse Owens rather than Hitler the hero of *Olympia* (1938), because in this case at least aesthetics determine politics. The history of films is in great part the history of our attitudes toward our bodies, as they have been expressed and as we have attempted to imitate the fleeting film images. *The Exorcist* (William Friedkin, 1973) may be the most elaborate version of the way films view the body. It is a story of demonic possession in which physical-sexual evil invades a girl on the verge of gaining adult sexuality. One of the murder victims is a homosexual director, and the nominal hero, a priest-psychiatrist, has his own problems with diverted sexuality. The demonic voice is supplied by Mercedes McCambridge—an unconscious tribute to the hidden self that sound film made possible. *The Exorcist* is more about the way movies view the body than it is about Christian doctrine. As Jekyll and Hyde were countered by Astaire and Rogers, so the true counterpart to *The Exorcist* are the Kung Fu films, with their emphasis on the ability of the trained body —available to all who will learn—to overcome great odds, using only inner force, a pure heart, mind, and body. We watch movies alone in the dark—and we reach out to the human image on the screen for solace and support. Whatever changes in the history of attitudes toward the body have occurred in the twentieth century, whatever releases from Victorianism and new stylizations of the self have been evolved, movies play an essential role in their creation.‡

ACTORS AND OBJECTS

Body images do not come only from the actors in films. They also come from our sense of the varieties of film enclosure and film openness, from cars and trains and vehicles of all sorts, from houses and rooms, and all kinds of spaces. My earlier distinction between the open and the closed film can be applied as well to those more recalcitrant objects, filmed actors. In the open films we experience character momentarily included by the limits of the film, with a life that extends beyond those limits. We believe that characters in such films pre-exist the specific events of the story and will exist after the story has completed its particular rhythm. In Renoir's *Boudu Saved from Drowning* (1931), for example, the main character enters the world of the film because Lestingois, the bookstore owner, decides to save him from committing suicide in the Seine. Lestingois brings Boudu into his life, into his house, and attempts to teach the clochard the benefits of bourgeois society: sleeping on a bed, wearing a tie, eating butter rather than lard. Boudu, of course, teaches Lestingois much more. At the end of the film Boudu has won a lottery and is about to marry Anne-Marie, the Lestingois' maid, who had previously been having an affair with Lestingois. (Boudu had meanwhile seduced Madame Lestingois.) While

‡ Kung Fu films are usually considered to be necessarily low-level genre films. But the link between their themes and basic film themes makes me think that merely because there has been no truly "great" Kung Fu film does not mean that none is possible. Perhaps a little self-consciousness is all that is required, for the Kung Fu film seems to be the natural heir of the musical.

floating down the river in a canoe with the rest of the wedding party, Boudu reaches out for a water lily. The boat overturns and he floats away, reaches the bank out of sight, exchanges his tuxedo for a scarecrow's clothes and goes on his way. There is no premeditation in his action. He has participated in the film to the extent of his interest and now he leaves. Only his hat still floats down the river. The relationship between the world of Lestingois and its architecturally imposed limits and the world of Boudu and its trails, rivers, and wanderings in and out of the camera frame defines the sense of character possible in Renoir's world and in the world of the open film in general. We see their place in a story, but they also imply a nature larger than the immediate purposes of the plot. At one point in *Boudu,* for example, Anne-Marie goes to a closet and reaches to the top shelf, where she has hidden some candy. She eats the candy and smiles to herself and then walks out of the frame. The action has nothing to do with the progress of the plot. But it does tell us something about Anne-Marie's character; nothing verifiable, just the fact that even she has a character that is not totally defined by the plot. Lestingois' bookshop is a world where definitions are too easy, however benevolently they are meant, while Boudu represents the uncategorizable, unplottable part of human nature. In his attitude toward character, Renoir is closer to Boudu than to Lestingois. His characters often talk, think, or act solely for themselves, enhancing our sense of their separate existence, rather than reaffirming their place in a preordained scheme of theme and story.

The open film emphasizes the continuity and the surprises of character. The closed film, on the other hand, considers character to be only another element in the visual pattern of the film. The inside of the open-film character is potential and variety; the inside of the closed-film character is limitation and repression. The open film deals with will, while the closed film deals with fate. Lang and Hitchcock place the character within a world of tyrannical forms—whether social institutions, legal and illegal conspiracies, the machinations of a faceless fate, or the uncontrollable forces from within the self. Character has no potential beyond what the film illustrates. It is character manipulated, because the closed film is a totally coherent system in which visual effects echo and re-echo, creating an aesthetic order that parallels the order in which their characters are caught.

One freedom possible to the character in open films is the ability to interpret the world in which he finds himself instead of being yet another object in the imposed interpretation of the director. Rauffenstein (in Renoir's *La Grande Illusion*) deliberately cutting a geranium to symbolize his feeling about the death of Boeldieu, and Katrin (in Rossellini's *Stromboli*) wearing shoes and painting a tree on the wall of her house both express an effort to control their worlds through their own will that is not available to the confused characters in a film by Lang or Hitchcock. Because of the visual nature of film, interpreting or being interpretable are both external process. But the ability to interpret implies a self-aware distance from the world of the film. The inability to interpret, the lack of interest in interpretation, makes the character subordinate to the larger truth of the plot of the film, in the same way that it makes the actor subordinate to the larger vision of the director. Closed-film directors therefore traditionally treat their actors "badly." They manipulate them and move around in accordance with the larger needs of story and scene: Hitchcock can kill off Janet Leigh a third of the way through *Psycho* because being a star outside the film means nothing in the scheme of Hitchcock's plot.*

Hitchcock's famous remark that "actors are cattle" similarly underlines the desire to make actors *mean* exactly what you have predetermined that they ought to mean; in the same way that the meaning of objects is limited, and thereby controlled, the individual is framed by society. Renoir, however, has usually emphasized improvisation; he called *Boudu,* one of his first films with sound, "an exercise around an actor" (Michel Simon). The contrast is clear in the differing attitudes toward the use of nonprofessional actors. Lang and Hitchcock, following Eisen-

---

* Historically, I might distinguish three varieties of the directorial imposition of meaning on the actor/character. In the first, exemplified by Lang and Hitchcock, the director includes the actor as another object in his world; in the second, exemplified by Howard Hawks and Ernst Lubitsch, the actor has an image of his own (like Cary Grant or Jack Benny) but essentially serves as an emissary of the director's purposes; in the third, the Kazan-Brando relationship I will discuss further below, the motion of the actor and the formal commitment of the director may be in specific thematic conflict.

stein and Pudovkin, choose such actors, when they have them at all, for their faces, the *typical* quality of their looks, whereas Renoir, Rossellini, and the neo-realists in general choose non-professionals on the basis of their *individual* suitability. Eisenstein's basic motive is to short-circuit the individualism of the professional actor (in a self-conscious polemic against Stanislavsky) and emphasize group or collective qualities. But, when Rossellini casts a French post office employee (Jean-Marie Patte) as Louis XIV, he is guided by his belief in their similar personal characteristics and manner and he emphasizes the interplay between individual and role. Rossellini's use of nonprofessional individuals extends outside the film frame, whereas Eisenstein's and Pudovkin's nonprofessionals submerge their individual natures in the film's depiction of more general and self-contained truth.†

The closed film therefore adheres to a closed view of the self, in which there are constant dangers to integrity from without and from within. Renoir, in his early sound films, experiments with sound as a possible freedom from the tyranny of the physical image. But Lang in *M* uses sound as a trap to parallel the way his main character, Beckert (Peter Lorre), is trapped by the demands of his mind and body. One of Lang's primary themes is the vulnerability of the self through the body, another version of the trap of visibility. Siegfried is an appropriate hero for Lang's silent period because he is invulnerable except for one spot on his body, and even the mental power of Dr. Mabuse cannot prevent him from falling when he is attracted to a woman. Since closed-film characters have no life outside the film, they are in constant danger from themselves in a way that can never be finally resolved. Open-film characters can include their sexuality in a complex view of self and society. But because society in the closed film functions more as psychic projection than external force, it is finally inescapable.

† The essentially formal relationships outlined above are also evident in the process of the film's making. Lang's first wife, Thea von Harbou, was his scriptwriter; between the two of them they shaped the world of the film. Renoir's first wife, Catherine Hessling, was his first star; between the two of them they stretched the film as part of their relationship. Lang, therefore, has always emphasized his control over his actors, while Renoir could experiment with improvisation. Hitchcock's wife, Alma Reville, has served as both scriptwriter and editor.

Closed-film characters mirror our fears about our inner natures and their separation from our physical selves; open-film characters are more like other people. Closed-film acting is therefore more schematic and mythic, while open-film acting draws upon an actor's individual nature. When Renoir directs, for example, he may follow an actor or an actress, and structure the film around the character rather than absorb the character into the pre-existing structure. As Rossellini has explained, "I always begin with a closeup, since it is the camera movement which follows the actor that discovers the world around him." The potentials of the actor's personality mean much more to Renoir and Rossellini in their creation of a film than they do to Lang, Welles, or Hitchcock, who are much more interested in the face and body of the actor, even to the point of casting either weak male leads or strong actors in the role of bystanders. So sexuality itself remains a theme of the closed film when it is about the fear of the body, and a theme of the open film when it is about the place of sex in society. The natural libertinism of *Boudu* complements the involuntary sex crimes of Beckert in *M*.

Clothing as an extension of a character's body also plays different roles in open and closed films. In the open film, clothing is costume, to be changed for different occasions. In the closed film, it often functions as a limit, the protection that has become confinement. Closed films rarely indulge in disguise as much as open films because disguise involves a more playful sense of role than closed films allow. By the 1950s the closed-film pressure—the manipulation of the actor's image, the preoccupation with the vulnerability of the body—makes clothing a powerful expression of character. I have already spoken about the use of jackets in *On the Waterfront* to represent obligation and maturity. Similarly Brando in *The Wild One* (Laslo Benedek, 1953) rides a motorcycle to assert a freedom and a will that defines his kind of rebellion. But equally defining is his leather jacket, his hat, his gloves, and his sunglasses, all protective, keeping the vulnerable self inside. The opposition gang, led by Lee Marvin (appropriately named Chino), with their more casual and soft clothes, present more comic and less heroic figures because they do not embody the same tension between will and repression. Brando's immobile face is an effort to get behind the frailties within. Hitchcock can deal with this self-imposed restriction because an important part of even his most melodramatic films is comedy. In the later films of Lang's career, his characters are becoming more and more like props, with hardly a wrinkle of expression crossing their faces. To accomplish his revenge, Glenn Ford in *The Big Heat* (1953) blanks out his face and emotions almost entirely—the total purification of Bogart's more sentimental "cool." A preoccupation with fate, with the establishment, with the conspiracies that will not allow one self-expression, may allow a sense of release through attack and a fantasy escape through identifying with the hero's final success. But when that fate becomes overpowering, as it does, for example, in Lang's *Beyond a Reasonable Doubt* (1956), the characters have no shred of will that can make them kin to the audience except the drive to avenge and revenge.

Even in films with visually open settings, the vulnerable character seeks to close himself off and prevent his vulnerability from being known. After World War Two the vulnerability is almost always sexual and emotional—the woman who makes the man forsake his gang (*The Wild One, On the Waterfront*), the wife whose murder begins the quest for revenge (*The Big Heat; Cornered,* Edward Dmytryk, 1945). The cold-faced heroes of the 1950s—Dana Andrews, Glenn Ford, Dick Powell, Ralph Meeker—off seeking revenge, their emotions shut into an expressionless mask—are close kin to the aggressive dressers like Brando, or their costumed descendants like Peter Fonda and Dennis Hopper in *Easy Rider*. No matter what kind of open road lies before Brando in *The Wild One* or Fonda and Hopper in *Easy Rider,* they are marked and limited by their attitude toward their clothes. All three refuse to be vulnerable; all three remain tied to their self-defined and self-limited conceptions of themselves. They have no sense of self-conscious play about their costumes, as do the characters in Renoir's *The Rules of the Game* or Louis XIV in Rossellini's *The Rise of Louis XIV*. They believe instead that they are in a fight to the death against people with other kinds of costumes. Terrified by the potential of open space they limit themselves by their clothes, as trapped as Monroe was by her body.

The basic distinction between the closed-film or machine view

of the self (worked by someone else) and the open-film or
self-moved view of the self (in which motion comes from within)
affects the treatment of many other themes as well. In line with
the closed view of character as limitation, it is in Langian-style
films that we first get any exploration of the problems of race and
occupation. The closed film considers color, like uniform, to be a
limit that can be fought against but finally never overcome, unless in the world of fantasy. The passing-for-white films of the
postwar period, such as *Lost Boundaries* (Alfred Werker, 1949)
and *Pinky* (Elia Kazan, 1949), concentrated on the simultaneous
freedom and trap of color in a manner not much beyond the old
stereotypes. Like anti-Semitism in *Gentleman's Agreement* (Kazan,
1947), the color problem was a problem of individual surfaces—
looking black or Jewish—rather than a problem of perspective
and social justice. At its best, however, the closed style could
produce films like Joseph Mankiewicz's *No Way Out* (1950), in
which Sidney Poitier plays a young intern who tries to prove he
did not kill the brother of a petty crook (Richard Widmark) by
giving him a spinal tap. For its time and for a long time after, *No
Way Out* is an excellent film about black-white relations. But its
conceptual limits are in great part the limit of its aesthetic form.
The title gives the basic premise away. Once it is assumed that
'there is no way out, what can be done? The basic attack of the
film is on the white liberal (Steve McNally) who is the chief
resident and believes that color is irrelevant and a man should be
treated according to his ability. But the film points out very
strongly that color (and class) must be considered; they cannot
be ignored. As long as the aesthetic by which films are made
implies that character is repression, it is difficult to envision a film
that treats black and white problems except as a function of
visibility. The only freedom is the self-awareness of limitation, and
so the chief resident's maid (Amanda Randolph) and the intern's
wife (Mildred Joanne Smith) keep up a brave front until the
whites leave: "You can cry, honey, they're gone." (Interestingly
enough, one of the most prejudiced characters in *No Way Out* is
deaf, and Poitier finally defeats the avenging Widmark because the
lights have been turned out.)

Films have always been obsessed with visual minority groups
for the same reasons that fiction has been obsessed with verbal

minorities. With this reasoning, one might argue that films created visual stereotypes of race and class much more than they helped to liberate us from them. But in the open film, where character is part of a life beyond the limits of the film, race and class tend to be defined in terms of the individual's efforts to include those definitions and move on, instead of being trapped by them. The most effective film efforts to present black life have, I think, been on television, especially in television commercials, where normality—the continuity of family life—allied with the momentary artifice of the commercial allows a breaking of limits films rarely achieve. The general demise of the closed film with the advent of wide screen and the expanded use of color has yet to produce the kind of socially open film we might hope for. But before that can happen, it is essential to see the ways in which the aesthetic of film has determined its treatment of such problems. The closed-film definition of society as a paranoid monolithic structure is specially suited to a fatalistic interpretation of race, class, and character. The open-film definition of society as a momentary frame, like the film itself, that is relevant so long as it is useful, interesting, and entertaining, has the aesthetic potential to change our definitions of society from exclusive to inclusive. In closed films characters tend to face the camera; in open films they tend to face each other.

FILMS AND HUMAN NATURE

The closed film concentrates especially on the double character; the open film on the theatrical character. The double character is plain on the surface and tangled within. Split between mind and body, he is intent on making himself into only his surface—calm and respectable—but he is fatally manipulated by controlling forces from without or uncontrollable forces from within. The theatrical character is more self-stylized and self-conscious. He considers the possibilities of the self to be a freedom rather than a prison. Able to create situations, he is the master of costume and appearances who wills his nature to be a certain way, himself both subject and object. But the double character cannot pick and choose among the possibilities of his nature. He regards the variety of his character as a threat, an eruption from the depths, an uncontrolled revelation. Beckert, the bourgeois in Lang's *M* who murders little girls, both indulges his passion and hates himself for it. Theatrical character, open-film character, attempts to express the potential in character, the freedom of costume and style. Double character, closed-film character, expresses the conflicts in character, the need for repressions and limits without which all will be destroyed. The essence of the double character is that he can't help himself, for the closed film is the theater of underfeelings, the normal person who finds himself capable of murder.

The character in the film becomes for the audience the individual in society, and the different types of character native to the open and closed films imply distinct attitudes about the world as well. When character can be created by will, as it is in the open film, and actors can be allowed to improvise, the director feels comfortable with nature. He sees how it might be changed, varied, and heightened, how character and society itself can be reformable, natural growths. But when, in the closed film and double character, the will is weak and its end is the repression of frightening potential, the director implies a cautious attitude toward nature, a need to control the image and the actors by enclosed sets and precise lighting, and the belief that society is always an imposition on a world of unpredictable violence and darkness. As I have suggested above, the technological innovations of the late 1950s and early 1960s helped create a historical moment of synthesis in which the aesthetic of the closed film was absorbed in that of the open film and new possibilities of theme and method opened up. The pessimism of the closed film and the optimism of the open film about character crossbred as well. Before examining the new attitude let me first ground the double and the theatrical character historically and discuss the appeal each makes to the audience.

THE DOUBLE

As many studies have shown, the double is a basic image of nineteenth-century literature. It arises most clearly from German romanticism as a way of expressing the divided nature of the German character, what Goethe called the "two souls" within him. The French variety, found in Baudelaire, emphasizes the double nature of the self in society. Since Baudelaire's dandy dresses up in order that he may step back from involvement in society, he is therefore more akin to what I have called the theatrical character. The American version—in writers like Poe and Hawthorne—is much more like the German and shows their common roots in the eighteenth-century novel, where the conflict between self and society was resolved not by stylization but by repression.

The double is only an important subtheme in the body of nineteenth-century literature. In film it has been the most prevalent way of defining human nature. The double expresses in terms of theme and plot something of the inner aesthetic of films, the double exposure, the fleeting insubstantiality of the image, its potential lack of authority even at the moment of greatest assertion. This simultaneous reality and transience of the film image can imply that character itself, so palpably before you, is merely a construction. Suitably for the strongest historical sources of the image, the first films to elaborate the theme of the double were German. Stellan Rye's *The Student of Prague* (1913) (and Henrik Galeen's 1926 version) drew on German romanticism and Poe's "William Wilson" to tell a story that ended with the double and the original killing each other. Fritz Lang's *Metropolis* (1926) includes a character named Maria, a saintly preacher to the workers, who is doubled by a robot programmed by the managers of Metropolis to stir up the workers so that repression can begin. Each represents the split in a single self. In *The Student of Prague,* as in Poe's story, the relationship between original and double is competitive: each seeks to best the other in worldly and personal success. In *Metropolis,* Maria's double is specifically seductive while the saintly Maria attracts only by her purity; the robot dances lewdly before a group of tuxedoed men, whereas the equivalent scene for Maria involves her rescue of the children of the workers from their flooding city. Maria is a mother; the robot is a sexual woman.‡

Although German films are the first to exploit the double explicitly, its presence in later films shows the attraction it had for filmmakers of all sorts, because it could express something of the

‡ This theme in German films has been amply documented by Lotte Eisner in *The Haunted Screen* and Siegfried Kracauer in *From Caligari to Hitler.*

special nature of film form and the role of the actor within that form. The novel in the eighteenth century had been born in part to express a sense of character that the stage could not, character from within, character perceived as an inner conflict. Films followed fiction in this attempt to portray a different kind of person than we had been used to in art—neither the stylized posturer of the stage nor the static figure of sculpture and drama, but a moving and changing person. It is appropriate, then, that films made their first attempts to explore character through the visible double, the obviously split self, for there alone could films draw on their special nature to define their difference from the theatrical tradition that in so many other ways had such a strong hold over them. Within the gloom of these early film sets, so obviously derived from expressionist drama and painting, could live a sense of character that dramatic and artistic forms could neither express nor encompass.

Sound internalizes the visual doubles of silent films. The monsters of Lang's *Destiny, Metropolis,* and the Mabuse films became in *M* the torments of a psychotic killer. The double character becomes self-consciously afraid of his own body and calls on society to help repress his potentially destructive desires. The great horror film explosion of early sound—*Frankenstein* (1931), *Dracula* (1931), *Dr. Jekyll and Mr. Hyde* (1932), *King Kong* (1933)— dealt with conflicts between the physical self and the social self that seem to reflect the new-found complexities brought by sound. The seamless relation between the silent-film actor and his body had been split at the level of popular fantasy perhaps to the point of schizophrenia. Appropriately enough, Fredric March received an Academy Award in 1932 for his double performance in *Jekyll and Hyde*. In addition to the tumults of the body, sound also emphasized the pressures of society. When it is akin to that of Baudelaire's dandy, such a distanced doubling is usually comic, as it is, for example, in Herbert Marshall's high society criminal in Ernst Lubitsch's *Trouble in Paradise* (1932), but could easily verge into malevolence, as it does in Hitchcock's *Murder* (1930), in which the murderer is a transvestite actor who, like Lang's Haghi, finally kills himself in the middle of a performance. (Hitchcock often plays between the various possibilities of the criminal dandy. Robert Walker in *Strangers on a Train,* 1951, is a malevolent version and Cary Grant in *To Catch a Thief,* 1955, a benevolent one.) But more often the conflict between self and society is tragic and fatal. The conflict in *M* between Beckert's respectable exterior and his pathological sexual desires is finally presented as a conflict between the laws and the mercies of society, between the desire for revenge and the desire for understanding, between the demand for order and the demand for individual sympathy. Most of Lang's films imply that the repressions of society are actually a projection of the individual's desire to be controlled, to be protected from his own instincts. When in Lang's later films, such as *Man Hunt* (1941) and *Ministry of Fear* (1945), the menace of society is represented by the Nazis and therefore has at least a touch of historical reality, the films are much weaker. They divert the truth of the conflicts within by seeming to make it part of the real world. The double for Lang was a given of human nature, not an aberration due to circumstances.

Film doubles became even more populous in the 1940s, when World War Two created a cultural situation in which almost everyone found themselves leading several lives. The World at War as expressed in 1940s films was in many ways an escape from the confined social world of the 1930s. But at the same time, the new situations of war, the new demands on the individual, bred divisions within that corresponded to and strengthened the basic theme of the double. The kind of general paranoia about society and the forces of order that the double expressed in earlier films could—in the context of war, occupied countries, disrupted families, and men trained to murder—became a realistic response to the world that existed. Rather than a pathological state, the paranoia about the forces of repression and the schizophrenia of the double response to the demands of society and the self could be considered logical and appropriate interpretations of history.

One of the most powerful expressions of the double theme in this period is Alfred Hitchcock's *Shadow of a Doubt* (1943, script by Thornton Wilder). In it Joseph Cotten and Teresa Wright play Charles and Charlotte, uncle and niece, Uncle Charlie and Charlie. Uncle Charlie murders rich widows not for their money but for moral reasons of his own—to rid society of the people who are most parasitic on it. Pursued by the police, he comes to stay in a small town in California where his sister and her family live. To them he is Uncle Charlie, the messenger from the outside world of sophistication who brightens their drab lives. The visual texture of the film almost immediately establishes the special relationship he has with his niece. In the first scenes we see Uncle Charlie in bed and then later Charlie in another bed, but in a mirror position. Telepathic, sympathetic, they have a bond deeper than the merely familial. In the course of the film, Charlie changes from a teenager to a young woman, and a central object in her discovery of Uncle Charlie's evil nature is a wedding ring he has given her as a present. Growing up becomes inextricably linked to the knowledge of sex and murder. In the double structure of the film, Charlie's impulse both to protect Uncle Charlie and condemn him underlines their participation in each other's psychic lives. She is the goodness, the moral standards by which he believes himself justified to murder; he is the darkness that she glimpses within herself, specifically associated with her growing sexuality. Uncle Charlie brings with him the knowledge of the outside world as well. The date of the action is explicitly 1941, and Uncle Charlie looks back to the world of his parents as a repository of lost values. But when Charlie has discovered his secret, he forces her to recognize that her own idyllic life is a dream. After a small town of picket fences and jolly policemen, he takes her to a café (the 'Til Two) that she had never known existed, yet where a girl she recognizes from high school works as a waitress, and soldiers in uniform sit with their dates. Charlie is forced to look out of her dream life into the true nightmare world beyond, as she must grow out of her sexual innocence into knowledge, finally to kill Uncle Charlie before he kills her. "Every once in a while the world goes crazy—like your Uncle Charlie," says a character at the end of the film. Was Charlie right to kill Uncle Charlie? Was Uncle Charlie right to kill the widows? Is World War Two a moral war, or just an excuse to indulge the evil within? The brilliance of *Shadow of a Doubt* is that it raises such questions without ever resolving them. Charlie has finally killed Uncle Charlie, but only as the Student of Prague or William Wilson killed the double that was actually himself.

In Hitchcock's elaborate return to the double theme in *Strangers on a Train* (1951), the resonances have become more schematic and therefore somewhat less compelling. The double nature of innocence and guilt for Hitchcock is an image of the relationship between audience and film, the desire of the audience to participate in murder and violence while seeking to avoid any responsibility. The innocent bystander is pulled into the plot, and Hitchcock's audience is pulled into the film, by his own inner darkness. Hitchcock's doubles expose the necessarily mixed motives behind every action, the guilt that arises from the desire, through movies, to experience the forbidden without being scarred or punished. When, in *Strangers on a Train,* we are asked to empathize with the social climber Guy (Farley Granger) while he is lured into an exchange of murders by the upperclass Bruno (Robert Walker), our fascination with Bruno so outweighs the blandness of the values and view of life held by Guy that there is little combat, little tension between the opposite selves that together, in Guy and Bruno, form a single personality. The loss perceived by Charlie at the end of *Shadow of a Doubt* has become the self-congratulation of Guy at the end of *Strangers on a Train,* and a final comic clergyman marks the change. Charlie has learned what in Uncle Charlie attracted her; Guy has no idea—perhaps because the homosexual misogyny of Uncle Charlie has become much more overt in Bruno. Hitchcock can still make enticing films about the theme of intertwined guilt and innocence, but the specific projection of that theme through doubled, twinned, or complementary characters no longer seems to be so defining. Hitchcock's socially "normal" characters become blander and blander, his deviants and doubles become more and more extreme, and the tension, by the 1960s and 1970s, in films like *Marnie* and *Topaz* can be treated only as comedy until Hitchcock himself appears in *Frenzy* as both corpse and bystander.

Shadow of a Doubt is a brilliant example of the complex play possible with the theme of the double. But the anxiety of Americans and Europeans forced to play so many often opposing psychic and social roles comes out in a variety of other ways in the films of the 1940s. Sometimes the emphasis is on character, other times on context, and sometimes on a combination of the two. How can one collect all the relevant cultural data? Let me just mention some examples: the vogue for Jack the Ripper films—the calm, upper-class man who is a brutal murderer; Charlie McCarthy and

Edgar Bergen, translated from the radio to the screen, the master
and the back-talking puppet; Superman, Batman and Robin, the
Green Hornet—all late 1930s and early 1940s characters with
double identities, the "respectable" identity usually being socially
upper-class or that of a reporter; the continued success of Jekyll
and Hyde films with Victor Fleming's version (1941, with Spencer
Tracy). Also in 1941 Hollywood created its own gothic character
in *The Wolf Man,* with Lon Chaney. In the film Chaney's
specific problem is the contrast between his beefy American look
and the dapper manners of his elegant English father (Claude
Rains). The wolf-man transformation allows him to free himself
from his father's yoke (he is a much younger son) and release
his own sexual feelings. Thus the Jekyll and Hyde elements of
lower-class sexuality are restated once again in a myth of transformation, a discovery of the double. But here, even more than
in Jekyll and Hyde, the sympathies are mainly for the monster.
The final scene, in which the werewolf is murdered by the un-
knowing father, restates the necessary fate of anyone who dares
to go against society's decisions about the values of personal instincts.* The message is not so much that assertion never works,
but that there is always something inside you that either prevents
success or says that its achievement is necessarily inhuman. As in
the many spiritualist films of the 1940s, the gift of knowledge
always brings with it a fatal destiny. The other side of films like
The Wizard of Oz, in which the dream liberates you to realize
you should never have left home, are films like Lang's *The Woman
in the Window* (1944), in which the murder turns out to be a
dream and the audience must face the possibility that we all can
dream of murder and may someday commit one. The many
biographical films popular in the 1940s may have been an effort
to find models for a complete and coherent life. But the stronger
fascination is with characters who return home to discover that
their wives, families, and identities have been taken over by
someone else (*The Man with My Face,* Edward J. Montagne,
1951) or in which twins either conflict with or kill one another
(*A Stolen Life,* Curtis Bernhardt, 1946, with Bette Davis). In

* The script is by Robert Siodmak, a product of the Ufa studies of the
1920s, where Lang and Hitchcock also began their careers. It was directed
by George Waggner.

films generally, and perhaps in the 1940s and 1950s specifically, the power of purging anxieties through presenting the most terrifying fantasies on screen may be more compelling than the power to present good examples for the audience to follow.

The appeal of the theme of the double, whether the doubling is within one person or projected into two characters, is to our sense of the split within, between emotions and intellect, private desires and public moral imperatives. As in *The Wolf Man,* we are torn between a loathing for it and a desire that it assume its rightful inheritance. By the 1950s the tension between those two selves has become somewhat shopworn for films that pretended to be pictures of contemporary life. When reality presented a suitable situation, the closed-film exploration of the double character could be very effective. Edward Dmytryk, a director whose films show the definite visual impact of the shadows of expressionism, was the appropriate person to film *The Sniper* (Edward Dmytryk, 1952), a story of a World War Two veteran who cracked under the strain of the enforced normality of the 1950s and began killing women. I have already referred to the loss of closed-film vitality in Charles Laughton's *The Night of the Hunter* (1955). The film may also be a convenient marking place for the diminished vitality of the theme of the double because it presents the conflict between guilt and innocence essentially as a children's story. The character of Robert Mitchum in *The Night of the Hunter* is a comic-strip Uncle Charlie. He is a minister who marries and then murders a woman (Shelley Winters) whose imprisoned husband has hidden money from a bank robbery. On one of Mitchum's hands is tattooed the word LOVE, and on the other, HATE—one letter per finger—and he is constantly interlacing them. The embodiment of evil, Mitchum is constantly both preaching against and manipulating sexuality—as befits his status as a double character. As usual, sexuality in the film is an impulse allied with murder and violence. The same women who flirted with Mitchum when he was respectable want to hang him when he's not. In essence *The Night of the Hunter* is a film about the need to reject sexuality before one grows up enough to be tempted. Two children flee the Frankenstein-like rampages of Mitchum and land finally at the home of Lillian Gish, who specializes in taking in homeless children. Gish's family is the family without a grown man, the family without the problems of sexuality, a harkening back to the good Maria of *Metropolis.* The family is threatened only when Mitchum arrives to pursue the children once again, and he gets his main entry into the family by coming on to Ruby, another child Gish is taking care of, when she goes to town to shop and be lured by the charms of the city. The process of the film is basically from Mitchum to Gish, from morbid antisexuality to reasonable and moral antisexuality, from a violent Old Testament religion to a calming New Testament religion. As a character says in *Forbidden Planet,* "We are all monsters in our subconscious. That's why we have laws and religion." *The Night of the Hunter* is a parable about growing up that rejects growing up unless the problems—both private and public—can be avoided. Gish's screen image has always been beyond sexuality. By having the silent-star Gish defeat the 1940s and 1950s star Mitchum, it seems to reject the world in which Mitchum's personality took shape and to return instead to an Eden of aesthetic innocence. Although made in 1955, its emphasis on the romance of the studio set, the safety and articulation of the enclosed world, seems remarkably archaic now, a dream made possible by its style.

The childlike mythmaking of *The Night of the Hunter* reflects what happens to the monster film in general in the 1950s. In such an undistinguished film as *I Was a Teenage Frankenstein* (Herbert Strock, 1958) the double theme's loss of emotional power has become even more apparent, although a bare outline of the film's actions shows the paradigmatic nature of its concerns. The last line in the film is "I'll never forget his face after the accident." The antisocial monster has become the teenager, and teenagers in 1950s films always seem more misunderstood than truly threatening. True to form, this teenage monster has died without really rampaging and the only element of true horror quality in the film is his burnt, dripping face with its one distended eye. The last and most important stage of his transformation by the Dr. Frankenstein of the film (Whit Bissell) involves getting a new face so that he can walk among people without being ashamed. The convenient source of the face is a teenager discovered in a lover's lane. Shortly after the final operation, we see the monster (Gary Conway) fondly studying his new face in the mirror. What an image of Hollywood's own process of transformation: beneath the sweet handsomeness is still the monster. But the once powerful theme of the double, the true self within and the false self without, has been reduced to doing service for the teenage worry about acne.

THE THEATRICAL CHARACTER

I Was a Teenage Frankenstein is a debased version of the basic Hollywood myth of transformation. Like most of the examples I have mentioned, the transformation is involuntary. But there is a voluntary process as well, in which the different aspects of the self are not so much at war as they are in league. The theatrical character, the character who doubles himself as an act of will, first appears most strongly in sound films. In silent films the removal of clothes could signify an essential psychological act, either to make oneself more natural, as in DeMille's *Male and Female* (1919), or less protected, as in Murnau's *The Last Laugh* (1924). But sound allowed verbal distancing and self-conscious stylization. To a certain degree the destructive double, the inarticulate self overcoming and destroying the articulate, is a legacy of silent film, while the theatrical character, the witty banterer playing the game of social identity, is a creature of sound.

The character who could play with his identity and stylize himself for greater freedom is in the 1930s almost always either a member of the upper class or, better, someone pretending to be upper class. Theater for such people is a kind of freedom that is unavailable for the other members of society. Whether the aristocrat is Cary Grant, Katharine Hepburn, or Pierre Fresnay's Boeldieu in *La Grande Illusion,* the sense of self as theater, as play, is paramount. It involves a distancing of emotions, an unwillingness to be the victim of inner feelings in the way that less stylized characters are. Critics often wonder that Renoir in so many of his films of the 1930s should be fond of his aristocratic characters—Boeldieu, Louis XVI in *La Marseillaise,* Robert de la Chesnaye in *The Rules of the Game.* But the fascination with the stylized character must come inevitably when sound adds to film the potential of self-irony. The theatrical character does not belong to a social class so much as he is a class unto himself, preserving in style what history has left behind.

As World War Two draws closer, however, self-contained style becomes more a trap than a possible protection and extension of the self. The flamboyance of Rosenthal (Marcel Dalio) in Renoir's *La Grande Illusion* turns into the aristocratic calm, the Buddhist imperturbability of La Chesnaye (Marcel Dalio) in *The Rules of the Game*. La Chesnaye's liking for eighteenth-century style leads finally to an effort to quiet emotions, smooth over conflict, and retreat into a world of rules. He finally leads his guests back into his country house, covering up the murder of André Jurieu. Renoir's American films carry with them an even greater sense of potential fate and enclosure, characters fighting against the pressures of society and nature, like Octave, the character played by Renoir in *The Rules of the Game,* trying vainly to get out of his bear costume. The banter of society, the masks assumed to divert, have begun to constrict and limit, and Bogart's mask of cool control must finally open to reveal the sentimentality within. Eccentricity, even in its own special world, was suspect in a society organized for war. The eccentric Custer in *They Died with Their Boots On* (1941) or Alvin York in *Sergeant York* (Howard Hawks, 1941) find that their individualism flourishes best in the Army. Bogart as the head of a mob of American gangsters in *All Through the Night* (Vincent Sherman, 1942) joins forces with the police to fight Nazi fifth columnists. The eccentric professors working on an encyclopedia of all knowledge in *Ball of Fire* (Hawks, 1941) find that they must enter the world outside and defeat the gangsters who are oppressing and condescending to them. Like Hitchcock's outsiders in *Lifeboat* (1941), the eccentrics, the self-stylizers, can no longer afford the luxury of personal style that seemed so effective in the 1930s, but must band together against a common enemy.

Ernst Lubitsch's *To Be or Not to Be* (1942) brilliantly elaborates the freedom of the theatrical character defined specifically as a professional actor. Jack Benny plays Joseph Tura, "the greatest Shakespearean actor in Poland," and Carole Lombard plays his wife, Maria, whose greater fame constantly puts Benny in a snit. But these comic jealousies and the backstage romantic farce are set just before and during the Nazi Occupation of Poland. Tura's company had planned to put on a show satirizing the Nazis, but were prevented from doing so by the war. Throughout the film, Lubitsch and his scriptwriter Edwin Justus Mayer play between the politics outside and the personalities inside the theater world, where the actor who was to play Hitler is otherwise only an extra. Through a complicated series of events, Benny, Lombard, and the other actors must put on the costumes of their thwarted anti-Nazi play in order to save the lives of Polish underground workers in real life. On stage Tura is the perfect ham, but offstage he can play the collaborationist Dr. Siletsky with perfect control and invention. Reality, in the shape of history, has invaded the world of theater and style. As the "real" Dr. Siletsky says, in his effort to seduce Maria Tura to his bed and the Nazi cause, "In the theater it's important that you choose the right part. In real life it's more important to choose the right side." But Lombard as Maria has a larger vision of the relation between theater and life: "I once played a spy," she responds, "but I got shot in the last act." Style is perspective and Lubitsch in *To Be or Not to Be* shows that theater need not be a refuge, but can reach out, absorb, and even control the bad actors of real life. The recognition that the social self is a creation of theater allows the theatrical character to make better moral decisions than the unself-conscious inhabitants of reality could ever make. It is appropriate that the prime villain, Dr. Siletsky, is exposed by the fact that he has never heard of Maria Tura, that is, by his ignorance of theater. Like Lang's Haghi and Hitchcock's Mr. Memory, he is finally trapped and killed onstage. To be or not to be is a false choice because it ignores the intermediate reality of art.

Lubitsch allows the self-consciousness of the theatrical character to be an effective way of discovering the values of play-acting in everyday life. But that sense of style must be supported by a group and also be essentially comic. Such flexibility for the individual has otherwise become too much of a luxury. In many other films of the 1940s, where the tone is more somber, the self-consciousness of the theatrical character becomes assimilated to the prevailing mode of the riven double character, with usually pessimistic results. In *A Double Life* (George Cukor,

1947), for example, Ronald Colman is an actor whose role as Othello begins to take over his offstage life. Colman's theatrical life—"the way he has of becoming someone else every night" —prevents him from truly knowing himself. Like the underground sexuality of the double character, the real self and the stage self unite only at their worst potential: "You're two men now, grappling for control, you and Othello." Consider the difference between this line from the film and the somewhat similar one I quoted from *Dinner at Eight:* "You're two people really. One's magnificent and the other's very shoddy." In the earlier film the interplay between Barrymore's offstage and onstage personalities could enrich the plot and his own characterization. But in the later the stage self represents limiting and ultimately destructive self-consciousness. In the same way that the inner exuberant self that so many musicals sought to release became something to be repressed in the late 1940s and early 1950s, so, too, the expansiveness allowed by acting and stylization within a film becomes in the same period a deadly and irresponsible retreat from the more important demands of everyday life. Like Fredric March, Colman also received an Academy Award for his double impersonation.

This very negative view of the role-playing part of the personality is expanded in the 1950s by the show business biographies, in which success on the stage always means failure in private life. A particularly Byzantine example of the relations between actor and character are the two films based on the life of Al Jolson, *The Jolson Story* (Alfred Green, 1946) and *Jolson Sings Again* (Henry Levin, 1949), both starring Larry Parks. *The Jolson Story* is straightforward show-business biography, a restaging of triumphs and tragedies, with the added teaser that, although Parks is mouthing, Jolson is doing his own singing. *Jolson Sings Again* is the story of the making of *The Jolson Story*. After Jolson collapses on a worldwide army singing tour, he is nursed back to health, marries his nurse, and is gradually persuaded to make a comeback by singing at a Community Chest benefit. Naturally, he comes on last, when most of the audience has left. But a producer who likes his work, and coincidentally has been offered a story based on Jolson's life the previous week, sees Jolson and loves him. Jolson is skeptical. The recordings are old: how can he act his twenty-year-old self? You'll rerecord, says the producer, and we'll use someone else. Jolson records and in the next scene he's in a screening room. Now come the complications. The lights go out and on screen is an actor in blackface singing the song Jolson has just recorded. Jolson is impressed, and the smiling producer says, "I'd like you to meet Larry Parks." Larry Parks playing the elder Jolson thereupon shakes hands with Larry Parks as Larry Parks; Jolson as played by Parks has watched Parks playing Jolson mouthing words sung by Jolson. And, while he watches, Parks playing Jolson in the screening room is so pleased that he begins to mouth the words that Parks playing Jolson is mouthing on the screen. The first words spoken by Jolson in *The Jazz Singer,* the disjuncture between the actor and voice they memorialize, between the cantor singing for a special group and the popular singer reaching out to a nationwide audience, have come a long way to this double and redoubled scene. To add a final touch, in the back of the screening room, unnoticed by the actors in the scene, is the real Jolson, looking on with approval.

But the schizoid exuberance of *Jolson Sings Again* was a whistling in the dark. It is depressing to look back on such films with their sleight-of-hand view of the theatrical self, and connect them with historical hindsight to the appearance of Larry Parks before the House Committee on Un-American Activities, where he, like so many others, was forced to insist that he was never of two minds about anything, especially America, and that one led three lives only to be useful to one's country and with that country's constant conniving and approval. The fear of doubleness and the identification of theatricality, the stylizing of self, with more malevolent images of the uncontrollable inner self is a constant of the period from 1945 to 1959.

The 1930s and 1940s had concentrated on the lower-class antisocial criminal. But the criminal of the 1950s was more often an intellectual who had gone bad or a psychopath. The fear of the body extended to a fear of the mind as well. Because your body was so weak, your emotions so malleable, your brain could be stolen from you or at least washed. The monster within, the nice neighbor whose heart held a murderer, easily transformed into the nice neighbor who was a secret Communist.

The attack made on the American actor by the postwar government—and postwar society in general—as a potential danger to the stability of American values was in essence an attack upon individual energy and eccentricity. It assumed, like the westerns and musicals of the period I have discussed, that the best values came from the structure of society rather than from the individuals who made up the society. The image of the politically delinquent actor that emerged time and again in the HUAC hearings was the image of the child, the innocent, the clown caught in matters he knew nothing about.

The image suited the times and, more tragically, the conception many actors had of their profession. Even such a stalwart professional as Paul Muni considered acting to be something no true adult would do, like the comic disguises of Alec Guinness in *Kind Hearts and Coronets* (Robert Hamer, 1949). Accordingly, film biographies of artists asserted the superiority of one's work to one's life. Toulouse-Lautrec, in John Huston's *Moulin Rouge* (1952), cautions against ever meeting someone whose work one admires—"What they do is always better than what they are"—and such films as Vincente Minnelli's *Lust for Life* (1956, about Van Gogh) confirmed the Romantic belief that creativity took a terrible toll on the self and should be approached, if at all, only at a distance. But the film actor had no product but his personality. The show business biography or the artist biography that contrasted personal failure with public success was therefore not merely a means of simultaneously teasing and appeasing the audience. Its values truly reflected the belief that actors were worse off than audiences, that their function was to be a scapegoat, entertaining at great personal cost. Actors, acting, film, theater, art in general did not expand the sensibilities of the audience; they allowed the audience a brief respite in their more important outside lives, where the real business of society was conducted.†

† A later Jekyll and Hyde reading of the same themes is Jerry Lewis' *The Nutty Professor* (1963), in which the ugly but intelligent professor by means of chemicals turns into the handsome but mean-spirited singer Buddy Love. Obviously Lewis' own attitude toward his former partner Dean Martin influences his film, as does his dual role of actor and director. But Lewis' real pedigree as a 1950s personality type appears in the contrast between his pontificating talk-show self and his out-of-control film

Two main styles of acting seemed possible in American films in the cultural situation of the 1950s. One was the enclosed self of characters like Glenn Ford's Bannion in Lang's *The Big Heat*. The other was the enclosed style of Marlon Brando and James Dean, a more vulnerable kind of characterization, associated especially with the Method and the Actors Studio, but influenced as well by Italian neo-realism and the sense of emotion under pressure projected by performers such as Anna Magnani, John Garfield, Alan Ladd, and Bogart. The Method had been created as a style of stage acting. But in retrospect it seems to have had more influence as a style of film acting. The routine at the Actors Studio—the individual classes, improvisations, and scenes—also trained actors in the discontinuities appropriate to film style. The Method emphasized the pool of real personal behavior at the actor's command, and the actors became adept at whipping up the appropriate feeling for any scene. So they moved easily into movies, where sound engineers could pick up the most inaudible anguish or cameramen focus on the most fleeting gesture. Compared to the vengeful cool of the self-contained actors, the Method actors and actresses explored the traps and explosions of emotion. They brought into films experiences and feelings that official culture either ignored or actively attacked. By representing and articulating the feelings of insecurity and impotent rage felt by so many in what was being billed as a secure and settled society, Brando and Dean allowed their audience a sense of release. By identifying with them, the audience could organize its confusions. By seeing their apparent reconciliations with society (in *East of Eden, Rebel Without a Cause,* and *On the Waterfront,* for example), their fans could experience the pleasures of both rebellion and reconciliation without the threat of having to be more than passive observers.

The new importance of the actor may have reflected the

---

self, a descendant of Danny Kaye's ability in films like *The Inspector General* (Henry Koster, 1949) or *The Court Jester* (Norman Panama and Melvin Frank, 1956) to go from one personality to another at the snap of a finger. Kaye also stands behind Lewis' impersonation of the body that escaped from the mind's control. The dead comedian-singer brother inside the live, shy, intellectual brother are both portrayed by Kaye in *Wonder Man* (H. Bruce Humberstone, 1945). Perhaps their ultimate source is the Lewis-like Hyde of Fredric March in Mamoulian's film, the lumpen Jewish self beneath the debonair exterior.

economic fact that, with the end of contract playing, they negotiated directly for each film. But the burden on the actual human beings who were these stars must have been enormous. They had developed their talent for acting only to discover that they were being worshipped for something inside them that seemed outside their conscious control. An actor in the older, more external style would have found it much easier to take. But both Brando and Dean already considered their acting skills to be the product of psychic weakness, and Brando at various times had counseled both Dean and Montgomery Clift to see psychiatrists. They had searched their own experience and the observed experience of others to create characters whose performability gave them some control over the threatening forces within, and their audiences reveled in the paradox of their consummate command of despair and aimless rebellion until it became some pure form of the misguided and uncontrollable. Glenn Ford's frozen face intent on revenging the murder of his wife was matched by the image of Brando at the end of *On the Waterfront,* his windbreaker zippered tightly to keep the blood invisible inside. In the psychic history of the 1950s it is necessary that Ford's wife in *The Big Heat* is played by Jocelyn Brando.

But with the success of Brando, Dean, Clift, and other new young actors in achieving that tense balance between emotion and repression came the more unsupportable image nurtured by the fan clubs, the publicity, and the cults, while the studios responded with charges of "temperament." Self-protection and retreat became the answer in private life as well. After the great Elia Kazan films of the 1950s and his own *One-Eyed Jacks* (1961), Brando protected himself by plunging into roles that demanded some kind of disguise. Always insistent on doing his own makeup, he began putting on false noses and working up a variety of new accents, demonstrating his virtuosity, covering the threatening nakedness of his early emotional power. Clift and Dean would not make even that choice. After a serious car accident, Clift's sensitive face was immobilized by plastic surgery. Dean died in a car crash at twenty-four, after only three important roles (*East of Eden, Rebel Without a Cause, Giant*). A cult quickly followed. Death had purified what Dean represented, and the living person could no longer give any trouble to those who sought personal salvation through a fragment of his car or a chip from his tombstone.

Dean, Clift, and Brando were only the most visible representatives of a change in the style of American acting and the necessarily related change in the American psychic landscape as well. Renoir and the open film had emphasized the individual, self-moved quality of the actor. But the Method had introduced the actor and his personality as a powerful counterforce to the shaping and organizing power of the director. Kazan's directorial style, for example, may have owed a great debt to closed-film and proscenium-stage styles, especially in his manipulation of situation and physical milieu. But, by always choosing strong central actors, Kazan built in an ambivalence, playing God with the sensibility of a victim. The structure of the film was coercive, but the personality of the actor potentially existed beyond its limits, like Zapata's image and meaning enduring beyond the fatal failures within *Viva Zapata!* (1952). Our recognition that Zapata has been corrupted by power is projected more by Brando than conveyed by Kazan. The political implications of the closed style bred the ambivalent films of such personal anarchists as Kazan, Nicholas Ray, and Samuel Fuller. Fuller's financial difficulty in hiring strong stars leaves his films often awkwardly unbalanced, with strongly focused roles being played by weak actors and actresses. Only *Pickup on South Street* (1953) truly realizes its power, through the central part played by Richard Widmark. Kazan needed Brando, Dean, or Widmark to define his own perspective, as Ray needed Bogart, Ryan, or Dean.

The childlike or childish rebel was a major figure of the 1950s —the sullenness of Brando and Dean, the shyness of Clift, the innocent sexual assertion of Elizabeth Taylor and Marilyn Monroe—because the actor had been identified as a child in the eyes of society. The search for a true father was naturally a major theme, going back to *Red River,* where John Wayne was the father and Clift the adoptive son, Wayne the lone entrepreneur and Clift the tentative seeker for community, Wayne the moral absolutist and Clift the relativist and compromiser. The paradigm emerged in many versions during the 1950s, down to Paul Newman searching for a true father as Billy the Kid in Arthur Penn's *The Left-Handed Gun* (1958). But the energy for its vitality came in great part from the dramatization of the aesthetic tension between actor and director. When, in *One-Eyed Jacks* (1961), Brando finally kills his traitorous ex-partner "Dad" Longworth (Karl Malden, the "Father Barry" in *On the Water-front*), the fact that Brando is the film's director dictates both conflict and resolution.‡ In American films of the 1950s the ambivalence about the place in society of acting and the actor reflects national conflicts over the relative demands of individual and social values. The implied conflict between actor and director reproduces those terms within the individual film. I do not have the space here to discuss whether such ambivalence is a charac-teristic of the 1950s or an essential part of popular culture in any period. Did the films of the 1950s, by articulating the problems, help to purge the conflicts and move the American audience into the 1960s? Zapata may have been killed, Kazan may have named names to the House Committee on Un-Ameri-can Activities. But the horse, the image, Brando as a star, live beyond the film—perhaps to infuse the more personal politics of the 1960s. The varieties of escapism seem more complex than we have allowed. The answers to such questions must come from a cultural criticism that is as sensitive to the history and meaning of film form as it is to the political, economic, and social history from which the film audience briefly retires into its purer but obvi-ously similar world.

John Frankenheimer's *Seconds* (1966) is for me the most brilliant exposition of the interpenetration of the general theme of personal identity in the American film with the theme of the film actor and the special nature of his personality. Franken-heimer is not really a Hollywood director or a 1950s director. His early films, like *The Manchurian Candidate,* show how he draws upon and elaborates the experimentation with a more

‡ I have spoken about the mutually defining contrast between director and actor, but the contrast can work within a film as well. The same forces that shaped the acting style of Montgomery Clift in *Red River* seem to have touched John Wayne as well. Maurice Zolotow writes, "He had, with this film, found himself, found his style, found his presence, adapted his personal tensions and emotional struggles to his technique, and he could use his feelings for his own sons, Pat and Mike, and be the son of his father, and project it into his characterization."

naturalistic, urban drama that was being carried on by such programs as Studio One, Playhouse 90, and the Philco Television Theater. Frankenheimer's attitude toward the actor was therefore a television concentration on the actor's face and its potential depths, especially its anguish and conflict, that is more akin to the Kazan-Brando tension than the Lang-Glenn Ford repression. Both *The Manchurian Candidate* and *Seconds* are about the change of identity, either unwilled, as in the brainwashing of Laurence Harvey in the one, or self-willed, as in the decision to take on a new body and a new identity as a "second chance," in the other. The credit sequence by Saul Bass for *Seconds* sets the mood of the film: distorted parts of the body appear behind the words, floating in and out of our vision. In the general visual style of the film Frankenheimer isolates parts of the face and parts of the body and gives the impression of the body as an assemblage; he assembles time through the jumpcuts of montage as well—a perfect formal equivalent to the creation of a new personality that allows a Scarsdale banker in his fifties to become a Malibu artist in his thirties. Overseeing the whole operation is the head of the company, played by Will Geer, the embodiment of the Yankee entrepreneur, adept at giving the impression that, next to helping you and helping his country, making money is a minor consideration. When the film first appeared, many criticized the result of the transformation: the new self is played by Rock Hudson. But that is exactly the point. The desire to become another person, to escape from the mess of one's life, from the death of desire and ideals, has been created by the movies. But once we have been forced to face the inadequacy of our nonmovie lives we can do nothing. Hudson comes out of the operation with his stitches unhealed. Like Mitchum in *The Night of the Hunter,* he is another image of Frankenstein, and, in the remanufacture of his face, we cannot help but wonder how much of the real Hudson's face was made the same way, to define that necessarily unachievable ideal of beauty. As the film clearly shows, the desire to be another person is basically infantile and irresponsible: the tape recording of Hudson's pretransformation desires begins, "I want a ball—a big, big red ball." When he goes back in his new form to visit his former wife, he is surprised to find she has a life of her own, and when he asks about his old self, pretending to be a friend, she says, "I never knew what he wanted. I don't think he ever knew." Hudson has botched the Malibu transformation and wants to try again; this time he will be able to deal with his new self responsibly. But there is no third chance, and the film ends with Hudson being wheeled to an operating room, where he is to become spare parts for yet another person's dreams. In the last shots, while the brain drill whirs closer and closer in the background, we glimpse a man and a child and a dog walking on a beach, and then there is blackness. It is the dead end of the movie dream of transformation. *Seconds* faces both ways. Caught between the ideal dream and the real inadequacy, it seems to counsel quietism and resignation; only the weak and immature want to change their lives. But the sense of an expanded self inspired by movies still abides, if only in the dream of music within fitfully fostered by such musicals as *The Music Man*.

Away from the pressures of cold war America and the fear of individual energy, however, the potentials of stylization, in both setting and personality, flower in the foreign films of the 1950s, spurred by directors like Renoir and Max Ophuls, who left Hollywood to work again in Europe. In contrast to Renoir, Ophuls is essentially a closed set director, more interested in the confinement of the film world than the growth that limits may foster. Renoir's *The Golden Coach* (1953) and Ophuls' *Lola Montès* (1955) offer an interesting contrast in their attitude toward the actor. For both Lola (Martine Carroll) and Camilla (Anna Magnani) the stage is their personal place, where they realize themselves best. But whereas Lola is presented as a waxwork statue, an idol to be venerated by her audience, Camilla is actively engaged with her audience, imploring them, arguing with them, and inviting them to share in the magic of theater. The difference between the two is crucial: Lola is an image from high culture. She has affairs with Franz Lizst and the King of Bavaria. She is a "dream figure for normal women" now reduced to being a sideshow in a circus where a ringmaster invites all to come watch her life and pay a dollar to kiss her hand. Camilla is a popular artist to begin with, a member of an eighteenth-century commedia dell'arte company traveling in Peru.

Lola, with her sphinxlike silence, is like a silent-film star; Camilla, with her raucous loquacity, is like a sound-film star, at once closer to her surroundings and more human herself. Lola has a public; Camilla has an audience. Lola is one display within a whole world of theater that with its oppressive objects threatens to overwhelm her; Camilla is the center of her theater, the motive and cohering force of the film in which she is a part. Ophuls finally remains superior to Lola; his camera ruthlessly exposes the façades within which she lives and finally draws back from her while the crowds press forward. Renoir structures his film around Camilla; his camera follows her until the last scene, when she steps from the film onto the stage and pays tribute to the world of theater, "those two little hours when you become another person, your true self."

The sensibility of the actress in *Lola Montès* follows the dictates of the general closed-film way of viewing the actor: she is basically narcissistic; she offers nothing to her public but an object to be adored. She expands no sensibility; she feeds only her own. Camilla's mood, on the other hand, is directly responsive to the audience. At the inn or the palace, when she is onstage, she is not self-absorbed so much as she is the extension of the antennas of the audience's sensibilities. The contact with an audience energizes Camilla (and Renoir), whereas for Lola (and Ophuls) the audience is to be manipulated in the cause of entertainment. Lola is so trapped in a world of objects that at the end of the film we can hardly see her for the crowds of people and things; but Camilla controls the objects of her world, assigns meaning to the Golden Coach over which all the other characters are arguing, and becomes thereby the creator of social and artistic coherence. Lola for Ophuls represents the limitations of acting, its false allure and its fraudulent sense of self. Camilla for Renoir represents the belief both that acting is an expression of the self and that the theater is a place where personality can flourish and expand rather than be reduced. We may admire Lola's style, but we like to be in Camilla's presence.

Renoir's insight into the possibilities of the theatrical personality is an insight typical of the open film, with its sensitivity to the parts of character that extend beyond the momentary frame of the film. Like Fellini, in such works as *La Strada* (1954) and

Nights of Cabiria (1957), Renoir is attempting to break away from the older conventions of film narrative by basing his films more on individual characters than plots in which characters are embedded. *Nights of Cabiria,* for example, is much more about Cabiria, the prostitute, than it is about any structured beginning-middle-end plot, creating a narrative from Cabiria's relationships rather than from any progression of events that happen to her. In a highly emblematic scene Cabiria is picked up by an actor and taken to his luxurious home, where, by a turn of events, she must sit in a bathroom alone and watch the actor and his girl-friend through a keyhole. Later, she is hypnotized onstage and becomes highly emotional, embarrassing the hypnotist. In fact, she is the actor manqué, more in touch with her emotions, more able to reach an audience, than the professional actor or the vaudeville hypnotist. The film does not really end. Betrayed by yet another man, Cabiria walks down a road among trees. Around her appear young men playing guitars and accordions, couples arm-in-arm and dancing. While she walks, one clownlike tear falls from her eye. A more melancholic Camilla, she too has created the coherence of the occasion, even though she must finally be alone. But, in contrast to the solitude of Lola, she takes satisfaction in the sense of expanded reality her life gives her and she can give in turn to her customers and to her audience.

The central character of Rossellini's *General della Rovere* (1959) is portrayed in a similar way. Played by Vittorio de Sica (another interesting example of the actor-direction tension in these films), he is a gambler and con man named Bardone, alias Grimaldi, who is forced by the Germans to assume the name and character of General della Rovere, a high Italian Resistance officer, to escape being put in jail himself. The real della Rovere has been mistakenly shot, despite a plan to trail him and learn the secrets of the Resistance. At first Bardone enjoys the role, for it is the perfect complement to his consciously showy personality. He is put into prison so that he can find out the names of Resistance members, and he luxuriates in the applause of the other prisoners for "his" exploits. But gradually Bardone realizes that the role of della Rovere shows only more clearly the emptiness of his real character, the disparity between his distinguished good looks and what he really is. The end of the process occurs when Bardone is included in a group of ten men to be executed the next morning so that he can finger the high Resistance official among them. During the night, the man makes himself known to Bardone, but the next morning Bardone refuses to tell the German commandant and almost runs toward execution, leaving the startled German a note for della Rovere's wife that reads "I love you. Viva Italy." The theatricality and flamboyance of the gesture is essential. Bardone has left his own nature behind to assume the ideal identity of della Rovere. Artifice, role-playing, the assumption of disguise are not necessarily limits on the self, but may be a way of both heightening ordinary lives and achieving some kind of final moral truth.

General della Rovere brings the open film's fascination with the possibilities of the theatrical character more firmly into everyday life. The general fear of the actor in the American 1950s appears in the European films as a preoccupation with acting as a possible way of life. The films of Renoir and Fellini in this period are fascinated by the popular rather than the elitist art of film and so they concentrate on characters who attempt to connect with an audience instead of expecting the audience to come to them. The actors in their films are not like stage actors who maintain a separation between stage and audience, but more like film actors who attempt to bridge that gap through emotion, empathy, and a sacrifice of part of their personal selves. For Shakespeare's audience, the idea that the world is a stage could be a new revelation. But for us, at a time when theater is a special occasion, it takes film to show us that we are actors in everyday life—not stage actors, but film actors, taking parts and playing roles to our expansion rather than our limit. The open films of the 1950s emphasize the potentially liberating effects of self-conscious acting. But the expansion is usually in the special world of the past or the world of the social outcast. The possibility that self-stylization can be liberating in a naturalistic world, a world like the one the audience sees around it everyday, the possibility that character need not be circumscribed and repressed for the purposes of personal safety and social order, requires a synthesis of the insights of the open and closed film, a new generation of directors, stars, and scriptwriters.

CHARACTER AND CONNECTION: EUROPEAN AND AMERICAN FILMS OF THE 1960s AND 1970s

In the preceding sections I have described the new synthesis that films seemed struggling toward from the late 1950s until now: the breakdown of traditional methods of visual narrative, the self-consciousness about genre and film creation generally, and the rising importance of a provisional and often partially improvisatory film, a film that teaches the audience about itself as we watch, so that when we reach the end, we often feel we want to see it again. The melodramatic and imagistic connections of the silent film give way in sound to a new mode of connection through the invisible world. Sound films still retain a respect for articulated plot and the sound often serves only to hammer the narrative together even more tightly, with characters (and actors) who emphasized style and the exterior self. The opening up of film narrative in the 1960s derives essentially from an effort to expand the film sense of character, to transcend the more restricted images of the past, the doubled and theatrical characters, and explore the ability of character to furnish a new kind of cinematic narrative coherence. One element that all the "new" filmmakers share—"new" only because the filmgoing public was beginning insensibly to realize things had changed—is their emphasis on the actor and through the actor on the human face. At no time since the silent films had the unadorned face been so important as it became in the late 1950s and early 1960s. Renoir and Fellini approached this face—in Anna Magnani and Giulietta Masina—through the stage actor and mime; Truffaut and the Americans approached it through more naturalistic and contemporary images; Godard wrote an essay in its praise; Bergman wove together the symbolic and the natural character with interpenetrating mystery. But the impact was the same: all used the empathy between the face on the screen and the face in the mirror to make new connections. Until the late 1950s, acting had been one element in the pattern of a film. From the late 1950s on, acting has a more essential role in generating the entire pattern, not because the actor means something specific to the audience—like an older archetypal or stereotypical figure—but because the new actors appeared to have a wealth of possibility within, a complexity beyond the surface. Rather than the barrier that the faces of both closed film and Method actors presented to the audiences of the American 1950s, the faces of the new actors were provisional bars, fences to cross, indications of hidden and more fruitful worlds. The concept of a real movie face had been redefined, often through unconventional looks like those of Jeanne Moreau or Jean-Paul Belmondo, to prevent the audience from stopping at the surface and to make them wonder what in this face and behind it was worth exploring.

The New Wave especially derives its presentation of the enigma of character from the potential of character to escape total interpretation. Society may impose forms to which the character cannot measure up. But the filmmaker presents himself as a possible intermediary between the character and the world, not as in Kazan's directorial competition with the actor, but as a more self-aware co-conspirator. So many of the early films of Truffaut and Godard focus on faces, through an interview or a conversation, with the camera's gaze directed to one person alone, while the words of the other move on the soundtrack. The disjunctures of conversation imply the continuities of character. The psychiatrist questioning the young Antoine Doinel in Truffaut's *The 400 Blows,* the philosopher talking to Nana in Godard's *Vivre sa vie,* the nurse Alma interrogating the silent Elisabet in Bergman's *Persona*—all are efforts to penetrate an enigma of character that we finally perceive as more mysterious than incomplete. There are few answers to the words and the sounds. But there is a human presence on the screen that implies the body beyond the frame, the character that still exists after the film has been completed. From the American genre films these directors took the flat faces of the actors and turned them into vessels for the imagination of the audience. The director, no longer so totally intent on creating a property, could use his conscious awareness of the past appearances of an actor to make the inner potential more visible, to turn the face from a blank wall into at least a dim window. Consider, for example, the differences between the way Godard uses Belmondo in *Breathless* and De Broca uses Belmondo in *That Man from Rio* (1964); or the difference between the way Ford uses John Wayne and the way Andrew MacLaglen uses John Wayne in *McClintock* (1963). Godard's Belmondo is a character whose self-stylization (as Bogart) hides a complex past, a world of psychic wounds related in part to the Algerian War that the film would only reduce if it attempted to portray them visually. De Broca uses Belmondo as a kind of comic Brando, posturing and adventuring, without a past or a self deeper than the particular predicament in which he finds himself—in short, a fantasy figure, in line with the genre fantasy figures of the past. In the same way, Wayne in a film by Ford or Hawks will carry with him the weight of accumulated character as an enrichment, while Wayne in a less expert, less aware film will carry with him merely a gesture to his "meaning" as an actor. In one film we feel the expansion that film contact with an actor's personality can bring; in another we feel the brief and superficial pleasures of the waxworks.

The collusion between actor and director becomes in the 1960s much more prevalent a mode than the manipulation of actor by director. Not that the actor is always given his head to improvise whatever he wants. But the kind of stories and situations typical of these films (and many films now) involve a following of a character, an exploration of a relationship, rather than a neatly articulated plot. Truffaut, for example, suiting his more self-conscious style, frequently concentrates on his autobiographical relation to his characters, especially Antoine Doinel (played by Jean-Pierre Léaud). His role as both director and actor—playing a teacher in *The Wild Child* (1970), and a director in *Day for Night* (1974)—is a further extension of this theme. The essence of role-playing doubleness in Truffaut's films seems to be the split between fame and anonymity, the threat of the outside world and the comfort of self-containment. Edouard Saroyan (Charles Aznavour), the famous pianist in *Shoot the Piano Player*, becomes Charlie Kohler the café piano player in order to distance himself from the world of fame and tragedy he has experienced. The unseen narrator of the film, with his ready access to Charlie's mind, talks more than does Charlie himself, who tends to speak in monosyllables. Like Truffaut, Edouard/Charlie is the talented lowerclass boy in upperclass society who finds that solitude and isolation protect one against involvement and pain. To a great extent, therefore, Truffaut's view of his main characters involves a more melancholic reading of the relation between actor and role than the more exuberant and optimistic one of *The Golden Coach.* (Truffaut's production company is called Les Films du Carrosse.) The audience's view of character may be expanded, but the characters themselves are trapped, like the double Julie Christie in *Fahrenheit 451* (1966) or the double Catherine Deneuve in *Mississippi Mermaid* (1969). Only in *Day for Night* is some sense of exuberance maintained. The scene has shifted from a more naturalistic world to the special world of the film set, with its consoling mediation between actor and society. By putting himself in the film, Truffaut, like Renoir in *The Rules of the Game,* can experiment with control and freedom at the same time, with the balance pressed more toward the problems of control. Actors who become directors—like Brando in *One-Eyed Jacks,* Charles Laughton using Robert Mitchum in *The Night of the Hunter,* or John Cassavetes—naturally focus on the actor as myth, while directors who become actors reduce their power and develop a more ambivalent attitude toward both roles. When directors use their wives, however, their methods are more dictated by their affinities with open or closed forms. Roger Vadim treats Brigitte Bardot, Annette Vadim, and Jane Fonda as playful sexual objects, with little beyond their skin at all, while Godard explores the inner lives of Anna Karina and Anne Wiazemsky.*

With a strong central character or a story focus on characterization in general, the director, scriptwriter, and cameraman are free to experiment with more fragmented and episodic ways of telling a story. Godard in *Vivre sa vie* (1962) presents a naturalistic story, the life of a prostitute named Nana (with an obvious nod to Zola), in twelve scenes reminiscent of a silent film or a vaudeville show, aggressively fragmenting the narrative while he preserves the integrity of the enigmatic central figure. Godard does not employ Truffaut's binding narrator with its implicit allusion to the director's control. For Godard the formal qualities of the film and the continuity of characters should be enough. In

---

* For this reason, Bardot can be the same no matter what director she works for; but Karina and Liv Ullmann look superficial when they are directed by anyone else but Godard and Bergman, Karina becoming a high-fashion mannikin and Ullmann, even in Jan Troell's *The Immigrants* (1972) and *The New Land* (1973), a mask of tender anguish.

his later films he tries to break that down as well, when, for example, the star of *Two or Three Things I Know About Her* (1967) introduces herself as the character and the actress, or the garbage men in *Weekend* (1967) stop to deliver long Marxian statements directly at the camera. This kind of formal disruption is Godard's effort to translate a Brechtian alienation effect to film, to defeat formal necessity with ideological sincerity. But it is very difficult to accomplish in a film, because the film audience, as I have argued above, does not experience the relation between actor and role in the same way the stage audience does. The film actor cannot get over the footlights to us. On the stage the actor alienated from his role might imply, "I can step out of my imposed role and therefore you should be able to step out of your restrictive social roles as well and even outside the theater to fight tyranny." But, because the relation between a film actor's role and his own nature is so close, alienation in a film tends to be experienced as schizophrenia rather than freedom for the self. Only when Godard plays directly with established film images, as he does with Jane Fonda and Yves Montand in *Tout Va Bien* (1972), using the frame of our expectation of their pre-existing personalities, does he finally achieve effects truly akin to Brecht's methods.

The more intriguing and effective way to transmit character and meaning through film is to enhance the illusion rather than break it down. Brecht—and Godard—imply that to disrupt the emotional involvement with the actor allows the artist to get his message across more clearly—a somewhat puritanical view of the sugar-coating of art. But character itself is an implicit destroyer of external forms, whether those of tradition, art, or society. For example, Bergman, in *Persona* (1966), the story of a schizophrenic actress, uses the many allusions to acting and films to build a strong identification with both main characters, the actress (Liv Ullmann) and the nurse (Bibi Andersson). The audience has been placed in a complex emotional situation, not a complex verbal or intellectual situation. Although the visual elements of the film can be interpreted, they have little meaning apart from the way they reflect the nature of Bergman's characters. The story Bibi Andersson tells of her sexual experience on a beach is, in its erotic effects, almost a direct denial of the "greater" truth of the visual world. When Godard reproduces the storytelling situation in *Weekend,* however, he remains on the surface, still looking for ways of visually pinning down his meaning. Godard tries to enhance character by invoking and playing against past film methods of seeing character, while Bergman uses a self-consciousness of film form to try to get away from its usual ways of explaining people. Godard's exaggerated use of words and speeches are intent on achieving the same disruptive effect that Bergman is searching for when Bibi Andersson in *Persona* says "more words . . . and then nausea." The camera finally achieves sincerity when it looks into a mirror and sees itself.

The more self-conscious use of traditional actor images and film methods of representing character that characterizes the 1960s and 1970s expand both our ideas of what a story is and what character is. Neither Godard's nor Bergman's, nor any other approach, has been a total definition. Bergman's career has moved from a concentration on the director's control, to a concentration on the stylized character (the magician, the actress), to an experimentation with relationships in *Scenes from a Marriage* (1974). The television origins of *Scenes from a Marriage* underline the irrelevance of an ordered Aristotelian screenplay to the problems explored by these character-oriented films—the way in which dialogue is less exposition than mood, bargaining, and the raising and lowering of barriers. Jacques Rivette's *Céline et Julie vont au bateau* (1974) similarly uses an extended (3½-hour) film situation to explore a relationship, this time between two women, that also whimsically contrasts the separate realities of film and stage, the outside world of Paris and the inside world of a suburban mansion. The conversations and relationships explored by Eric Rohmer in such films as *My Night at Maude's* and *Chloë in the Afternoon* are the binding structures in more urban and milieu-oriented films like Robert Altman's *McCabe and Mrs. Miller* (1972) and *California Split* (1974), neither of which can cohere without a sense of relationship between the main characters. Through such plotless situations, the films of the 1960s and 1970s are essentially exploring the way we play ourselves, alone and with others, in situations of intimacy rather than situations of society and public exposure. Brando's role in *Last Tango in Paris* was the first time an actor played against his screen image to comment upon it, rather than as a source of comic reference. Through that self-consciousness Bertolucci could contrast the older double character and its self-induced repression with the newer self-delusions of the character played by Maria Schneider, while invoking as well the way stars like Brando have helped shape such images.

Robert Altman may be the most elaborate practitioner of this new formula: complex and realistic characters set down in a limited genre situation—the American version of the New Wave's limited character in an open situation. In *Images* (1971), the story of a schizophrenic girl (Susannah York), he invests the typical film story of the split personality with a psychological self-consciousness through which the main character tries to combat her delusions by will alone. Suitably for such a late version of the story, the audience is often unsure when she is hallucinating and when she is seeing accurately. The film is filled with cameras, stereopticons, and jigsaw puzzles—all emblems of the uncertainty of the visual world. The main character is herself much more verbally oriented, and the script is filled with puns and double meanings as if to set the effort of the actress/character to regain her sanity through verbal control against the visual mystifications of the director. Finally, to complete the round of doublings, in the final credits we learn that the characters in the film all have the names of the actors and actresses who play their opposites and that Susannah York herself is the author of the fairytale by which the main character explains her insanity. Within the film, however, the madness finally cannot be controlled by writing about it; the escape outside the confining house into the beautiful English countryside becomes the final trap; and the effort to attack the visual artifice of the camera itself is punished by the final deadly illusion. The director, necessarily, has won again, even though his subject matter has been the interweaving of genre conventions with what might be called the theme of the actor. *Images* in fact marks a shift in Altman's films from the meditation on genre conventions to an interest in the structures spawned by character; the world so intensely created by the psyche of one person in *Images* becomes the two-person picaresques of *McCabe and Mrs. Miller* and *California Split*. In *Nashville* (1975) this structure is expanded to interplay twenty-four characters, each with a personal story incomplete but integral to the total effect. The themes of *Nashville* extend still further Altman's interest both in the way character creates action and in the symbiotic relation between character and acting. Within the world of actors playing characters appear an actor and an actress—Elliott Gould and Julie Christie—playing "themselves," to complicate still further the already intricate relation within the film between the characters who perform on stage, the characters who want to be famous, the characters who have only private lives, and the characters who have only public lives.

The realization that acting can be part of an authentic personal style—a synthesis of the stage actor's self-conscious intelligence and the film actor's self-conscious emotion—appears with both comic and more serious force in a film like *The Sting* (George Roy Hill, 1974). Part of *The Sting* emphasizes entertainment (the Scott Joplin theme is "The Entertainer"), style, and decor. But another part exposes the roots of their allure: the American preoccupation with surfaces, with external importance, and with fame. Terry Malloy, the Brando character in *On the Waterfront,* could feel justified when he accused his brother Charley of letting him down, when he "had a chance to be somebody, instead of a bum, which is what I am." Terry's identity, defined as the possibility of being somebody, had been taken away. The 1950s answer was to establish his moral authority by a heroic gesture, talking to the Crime Commission, attacking the corrupt union boss, and leading the men to work with wobbly knees, broken ribs, and a battered face. But in *The Sting,* the two con men played by Paul Newman and Robert Redford can say of their prospective victim: "We had him years ago, when he decided to be somebody." In part the difference comes from a more acute awareness of the presence of the audience, the other people before whom the actor, the entertainer, displays himself. The stance of the 1950s was aggression and self-defense. Brando in *Last Tango in Paris* finally accepts his own screen image, his own surface, and creatively uses his face as a summary of its past. But the effort might have been unique. As he said to Bernardo Bertolucci, the director, "For the first time, I have felt a violation of my innermost self. It should be the last time." Brando's characters constantly feel the pressures of outside demands. The characters created by Newman and Redford, in *The Sting,* or in more somberly meant films like Newman's *Sometimes a Great Notion* (directed by Newman, 1972) and Redford's *Jeremiah Johnson* (Sidney Pollack, 1973), meet those demands with their own whimsy, control, and personal style. The possibility of many societies rather than just one, many styles rather than just one, many selves rather than just one, has begun to exist.

The most striking efforts made by films today are to explore human character and personal relations in ways prevented or warped by the methods of the past. Innovations in form and directorial control are less interesting than innovations in content and acting, whether in the more naturalistic modes of *Scenes from a Marriage* and *California Split,* or the social allegories of *The Poseidon Adventure* and *The Longest Yard.* Movies in general, whether American or foreign, still seem to be in a period of ferment, while the basic changes in film form and film style that occurred in the late 1950s and early 1960s are being absorbed, understood, varied, and improved upon. I have discussed the changes in terms of the physical objects in films, the growth of film conventions of narrative, and the possibilities of film acting. But the historical frame of the changes has always been the increasing humanization of the images we see on the screen, as the characters and the stories move closer and closer to what we consider to be our own lives. Movies have helped us to know and expand our lives as much as they have held a mirror up to them. Without the opening of films in the 1960s, the discovery that the old fantasy selves were no longer useful and new explorations of character were needed, the political atmosphere of the late 1960s would have been very different, if it would have existed at all. Within the repressed self of the closed-film hero, there were the seeds of a new way of defining human nature within society, not by repression until all that is left is a furtive inner life, but by expansion, expression, and play: all the virtues that it is in the basic nature of films to convey. In the terms of this study, the open film definition of character has attacked and perhaps defeated the closed-film definition of society.

Like all other arts, film structures our perceptions of the world in its own special way. It takes the familiar world from us and then returns it to us defamiliarized and new. If you have come this far with me, you know that my main interest has been in the varieties of connection within and across individual films, between films and their audiences, and between films and the culture they both inhabit and express. The cultural era we have come to holds within it the potential for new continuities between the individual, society, and culture at large that stand against the exclusive and elitist values of the past. Its ideals are in great part the ideals of the great films and the great filmmakers: synthesis rather than analysis, inclusion rather than exclusion, understanding rather than rejection. If these are possible ideals, they should apply to our appreciation and understanding of film as well. Unlike the more elitist arts, which appeal to the solitary self or the select group, movies at their best assert that art should transform individual life by making us into a new community through its power. The rules of an art are necessary only to enter its world. The aesthetic of movies embodies the new values possible in the breakdown of older ideas of artistic and political hierarchy. Whatever their stories, whatever their methods, movies show us how to be human in ways that the other arts cannot. Let us honor them by understanding all the ways they work their magic, and thereby force them to invent new ones. Once the frame has been acknowledged, it can be forgotten.

Index of Films

Director and date are cited only if they are omitted in the text.

General Index

R